INDIA BOOKVARSITY

LOTUS CHOICES

Editor: Mahendra Kulasrestha

Classics Revived
for an
Ultramodern World

GENIUS: Tagore Select

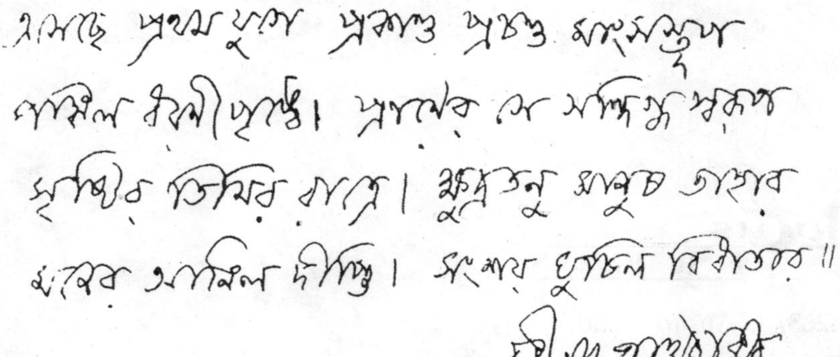

Latest

"It is possible to be both interested in the richness of India's own culture and heritage and take an interest in the cultures and achievements of the rest of the world, in exactly the way that Rabindranath Tagore discussed so eloquently and convincingly. There is no necessary conflict between 'the home' and 'the world' if we continue to stand on our own feet and look at the world with interest and involvement, rather than with docility and slavishness."

—Amartya Sen
15 Aug. 06

Lotus PRESS

4263/3, Ansari Road,
Darya Ganj, New Delhi-110002

GENIUS

TAGORE SELECT

Edited by: Mahendra Kulasrestha

Poet, writer, thinker,
musician, painter, educationist

Sources: Works of Tagore and **Tagore Centenary Volume,** V.V. Research Inst., Hoshiarpur, Pb.

All Art-work by Tagore

GENIUS: TAGORE SELECT
New First Edition 2006

Published by: **LOTUS PRESS**
4263/3, Ansari Road, Darya Ganj, New Delhi-110002
Ph: 30903912, 23290047
E-mail: lotus_press@sify.com

ISBN 81-8382-090-5

Laser typeset by: Computek System, Delhi-110032
Printed at: Gyan Sagar, New Delhi

'Life began its dubious chapter with an exaggeration of flesh. The little man came to solve the doubt from Creator's mind.'

—**Rabindranath Tagore**

Faces

Editorspeak

Recognising Tagore

Ever since I edited the *Tagore Centenary Volume* in 1962, I have the feeling that Rabindranath Tagore's contribution to Indian renaissance as well as world modernism has not been recognised. The feeling gets stronger as now I prepare to publish a representative work on him, which comprises Part I of the above entitled *The Genius of Tagore*, slightly rearranged and edited, adding some more significant material, mostly selections from his own writings and paintings, but not music, the most superior form of art according to him, because it cannot by any effort be included in a work depending on the printing-skill, though there is an article on the much ignored subject—and perhaps also disliked in his own beloved Bengal—a pity indeed to me.

The reason is simple: he was overshadowed by Gandhi. This was natural because political freedom was a greater priority of the times and various forces from Bengal herself, Punjab, Maharashtra, etc., were persistently promoting this cause and purpose. In fact, Bengal was the leader in this national activity also, as it was in socio-religious change, with the Brahmo Samaj as its first powerful expression, of which Rabindranath himself was an all-rounded near-complete product, and which, to my surprise, did not acquire as much acceptability as it deserved in Bengal itself and other parts of the country. In comparison, Arya Samaj, a Gujerati product like that of Gandhi in later times, acquired a near-national status in this area, and also contributed mightily to the freedom movement, with hefty Punjabi help, by providing not only the leadership but also the cadre of the movement.

That Rabindranath was not much in favour of strident political action, is well known. It was the same with Vivekananda—to him the supreme cause was eradication of poverty. He even forbid his followers to partake in the freedom movement—which Dayanand did not even think of doing. It is an interesting irony of the situation that the freedom fighters of the country always regarded Vivekananda as their inspiration-point. His chief disciple Sister Nivedita resigned from the Ramakrishna Mission to support the freedom movement while working for the spread of the Swami's mission, especially of teaching Indian women in the 3-r's as well as social regeneration, in strict observation of the Swami's desire.

I am always surprised at this fact that these two most important of Bengali reformers were so opposed to freedom movement, though it cannot be said that they were opponents of the freedom of India. This is, anyway, an academic problem for the present times and can be passed over. What remains is that both were complementary. My submission also is that the freedom part having been achieved, the other part of reconstruction, with modern inputs, is awaiting our attention.

It is here that Rabindranath is relevant. I would like to stress this point with all the will and energy at my command. While rereading his writings and looking at his paintings, I am surprised, again, at the basic quality and originality as well as analysis of his national and world situation, which has not yet been recognised, nay, even read and understood properly. I retain this feeling since I had the occasion to read his books of essays a long time ago, while very young, perhaps not even enough mature. My general impression at the time was that though the Nobel-winner **Gitanjali** was fine, very very fine indeed in view of its most unusual subject matter as well as the super-simple style of expression, which in no time drew attention, wild in certain cases, pushing the work for the most coveted prize; his more, much more, significant contribution lay in his remarkable essays. But as essays are generally not given the importance they rightfully deserve, these were totally ignored and remain so till date.

I am also surprised and intrigued at the nature of his paintings which remind one of Paul Klee and Kandinsky than the Bengal School of Art started at his own Santiniketan and spread all over the country during his lifetime itself. His paintings present an alarming contrast to the spirit which was expressed in **Gitanjali** and other poems. These he did during the last two decades of his life which may be taken as proof of the fact that, having experienced the ups and downs of life, he was now a totally changed man—a deeply sad, perturbed person who, if given another one or two decades, might become an iconoclast, looking at a new philosophy of life, God, etc. This was not to happen.

This important fact immediately places him in the entirely modern, avant garde, thinker-artist-human category. The truth he earned from life is most vocally expressed in his paintings which haunt one like the spirit of his famous story **Hungry Stones.**

For these reasons, though Rabindranath himself describes his status as that of a poet in **Ami Kobi**—I Am A Poet—I would prefer to call him primarily a Thinker—Aapni Bicharak—and a Painter, which also depicts the attitude of a thinking and deeply feeling person. I would also want to regard the later presentations of his life and work as more significant than his earlier work.

Rabindranath Tagore's analysis of world cultures, India's basically racial structure and caste system—where he so many years ago found a parellel with America and which perhaps was the best arrangement in the given circumstances, but in managing which we have failed—, his severe criticism of the 'Nation' philosophy and politics, his vision of a multicultural world-culture, etc., are and remain some of the best ideas thrown up by human intellect. This collection contains such articles presented in a separate section.

He was a most remarkable person by any measures. I've never liked beards, but his I found most enchanting. I strongly feel that he should be revived in modern times, and a holistic view of his work should be taken. His ideas await to be implemented not only in his own country but all over the world.

I end this note by presenting aspects of his charisma in the following notes:

THOUGH a Bengali, Tagore did not like Sakti worship, especially in the form of Kali, the fearful goddess. The Swadeshi leaders of Bengal were trying to transform Kali-worship into a form of national worship. They asked Rabindranath to write a hymn in furtherance of this effort but he refused. He rather tried to personify Kali as Lakshmi, the gentle goddess of love and good fortune.

●

TAGORE was a great lover of Nature—of rains and rivers, clouds and moonlight and dawn, trees and flowers and bees—but of mountains, little. About them he once told a friend: 'These massive screens of stones block the eye, they are rigid and unchanging, they narrow down the freedom of space.'

●

ONCE Tagore supposed himself to be the poetical incarnation of an imaginary old Vaishnava singer, Bhanu Singh, and published a collection of his songs. They mightily deceived the Vaishnava enthusiasts and a researcher was even awarded a Ph.D. from Germany for his treatise on ancient Vaishnava poetry in which Bhanu Singh had a major place.

●

ONCE Rabindranath was invited to R.C. Dutta's house to a marriage feast. As he arrived, people were garlanding Bankim

Chandra Chatterji. Bankim saw him and said: "You must garland him. Have you not read his *Invocation*?" In later times, Tagore set the famous poem, *Bande Mataram*, of Bankim to music.

●

RABINDRANATH edited a number of magazines, *Bharati*, *Sadhana* and so on. But he actually wrote them—from seventy-five to fifty per cent; outside contributors got little space in them.

●

UNLIKE Gandhiji's ashramas, free association of young men and women was a special feature of Santiniketan. Those who fell in love with each other and wanted marriage, had just to go to the Poet, bow to him, declare their intention and get his blessings. Marriages were celebrated, under his aegis, with due ceremony.

●

IN his last years, Tagore was greatly distressed by the religious bigotry of the Indian people. Once he told an English visitor that he would welcome even a wave of atheism over India, for it would act like a forest fire that sweeps away dead stuff and rubbish.

●

STATISTICALLY, Tagore's contribution to Muses is as follows:

150,000 lines of verse, including dramas
300,000 lines of prose—fiction, criticism, essays, etc.
3,000 songs
2,500 paintings.

Contents

A Thinker Par Excellence

A Few Great Stories

Paintings

Nobel Prize 1913

GITANJALI

Songs of Gold and Silver

The Story: Nobel Prize for *Gitanjali*

Edward Thompson

In 1912 the Bengal Literary Academy celebrated Rabindranath's jubilee. The Calcutta Town Hall was packed with a wildly enthusiastic audience, in which every branch of activity was fully represented.

The experience proved too much for him. He had been in intense pain for a long time, physical suffering having succeeded to his protracted mental distress; and for the next two years it seemed as if he must soon die. One thing that drove him to the West was the hope of recovering health. C. F. Andrews told me how wasted he looked. 'In fact, I can't believe that this robust fellow is the same person. I always have a picture of him as he looked then in London, wretched and broken.' On his return from England, after the visit which made him famous, he was persuaded to undergo an operation. An English specialist took the case, and handled it with a patience and kindness that the poet never forgot. Had operating not taken place, Andrews said, Rabindranath could not have lived out the year. He was saved; and never suffered again in the same way.

Illness followed his ovation in the Town Hall, prostrating him on the very morning when he should have sailed for England. His doctor forbade him to move, and enjoined a month's absolute rest.

'So I went to Shileida, and simply to while away time I translated those *Gitanjali* songs. For they were very dear to me, and I wanted to have the pleasure of going over them a second time. I felt sure my translations were only schoolboy exercises. So I showed them to Ajit, who said they were quite good. Also, on the steamer I went on translating, which gave me great pleasure.

'I reached London and stayed in a hotel. Here I suffered great disappointment. Everyone seemed like phantoms. The hotel used to empty after breakfast, and I watched the crowded streets. I was in despair and thought of coming back. It was not possible to know this humanity, or enter into the heart of another place.

'Then it occurred to me to try to get into touch with Rothenstein. I had met him at Abanindranath's place, but no one had told him I was a poet; he just knew me as one of the Tagore family. So I looked up his telephone number and rang him up; and he came at once, and got me better lodgings. You know that Vale of Health, in Hampstead—absurd name! Well, he got me a house there. He was my neighbour, and came often to see me.

'Then one day he said he had heard I was a poet. Could I give him any idea of my work? I told him I had some prose translations, but knew the English was not good. However, he took them. After a day or two, he came back quite excited, and said they were the most wonderful things he had ever seen. I thought he was an artist and did not understand literature; he saw that I didn't believe him.

'He had copies typed, and sent them to Yeats, Stopford Brooke, and Bradley. Bradley replied that he had never expected to find a real poet. The other two were very excited, too. So Rothenstein gave a reading at his house—Yeats read to a group of people—Miss May Sinclair and Nevinson were there. That was where I met Andrews. I had not met him before. Yeats read some very short poems, while I was miserable. How could these make any impression? I asked. They would glide over their minds. You know, your people are not demonstrative, and they made no sign. I was quite angry with Yeats for doing me this injustice! Next day letters came from Miss Sinclair and other people; I was startled by their tone. But gradually I saw they were quite sincere.'

The best of all of his own translations, the English *Gitanjali* is a haunted book. He had spent so much time with these versions, in India and on his voyage to England, that the book was essentially a new one; his personality had passed into it. Despite its name, it contains translations, not only from the Bengali *Gitanjali* but from a number of other works.

After a visit to America, following his English stay, he returned to India, in the autumn of 1913. The tide of fame was still running strongly, and had not attained its height. At the landing-stage in Bombay, he found a crowd waiting with garlands—he thought, for some official, but it was for him. He was mobbed with praise as he fled across India.

On the evening of a day in the first week of November, when I was staying at Santiniketan, suddenly a hubbub arose, and the masters rushed up with a sheaf of telegrams. 'We have great news. Mr. Tagore has won the Nobel Prize.' A minute later he entered. It was a time of great happiness for all. The boys did not know what the Nobel Prize was, but they understood that their Gurudeb had done something wonderful, as he was always doing.

They formed ranks and marched round the Ashrama, singing *Amader Santiniketan,* the school song. They would not go by the guesthouse a second time, but gathered at the door till the poet went to it. He was greeted with a frenzy of worship, one after another throwing himself down and touching his feet. He stood with hands to his face, palms together, deprecating their homage; and when Ajit Chakravarti flung himself down, he tried to stop him. Everyone shouted and sang. At last the boys dispersed and made a hung bonfire.

Rabindranath told me the award was not altogether a surprise. When in England, he had been asked to send copies of his books and press-cuttings to the Nobel Prize Committee.

Ezra Pound's
Review of *Gitanjali*

(Written in 1913)

The appearance of the poems of Rabindranath Tagore is, to my mind, very important. I am by no means sure that I can convince the reader of this importance. For proof I must refer him to the test. He must read it quietly. He would also do well to read it aloud, for this apparently simple English translation has been made by a great musician, by a great artist, who is familiar with a music subtler than our own.

It is a little over a month since **I went to Mr. Yeats' rooms and found him much excited over the advent of a great poet, someone 'greater than any of us.'**

Bengal is a nation of fifty million people. Superficially it would seem to be beset with phonographs and railways. Beneath this there would seem to subsist a culture not wholly unlike that of twelfth-century Provence. Mr. Tagore is their great poet and their great musician as well. He has made them their national song, their *Marseillaise,* if an Oriental nation can be said to have an equivalent to such an anthem. I have heard his *Golden Bengal,* with its music, and it is wholly Eastern, yet it has a curious power, a power to move the crowd. It is minor and subjective, yet has all the properties of action.

The next resemblance to medieval conditions is that Mr. Tagore teaches his songs and music to his jongleurs, who sing them throughout Bengal. He can boast with the best of the troubadours, 'I made it, the words and the notes.' Also, he sings them himself, I know, for I have heard him.

The forms of this poetry as they stand in the original Bengali are somewhere between the forms of Provencal canzone and the roundels and odes of the Pleiade. The rhyme arrangements are different, and they have rhymes in four syllables, something, that is, beyond the leonine. Their meters are more comparable to the latest development of *vers libre* than to anything else Western.

The language itself is a daughter of Sanskrit. It sounds more like good Greek than any language I know of. It is an inflected language, and therefore easy to rhyme in. You may couple words together as you do in Greek or German. Mr. Tagore tells me that there is scarcely a poem where you do not make some such word-combination. It is an ideal language for poets, it is fluid, and the order is flexible, and all this makes for precision.

The hundred poems in the present volume are all songs to sing. The tunes and the words are knit together, are made together, and Oriental music would seem to fit this purpose better than our own. Firstly, because it is unencumbered with a harmony. Secondly, from the nature of the *Ragini*, which are something in the nature of the Greek *Modes*. And in these *Raginis* there is a magic of association. For certain of these scales are used only for song in the evening, or for song in the rainy season, or at sunrise, so that a Bengali hearing any opening bar knows at once the place and atmosphere of the poem.

The precision of his language remains. I think this good fortune is unconscious. I do not think it is an accident. It is the sort of prose rhythm a man would use after years of word arranging. He would shun cacophony almost unwittingly.

The next easiest things to note are the occasional brilliant phrases, now like some pure Hellenic, in 'Morning with the golden basket in her right hand,' now like the last sophistication of De Gourmont or Baudelaire.

But beneath and about it all is this spirit of curious quiet. We have found our new Greece suddenly. As the sense of balance came back upon Europe in the days before the Renaissance, so it seems to me does this sense of a saner stillness come now to us in the midst of our clangour of medianisms.

I am not saying this hastily, nor in an emotional flurry, nor from a love of brandishing statement. I have had a month to think it over.

Hearing his first Greek professor, hearing for the first time the curious music of Theocritus, coming for the first time upon that classic composure which Dante had a little suggested in his description of limbo, Boccaccio must have felt, I think, a little differently from what we have felt here, we few who have been privileged to receive the work of Mr. Tagore before the public and heard it.

To find fitting comparison for the content of the volume before us, I am compelled to one sole book of my acquaintance, the *Paradiso* of Dante.

Ecco qui creascera li nostril amori.

Dante hears more than a thousand spirits, singing it as he comes into the fourth heaven. Yet the voice of the Brahmo Samaja is different, the mysticism is calm rather than fervid.

There is in Tagore the stillness of nature. The poems do not seem to have been produced by storm or by ignition, but seem to show the normal habit of his mind. He is at one with nature, and finds no contradictions. And this is in sharp contrast with the Western mode, where man must be shown attempting to master nature if we are to have 'great drama'. It is in contrast to the Hellenic representation of man as the sport of the gods, and both in the grip of destiny.

Oddly enough, I wrote some six months ago this passage, annent the introduction of humanism at the time of the Renaissance:

> Man is concerned with man and forgets the whole and the flowing... And we have in sequence, first the age of drama, and then the age of prose.

And this sort of humanism, having pretty well run its course, it seems to me we have the balance and corrective presented to us in this writing from Bengal.

I cannot prove it. Every true criticism of an important work of art must be a personal confession rather than a demonstration. Perhaps simple confession is the best criticism after all. I do not want to confuse Mr. Tagore's personality with his work, and yet the relation between the two is so close that perhaps I may not offend by the two statements, which I shall not attempt to explain.

When I leave Mr. Tagore I feel exactly as if I were a barbarian clothed in skins, and carrying a stone war-club, the kind, that is, where the stone is bound into a crotched stick with thongs. Perhaps you will get some hint of the curious quality of happiness which pervades his poems from the following incident:

Mr. Tagore was seated on a sofa, and just beginning to read to me in Bengali, when our hostess's little girl of three ran into the room, laughing and making a most infernal clatter. **Immediately the poet burst into laughter exactly like the child's.** It was startling and it was for a moment uncanny, I do not attempt to explain it. **Was he in some sudden and intimate connection with the child's gaiety, or was it merely some Oriental form of super-courtesy to prevent our hosts from guessing that he noticed an interruption? Was it a simple acknowledgement that the child's mirth was quite as important in the general scheme of things as was our discussion of international aesthetics?**

Thus it is that thy joy in me is so full.

Briefly, I find in these poems a sort of ultimate common sense, a reminder of a thing and of forty things of which we are never likely to lose sight in the confusion of our

Western life, in the racket of our cities, in the jabber of manufactured literature, in the vortex of advertisement.

There is the same sort of common sense in the first part of the New Testament, the same happiness in some of the psalms, but these are so apt to be spoiled for us by association; there are so many fools engaged in mispreaching them that it is pleasant to find their poetic quality in some work which does not bring into the spectrum of our thought John Calvin, the Bishop of London, and the loathly images of cant.

It these poems have a flaw, I do not admit that they have, but if they have a quality that will put them at a disadvantage with the general reader, it is that they are too pious. Yet I have nothing but pity for the reader who is unable to see that their piety is the poetic piety of Dante, and that it is beautiful.

I do not think I have ever undertaken so difficult a problem of criticism, for one can praise most poetry in a series of antitheses. **In the work of Tagore the source of the charm is in the subtle underflow. It is nothing else than his 'sense of life'. The sort of profound appreciation of it which leads Rodin to proclaim that 'Energy is Beauty'. It is the sort of appreciation of it that we find in Swinburne's ballad beginning: 'I found in dreams a palace of wind and flowers',** where he says in allegory: 'Now assuredly I see my lady is perfect, and transfigureth all sin and sorrow and death, making them fair as her eyelids be'.

For purely selfish reasons I want this book *Gitanjali* to be well received. Mr. Tagore's work does not consist wholly of such songs as these. There are plays and love-lyrics still hidden in the original, The task on which he has already set forth is the translation of his children's songs, and I am anxious to see them. When criticism fails one can do no more than go, personally, security for the work one is announcing.

Thou hast made me known to friends whom I knew not. Thou hast given me seats in houses not my own. Thou hast brought the distant near and made a brother of the stranger.

says Tagore, and he might have said most truly of his own writings, and indeed, of all great art, for it is only by the arts that strange people can come together in any friendly intimacy. By such expression they learn a mutual respect, and there is more marrow in such expression than in much propaganda for economic peace.

Rabindranath Tagore has done well for his nation in these poems. He has well served her Foreign Office. He has given us beauty that is distinctly Oriental, and though it is almost severe, it is free from that lusciousness, that overprofusion which, in so much South-Oriental work, repels us. His work is, above all things, quiet. It is sunny, 'fed with sun' and 'delighting in sunlight'.

One has in reading it a sense of even air, where many Orientals only make us aware of abundant vegetation. I will quote one poem, and bid you then to go to the book.

I have come to the river, she said, to float my lamp on the stream and when the daylight wanes in the west. I stood alone along tall grasses and watched the timid flame of her lamp uselessly drifting in the tide.

Gitanjali: Work of a Supreme Culture

W.B. Yeats

These translations from Rabindranath Tagore have stirred my blood as nothing has for years. For all I know, so abundant and simple is this poetry, the new Renaissance has been born in that country.

I have carried the manuscript of these translations about with me for days, reading it in railway trains, or on the top of omnibuses and in restaurants, and I have often had to close it lest some stranger would see how much it moved me. These lyrics display in their thought a world I have dreamed of all my life long. The work of a supreme culture, they yet appear as much the growth of the common soil as the grass and the rushes.

A tradition, where poetry and religion are the same thing, has passed through the centuries, gathering from learned and unlearned metaphor and emotion, and carried back again to the multitude the thought of the scholar and of the noble. These verses, as the generations pass, travellers will hum on the highway and men rowing upon rivers. Lovers, while they await one another, shall find, in murmuring them, this love of God a magic gulf wherein their own more bitter passion may bathe and renew its youth. Tagore, like the Indian civilization itself, has been content to discover the soul and surrender himself to its spontaneity.

An innocence, a simplicity that one does not find elsewhere in literature!

AMI KOBI

(I Am A Poet)

Rabindranath Tagore

It is not an easy thing to know one's true nature, what one really is. If God had not granted me this long life, this knowledge might have escaped me. In course of my life I have been attracted to a variety of activities, but the inmost me is not to be found in any of these. At the end of the journey I can see the curve of my life a little more clearly. Looking back, the only thing of which I feel fairly certain is that I am a poet.

I do not claim to be a theologian, a leader of men, a moral or religious preceptor. I had once written: I have no desire to be a leader of the New Bengal. I meant it. The messengers of Truth's white radiance, who purify earth, air and water, who guide me to the paths of peace, I honour them,—and I know that I am not of their company. But when that one radiance throws itself out joyously into the many, scatters its sheer splendour through the spectrum of this universal movement, then there I find my vocation—as a poet. I am a voice of the expressive many, the Infinite's self-variation, the endless, nameless joy, the passion of bliss that fathers forth all things.

To cherish this delight, at the centre of creation, to take into one's heart and to express it in all ways of one's being, that indeed has been my labour. I do not presume to lead men to their life's goal, to travel alongside is happiness enough for me. Some had called me a metaphysician, others have thrust me the doubtful role of a schoolmaster. But led by my love of play, I have been a truant ever—not for me is the teacher's job. I still remember the little boy setting out on his life's journey at the early hour of dawn—the light struggling to break through the veil of obscurity. The esctasy of that wonder, the eyes' happy interchange of light and darkness, has never ceased. The lotus pool of the child-heart stirred and shivered at the ungrasped mystery. It left me restless, a wanderer for ever.

And now that I have turned seventy, friends complain about my lightheartedness, it hurts their sense of propriety. I can hardly afford to waste my time trying to do what is not in my power to do. Through all the vicissitudes of these seventy years, I have come to the conclusion that I was meant to be a companion of the ever-changing. I do not know if I have achieved anything or if I shall leave anything worthwhile behind me. I crave not for permanence. He plays through me, but without attachment, and the playhouse which He builds is also the one which He pulls down or allows to fall by the wayside.

The wings of storm have swept away yesterevening's *alaponā* designs in our mango grove, and they have to be laid afresh. If I have been able to furnish a few toys to the world's playhouse, I shall not care for their preservation in perpetuity. The potsherd will one day be consigned to the scrapheap, anyway. Enough if I have been able to breathe life into these toys of Time and charged them with the rapture of Bliss at the heart of all that is. I ask for nothing more.

The expressive side of the *ashrama*—that, alone, is mine. It has of course its executive side, there are experts to look after that. What I had wished for was to release the human urge for self-expression, for form. And so I had looked for a forest retreat, a *tapovana,* as its proper ambience. Not in the midst of sordid citybuilt houses, but under the blue canopy, in this wide quadrangle from morn to eve have I wished to be a playmate of these boys and girls. To express, growing out of our common life, beauty's happy and blessed form, that was my real concern.

I have naturally had to introduce other utilitarian activities as well but you will not find me in these. I am where life is trying to express itself, anew. The classes that I have started or taught here are secondary—my real work has been to open up, in nature's vast playground, the tender grace of childhood, its budding effort, the first sweet rays of knowledge falling across its horizon. Otherwise I would have been swamped by the rubbish of routine, statute and syllabus.

My sole happiness, the only fulfilment, has been in trying to rouse young folk to the delight of the Player, to set them in tune with the dance of life itself. It is not in me to be more serious than that. Those who try to set me up on a pedestal, I tell them that I was born with my seat below, on the earth.

The Master of Games has mercifully released me from the role of the mature and the elder. In this dust, earth and grass, in these trees and forests, have I poured out my life. Those who are close to the lap of the earth, those who are made and shaped by her, who have learnt their first steps on the soil and who find final rest in her, of them all I am the friend. I am a poet, *ami kobi.*

—Translated by Dr. S.K. Ghose

Songs

THOU hast made me endless, such is thy pleasure. This frail vessel thou emptiest again and again, and fillest it ever with fresh life.

This little flute of a reed thou hast carried over hills and dales, and hast breathed through it melodies eternally new.

At the immortal touch of thy hands my little heart loses its limits in joy and gives birth to utterance ineffable.

Thy infinite gifts come to me only on these very small hands of mine. Ages pass, and still thou pourest, and still there is room to fill.

2

WHEN thou commandest me to sing it seems that my heart would break with pride; and I look to thy face, and tears come to my eyes.

All that is harsh and dissonant in my life melts into one sweet harmony—and my adoration spreads wings like a glad bird on its flight across the sea.

I know thou takest pleasure in my singing. I know that only as a singer I come before thy presence.

I touch by the edge of the far-spreading wing of my song thy feet which I could never aspire to reach.

Drunk with the joy of singing I forget myself and call thee friend who art my lord.

3

I KNOW not how thou singest, my master! I ever listen in silent amazement.

The light of thy music illumines the world. The life breath of thy music runs from sky to sky. The holy stream of thy music breaks through all stony obstacles and rushes on.

My heart longs to join in thy song, but vainly struggles for a voice. I would speak, but speech breaks not into song, and I cry out baffled.

Ah, thou hast made my heart captive in the endless meshes of thy music, my master!

4

LIFE of my life, I shall ever try to keep my body pure, knowing that thy living touch is upon all my limbs.

I shall ever try to keep all untruths out from my thoughts, knowing that thou art that truth which has kindled the light of reason in my mind.

I shall ever try to drive all evils away from my heart and keep my love in flower, knowing that thou hast thy seat in the inmost shrine of my heart.

And it shall be my endeavour to reveal thee in my actions, knowing it is thy power that gives me strength to act.

5

I ASK for a moment's indulgence to sit by thy side. The works that I have in hand I will finish afterwards.

Away from the sight of thy face my heart knows no rest nor respite, and my work becomes an endless toil in a shoreless sea of toil.

Today the summer has come at my window with its sighs and murmurs; and the bees are plying their minstrelsy at the court of the flowering grove.

Now it is time to sit quiet, face to face with thee, and to sing dedication of life in this silent and overflowing leisure.

6

PLUCK this little flower and take it, delay not! I fear lest it droop and drop into the dust.

It may not find a place in thy garland, but honour it with a touch of pain from thy hand and pluck it. I fear lest the day end before I am aware, and the time of offering go by.

Though its colour be not deep and its smell be faint, use this flower in thy service and pluck it while there is time.

7

MY song has put off her adornments. She has no pride of dress and decoration. Ornaments would mar our union; they would come between thee and me; their jingling would drown thy whispers.

My poet's vanity dies in shame before thy sight. 0 master poet, I have sat down at thy feet. Only let me make my life simple and straight, like a flute of reed for thee to fill with music.

8

THE child who is decked with prince's robes and who has jewelled chains round his neck loses all pleasure in his play; his dress hampers him at every step.

In fear that it may be frayed, or stained with dust, he keeps himself from the world, and is afraid even to move.

Mother, it is no gain, thy bondage of finery, if it keep one shut off from the healthful dust of the earth, if it rob one of the right of entrance to the great fair of common human life.

9

0 FOOL, to try to carry thyself upon thy own shoulders! 0 beggar, to come to beg at thy own door!

Leave all thy burdens on his hands who can bear all, and never look behind in regret.

Thy desire at once puts out the light from the lamp it touches with its breath. It is unholy—take not thy gifts through its unclean hands. Accept only what is offered by sacred love.

10

HERE is thy footstool and there rest thy feet where live the poorest, and lowliest, and lost.

When I try to bow to thee, my obeisance cannot reach down to the depth where thy feet rest among the poorest, and lowliest, and lost.

Pride can never approach to where thou walkest in the clothes of the humble among the poorest, and lowliest, and lost.

My heart can never find its way to where thou keepest company with the companionless among the poorest, the lowliest, and the lost.

11

LEAVE this chanting and singing and telling of beads! Whom dost thou worship in this lonely dark corner of a temple with doors all shut? Open thine eyes and see thy God is not before thee!

He is there where the tiller is tilling the hard ground and where the pathmaker is breaking stones. He is with them in sun and in shower, and his garment is covered with dust. Put off thy holy mantle and even like him come down on the dusty soil!

Deliverance? Where is this deliverance to be found? Our master himself has joyfully taken upon him the bonds of creation; he is bound with us all for ever.

Come out of thy meditation and leave aside thy flowers and incense! What harm is there if thy clothes become tattered and stained? Meet him and stand by him in toil and in sweat of thy brow.

12

THE time that my jounery takes is long and the way of it long.

I came out on the chariot of the first gleam of light, and pursued my voyage through the wildernesses of worlds leaving my track on many a star and planet.

It is the most distant course that comes nearest to thyself, and that training is the most intricate which leads to the utter simplicity of a tune.

The traveller has to knock at every alien door to come

to his own, and one has to wander through all the outer worlds to reach the innermost shrine at the end.

My eyes strayed far and wide before I shut them and said 'Here art thou!'

The question and the cry 'Oh, where?' melt into tears of a thousand streams and deluge the world with the flood of the assurance 'I am!'

13

THE song that I came to sing remains unsung to this day.

I have spent my days in stringing and in unstringing my instrument.

The time has not come true, the words have not been rightly set; only there is the agony of wishing in my heart.

The blossom has not opened; only the wind is sighing by.

I have not seen his face, nor have I listened to his voice; only I have heard his gentle footsteps from the road before my house.

The livelong day has passed in spreading his seat on the floor; but the lamp has not been lit and I cannot ask him into my house.

I live in the hope of meeting with him; but this meeting is not yet.

14

MY desires are many and my cry is pitiful, but ever didst thou save me by hard refusals; and this strong mercy has been wrought into my life through and through.

Day by day thou art making me worthy of the simple, great gifts that thou gavest to me unasked—this sky and the light, this body and the life and the mind—saving me from perils of overmuch desire.

There are times when I languidly linger and times when I awaken and hurry in search of my goal; but cruelly thou hidest thyself from before me.

Day by day thou art making me worthy of thy full acceptance by refusing me ever and anon, saving me from the perils of weak, uncertain desire.

15

I AM here to sing thee songs. In this hall of thine 1 have a corner seat.

In thy world 1 have no work to do; my useless life can only break out in tunes without a purpose.

When the hour strikes for thy silent worship at the dark temple of midnight, command me, my master, to stand before thee to sing.

When in the morning air the golden harp is tuned, honour me, commanding my presence.

16

I HAVE had my invitation to this world's festival, and thus my life has been blessed. My eyes have seen and my ears have heard.

It was my part at this feast to play upon my instrument, and I have done all I could.

Now, I ask, has the time come at last when I may go in and see thy face and offer thee my silent salutation?

17

I AM only waiting for love to give myself up at last into his hands. That is why it is so late and why I have been guilty of such omissions.

They come with their laws and their codes to bind me fast; but I evade them ever, for I am only waiting for love to give myself up at last into his hands.

People blame me and call me heedless; I doubt not they are right in their blame.

The market day is over and work is all done for the busy. Those who came to call me in vain have gone back in anger. I am only waiting for love to give myself up at last into his hands.

18

CLOUDS heap upon clouds and it darkens. Ah, love, why dost thou let me wait outside at the door all alone?

In the busy moments of the noontide work I am with the crowd, but on this dark lonely day it is only for thee that I hope.

If thou showest me not thy face, if thou leavest me wholly aside, I know not how I am to pass these long, rainy hours.

I keep gazing on the far-away gloom of the sky, and my heart wanders wailing with the restless wind.

19

IF thou speakest not I will fill my heart with thy silence and endure it. I will keep still and wait like the night with starry vigil and its head bent low with patience.

The morning will surely come, the darkness will vanish, and thy voice pour down in golden streams breaking through the sky.

Then thy words will take wing in songs from every one of my birds' nests, and thy melodies will break forth in flowers in all my forest groves.

20

ON the day when the lotus bloomed, alas, my mind was straying, and I knew it not. My basket was empty and the flower remained unheeded.

Only now and again a sadness fell upon me, and I started up from my dream and felt a sweet trace of a strange fragrance in the south wind.

That vague sweetness made my heart ache with longing and it seemed to me that it was the eager breath of the summer seeking for its completion.

I knew not then that it was so near, that it was mine, and that this perfect sweetness had blossomed in the depth of my own heart.

21

I MUST launch out my boat. The languid hours pass by on the shore—Alas for me!

The spring has done its flowering and taken leave. And now with the burden of faded futile flowers I wait and linger.

The waves have become clamorous, and upon the bank in the shady lane the yellow leaves flutter and fall.

What emptiness do you gaze upon! Do you not feel a thrill passing through the air with the notes of the far-away song floating from the other shore?

22

IN the deep shadows of the rainy July, with secret steps, thou walkest, silent as night, eluding all watchers.

Today the morning has closed its eyes, heedless of the insistent calls of the loud east wind, and a thick veil has been drawn over the ever-wakeful blue sky.

The woodlands have hushed their songs, and doors are all shut at every house. Thou art the solitary wayfarer in this deserted street. Oh my only friend, my best beloved, the gates are open in my house—do not pass by like a dream.

23

ART thou abroad on this stormy night on thy journey of love, my friend? The sky groans like one in despair.

I have no sleep tonight. Ever and again I open my door and look out on the darkness, my friend!

I can see nothing before me. I wonder where lies thy path!

By what dim shore of the ink-black river, by what far edge of the frowning forest, through what mazy depth of gloom art thou threading thy course to come to me, my friend?

24

IF the day is done, if birds sing no more, if the wind has flagged and tired, then draw the veil of darkness thick upon me, even as thou hast wrapt the earth with the coverlet of sleep and tenderly closed the petals of the drooping lotus at dusk.

From the traveller, whose sack of provisions is empty before the voyage is ended, whose garment is torn and dustladen, whose strength is exhausted, remove shame and poverty, and renew his life like a flower under the cover of thy kindly night.

25

IN the night of weariness let me give myself up to sleep without struggle, resting my trust upon thee.

Let me not force my flagging spirit into a poor preparation for thy worship.

It is thou who drawest the veil of night upon the tired eyes of the day to renew its sight in a fresher gladness of awakening.

26

HE came and sat by my side but I woke not. What a cursed sleep it was, 0 miserable me!

He came when the night was still; he had his harp in his hands, and my dreams became resonant with its melodies.

Alas, why are my nights all thus lost? Ah, why do I ever miss his sight whose breath touches my sleep?

27

LIGHT, oh where is the light? Kindle it with the burning fire of desire!

There is the lamp but never a flicker of a flame— is such thy fate, my heart? Ah, death were better by far for thee!

Misery knocks at thy door, and her message is that thy lord is wakeful, and he calls thee to the love-tryst through the darkness of night.

The sky is overcast with clouds and the rain is ceaseless.

I know not what this is that stirs in me— I know not its meaning.

A moment's flash of lightning drags down a deeper gloom on my sight, and my heart gropes for the path to where the music of the night calls me.

Light, oh where is the light? Kindle it with the burning fire of desire? It thunders and the wind rushes screaming through the void. The night is black as a black stone. Let not the hours pass by in the dark. Kindle the lamp of love with thy life.

28

OBSTINATE are the trammels, but my heart aches when I try to break them.

Freedom is all I want, but to hope for it I feel ashamed.

I am certain that priceless wealth is in thee, and that thou art my best friend, but I have not the heart to sweep away the tinsel that fills my room.

The shroud that covers me is a shroud of dust and death; I hate it, yet hug it in love.

My debts are large, my failures great, my shame secret and heavy; yet when 1 come to ask for my good, I quake in fear lest my prayer be granted.

29

HE whom I enclose with my name is weeping in this dungeon. I am ever busy building this wall all around; and as this wall goes up into the sky day by day I lose sight of my true being in its dark shadow.

I take pride in this great wall, and I plaster it with dust and sand lest a least hole should be left in this name; and for all the care I take I lose sight of my true being.

30

I CAME out alone on my way to my tryst. But who is this that follows me in the silent dark?

I move aside to avoid his presence but I escape him not.

He makes the dust rise from the earth with his swagger; he adds his loud voice to every word that I utter.

He is my own little self, my lord, he knows no shame; but I am ashamed to come to thy door in his company.

31

"PRISONER, tell me, who was it that bound you?'

'It was my master' said the prisoner. 'I thought I could outdo everybody in the world in wealth and power, and I amassed in my own treasure-house the money due to my king. When sleep overcame me I lay upon the bed that was for my lord, and on waking up I found I was a prisoner in my own treasure-house.'

'Prisoner, tell me, who was it that wrought this unbreakable chain?'

'It was I,' said the prisoner, 'who forged this chain very carefully. I thought my invincible power would hold the world captive, leaving me in a freedom undisturbed. Thus night and day I worked at the chain with huge fires and cruel hard strokes. When at last the work was done and the links were complete and unbreakable, I found that it held me in its grip.'

32

BY all means they try to hold me secure who love me in this world. But it is otherwise with thy love which is greater than theirs, and thou keepest me free.

Lest I forget them they never venture to leave me alone. But day passes by after day and thou art not seen.

If I call not thee in my prayers, if I keep not thee in my heart, thy love for me still waits for my love.

33

WHEN it was day they came into my house and said,

*We shall only take the smallest room here.'

They said, 'We shall help you in the worship of your God and humbly accept only our own share of his grace'; and then they took their seat in a corner and they sat quiet and meek.

But in the darkness of night I find they break into my sacred shrine, strong and turbulent, and snatch with unholy greed the offerings from God's altar.

34

LET only that little be left of me whereby I may name thee my all.

Let only that little be left of my will whereby I may feel thee on every side, and come to thee in everything, and offer to thee my love every moment.

Let only that little be left of me whereby I may never hide thee.

Let only that little of my fetters be left whereby I am bound with thy will, and thy purpose is carried out in my life—and that is the fetter of thy love.

35

WHERE the mind is without fear and the head is held high;

Where knowledge is free;

Where the world has not been broken up into fragments by narrow domestic walls;

Where words come out from the depth of truth;

Where tireless striving stretches its arms towards perfection.

Where the clear stream of reason has not lost its way into the dreary desert sand of dead habit;

Where the mind is led forward by thee into ever-widening thought and action—

Into that heaven of freedom, my Father, let my country awake

36

THIS is my prayer to thee, my lord—strike, strike at the root of penury in my heart.

Give me the strength lightly to bear my joys and sorrows.

Give me the strength to make my love fruitful in service.

Give me the strength never to disown the poor or bend my knees before insolent might.

Give me the strength to raise my mind high above daily trifles.

And give me the strength to surrender my strength to thy will with love.

37

I THOUGHT that my voyage had come to its end at the last limit of my power,—that the path before me was closed, that provisions were exhausted and the time come to take shelter in a silent obscurity.

But I find that thy will knows no end in me. And when old words die out on the tongue, new melodies break forth from the heart; and where the old tracks are lost, new country is revealed with its wonders.

38

THAT I want thee, only thee—let my heart repeat without end. All desires that distract me, day and night, are false and empty to the core.

As the night keeps hidden in its gloom the petition for light, even thus in the depth of my unconsciousness rings the cry—'I want thee, only thee.'

As the storm still seeks its end in peace when it strikes against peace with all its might, even thus my rebellion strikes against thy love and still its cry is—'I want thee, only thee.'

39

WHEN the heart is hard and parched up, come upon me with a shower of mercy.

When grace is lost from life, come with a burst of song.

When tumultuous work raises its din on all sides shutting me out from beyond, come to me, my lord of silence, with thy peace and rest.

When my beggarly heart sits crouched, shut up in a corner, break open the door, my king, and come with the ceremony of a king.

When desire blinds the mind with delusion and dust, 0 thou holy one, thou wakeful, come with thy light and thy thunder.

40

THE rain has held back for days and days, my God, in my arid heart. The horizon is fiercely naked—not the thinnest cover of a soft cloud, not the vaguest hint of a distant cool shower.

Send thy angry storm, dark with death, if it is thy wish, and with lashes of lightning startle the sky from end to end.

But call back, my lord, call back this pervading silent heat, still and keen and cruel, burning the heart with dire despair.

Let the cloud of grace bend low from above like the tearful look of the mother on the day of the father's wrath.

41

WHERE dost thou stand behind them all, my lover, hiding thyself in the shadows? They push thee and pass thee by on the dusty road, taking thee for naught. I wait here weary hours spreading my offerings for thee, while passers-by come and take my flowers, one by one, and my basket is nearly empty.

The morning time is past, and the noon. In the shade of evening my eyes are drowsy with sleep. Men going home glance at me and smile and fill me with shame. I sit like a beggar maid, drawing my skirt over my face, and when they ask me, what it is I want, I drop my eyes and answer them not.

Oh, how, indeed, could I tell them that for thee I wait,

and that thou hast promised to come. How could I utter for shame that I keep for my dowry this poverty. Ah, I hug this pride in the secret of my heart.

I sit on the grass and gaze upon the sky and dream of the sudden splendour of thy coming—all the lights ablaze, golden pennons flying over thy car, and they at the roadside standing agape, when they see thee come down from thy seat to raise me from the dust, and set at thy side this ragged beggar girl a tremble with shame and pride, like a creeper in a summer breeze.

But time glides on and still no sound of the wheels of thy chariot. Many a procession passes by with noise and shouts and glamour of glory. Is it only thou who wouldst stand in the shadow silent and behind them all? And only I who would wait and weep and wear out my heart in vain longing?

42

EARLY in the day it was whispered that we should sail in a boat, only thou and I, and never a soul in the world would know of this our pilgrimage to no country and to no end.

In that shoreless ocean, at thy silently listening smile my songs would swell in melodies, free as waves, free from all bondage of words.

Is the time not come yet? Are there works still to do? Lo, the evening has come down upon the shore and in the fading light the seabirds come flying to their nests.

Who knows when the chains will be off, and the boat, like the last glimmer of sunset, vanish into the night?

43

THE day was when I did not keep myself in readiness for thee; and entering my heart unbidden even as one of the common crowd, unknown to me, my king, thou didst press the signet of eternity upon many a fleeting moment of my life.

And today when by chance I light upon them and see thy signature, I find they have lain scattered in the dust mixed with the memory of joys and sorrows of my trivial days forgotten.

Thou didst not turn in contempt from my childish play among dust, and the steps that I heard in my playroom are the same that are echoing from star to star.

44

THIS is my delight, thus to wait and watch at the wayside where shadow chases light and the rain comes in the wake of the summer.

Messengers, with tidings from unknown skies, greet me and speed along the road. My heart is glad within, and the breath of the passing breeze is sweet.

From dawn till dusk I sit here before my door, and I know that of a sudden the happy moment will arrive when I shall see.

In the meanwhile I smile and I sing all alone. In the meanwhile the air is filling with the perfume of promise.

45

HAVE you not heard his silent steps? He comes, comes, ever comes.

Every moment and every age, every day and every night he comes, comes, ever comes.

Many a song have I sung in many a mood of mind, but all their notes have always proclaimed, 'He comes, comes, ever comes.'

In the fragrant days of sunny April through the forest path he comes, comes, ever comes.

In the rainy gloom of July nights on the thundering chariot of clouds he comes, comes, ever comes.

In sorrow after sorrow it is his steps that press upon my heart, and it is the golden touch of his feet that makes my joy to shine.

46

I KNOW not from what distant time thou art ever coming nearer to meet me. Thy sun and stars can never keep thee hidden from me for aye.

In many a morning and eve thy footsteps have been heard and thy messenger has come within my heart and called me in secret.

I know not why today my life is all astir, and a feeling of tremulous joy is passing through my heart.

It is as if the time were come to wind up my work. and I feel in the air a faint smell of thy sweet presence.

47

THE night is nearly spent waiting for him in vain. I fear lest in the morning he suddenly come to my door when I have fallen asleep wearied out. Oh friends, leave the way open to him—forbid him not.

If the sound of his steps does not wake me, do not try to rouse me, I pray. I wish not to be called from my sleep by the clamorous choir of birds, by the riot of wind at the festival of morning light. Let me sleep undisturbed even if my lord comes of a sudden to my door.

Ah, my sleep, precious sleep, which only waits for his touch to vanish. Ah, my closed eyes that would open their lids only to the light of his smile when he stands before me like a dream emerging from the darkness of sleep.

Let him appear before my sight as the first of all lights and all forms. The first thrill of joy to my awakened soul let it come from his glance. And let my return to myself be immediate return to him.

48

THE morning sea of silence broke into ripples of bird songs; and the flowers were all merry by the roadside; and the wealth of gold was scattered through the rift of the clouds while we busily went on our way and paid no heed.

We sang no glad songs nor played; we went not to the village for barter; we spoke not a word nor smiled; we lingered not on the way. We quickened our pace more and more as the time sped by.

The sun rose to the mid sky and doves cooed in the shade. Withered leaves danced and whirled in the hot air of noon. The shepherd boy drowsed and dreamed in the shadow of the banyan tree, and I laid myself down by the water and stretched my tired limbs on the grass.

My companions laughed at me in scorn; they held their heads high and hurried on; they never looked back nor rested; they vanished in the distant blue haze. They crossed many meadows and hills, and passed through strange, far-away countries. All honour to you, heroic host of the interminable path! Mockery and reproach pricked me to rise, but found no response in me. I gave myself up for lost in the depth of a glad humiliation—in the shadow of a dim delight.

The repose of the sun-embroidered green gloom slowly spread over my heart. I forgot for what I had travelled, and I surrendered my mind without struggle to the maze of shadows and songs.

At last, when I woke from my slumber and opened my eyes, I saw thee standing by me, flooding my sleep with thy smile. How I had feared that the path was long and wearisome, and the struggle to reach thee was hard!

49

YOU came down from your throne and stood at my cottage door.

I was singing all alone in a corner, and the melody caught your ear. You came down and stood at my cottage door.

Masters are many in your hall, and songs are sung there at all hours. But the simple carol of this novice struck at your love. One plaintive little strain mingled with the great music of the world, and with a flower for a prize you came down and stopped at my cottage door.

50

I HAD gone a-begging from door to door in the village path, when thy golden chariot appeared in the distance like a gorgeous dream and I wondered who was this King of all kings!

My hopes rose high and methought my evil days were at an end, and 1 stood waiting for alms to be given unasked and for wealth scattered on all sides in the dust.

The chariot stopped where I stood. Thy glance fell on me and thou earnest down with a smile. I felt that the luck of my life had come at last. Then of a sudden thou didst hold out thy right hand and say 'What hast thou to give to me?'

Ah, what a kingly jest was it to open thy palm to a beggar to beg! I was confused and stood undecided, and then from my wallet I slowly took out the least little grain of corn and gave it to thee.

But how great my surprise when at the day's end I emptied my bag on the floor to find a least little gram of gold among the poor heap. I bitterly wept and wished that I had the heart to give thee my all.

51

THE night darkened. Our day's works had been done. We thought that the last guest had arrived for the night and the doors in the village were all shut. Only some said the king was to come. We laughed and said 'No, it cannot be!'

It seemed there were knocks at the door and we said it was nothing but the wind. We put out the lamps and lay down to sleep. Only some said, 'It is the messenger!' We laughed and said 'No, it must be the wind!'

There came a sound in the dead of the night. We sleepily thought it was the distant thunder. The earth shook, the walls rocked, and it troubled us in our sleep. Only some said it was the sound of wheels. We said in a drowsy

murmur, 'No, it must be the rumbling of clouds!'

The night was still dark when the drum sounded. The voice came 'Wake up! delay not!' We pressed our hands on our hearts and shuddered with fear. Some said, 'Lo, there is the king's flag!' We stood up on our feet and cried, 'There is no time for delay!'

The king has come—but where are the lights, where are the wreaths? Where is the throne to seat him? Oh, shame! Oh utter shame! Where is the hall, the decorations? Someone has said, 'Vain is this cry! Greet him with empty hands, lead him into thy rooms all bare!'

Open the doors, let the conch-shells be sounded! In the depth of the night has come the king of our dark, dreary house. The thunder roars in the sky. The darkness shudders with lightning. Bring out thy tattered piece of mat and spread it in the courtyard. With the storm has come of a sudden our king of the fearful night.

52

I THOUGHT I should ask of thee—but I dared not—the rose wreath thou hadst on they neck. Thus I waited for the morning, when thou didst depart, to find a few fragments on the bed. And like a beggar I searched in the dawn only for a stray petal or two.

Ah me, what is it I find? What token left of thy love? It is no flower, no spices, no vase of perfumed water. It is thy mighty sword, flashing as a flame, heavy as a bolt of thunder. The young light of morning comes through the window and spreads itself upon thy bed. The morning bird twitters and asks, 'Woman, what hast thou got?' No, it is no flower, nor spices, nor vase of perfumed water—it is thy dreadful sword.

I sit and muse in wonder, what gift is this of thine. I can find no place where to hide it. I am ashamed to wear it, frail as I am, and it hurts me when I press it to my bosom. Yet shall I bear in my heart this honour of the burden of pain, this gift of thine.

From now there shall be no fear left for me in this world, and thou shall be victorious in all my strife. Thou hast left death for my companion and 1 shall crown him with my life. Thy sword is with me to cut asunder my bonds, and there shall be no fear left for me in the world.

From now I leave off all petty decorations. Lord of my heart, no more shall there be for me waiting and weeping in corners, no more coyness and sweetness of demeanour. Thou hast given me thy sword for adornment. No more doll's decorations for me!

53

BEAUTIFUL is thy wristlet, decked with stars and cunningly wrought in myriad-coloured jewels. But more beautiful to me thy sword with its curve of lightning like the outspread wings of the divine bird of Vishnu, perfectly poised in the angry red light of the sunset.

It quivers like the one last response of life in ecstasy of pain at the final stroke of death; it shines like the pure flame of being burning up earthly sense with one fierce flash.

Beautiful is thy wristlet, decked with starry gems; but thy sword, 0 lord of thunder, is wrought with uttermost beauty, terrible to behold or to think of.

55

I ASKED nothing from thee; I uttered not my name to thine ear. When thou took'st thy leave I stood silent. I was alone by the well where the shadow of the tree fell aslant, and the women had gone home with their brown earthen pitchers full to the brim. They called me and shouted, 'Come with us, the morning is wearing on to noon.' But I languidly lingered awhile lost in the midst of vague musings.

I heard not thy steps as thou camest. Thine eyes were sad when they fell on me; thy voice was tired as thou spokest low—'Ah, I am a thirsty traveller.' I started up from my day-dreams and poured water from my jar on thy joined palms.

The leaves rustled overhead; the cuckoo sang from the unseen dark, and perfume of *babla* flowers came from the bend of the road.

I stood speechless with shame when my name thou didst ask. Indeed, what had I done for thee to keep me in remembrance? But the memory that I could give water to thee to allay thy thirst will cling to my heart and endfold it in sweetness. The morning hour is late, the bird sings in weary notes, *neem* leaves rustle overhead and I sit and think and think.

55

LANGUOR is upon your heart and the slumber is still on your eyes.

Has not the word come to you that the flower is reigning in splendour among thorns? Wake, oh awaken! Let not the time pass in vain!

At the end of the stony path, in the country of virgin solitude, my friend is sitting all alone. Deceive him not. Wake, oh awaken!

What if the sky pants and trembles with the heat of the midday sun—what if the burning sand spreads its mantle of thirst—

Is there no joy in the deep of your heart? At every footfall of yours, will not the harp of the road break out in the sweet music of pain?

56

THUS it is that thy joy in me is so full. Thus it is that thou hast come down to me. 0 thou lord of all heavens, where would be thy love if I were not?

Thou hast taken me as thy partner of all this wealth. In my heart is the endless play of thy delight. In my life thy will is ever taking shape.

And for this, thou who art the King of kings hast decked thyself in beauty to captivate my heart. And for this thy love loses itself in the love of thy lover, and there art thou seen in the perfect union of two.

57

LIGHT, my light, the world-filling light, the eye-kissing light, heart-sweetening light!

Ah, the light dances, my darling, at the centre of my life; the light strikes, my darling, the chords of my love; the sky opens, the wind runs wild, laughter passes over the earth.

The butterflies spread their sails on the sea of light. Lilies and jasmines surge up on the crest of the waves of light.

The light is shattered into gold on every cloud, my darling, and it scatters gems in profusion.

Mirth spreads from leaf to leaf, my darling, and gladness without measure. The heaven's river has drowned its banks and the flood of joy is abroad.

58

LET all the strains of joy mingle in my last song—the joy that makes the earth flow over in the riotous excess of the grass, the joy that sets the twin brothers, life and death, dancing over the wide world, the joy that sweeps in with the tempest, shaking and waking all life with laughter, the joy that sits still with its tears on the open red lotus of pain, and the joy that throws everything it has upon the dust, and knows not a word.

59

YES, I know, this is nothing but thy love, 0 beloved of my heart—this golden light that dances upon the leaves, these idle clouds sailing across the sky, this passing breeze leaving its coolness upon my forehead.

The morning light has flooded my eyes—this is thy message to my heart. Thy face is bent from above, thy eyes look down on my eyes, and my heart has touched thy feet.

60

ON the seashore of endless worlds children meet. The infinite sky is motionless overhead and the restless water is boisterous. On the seashore of endless worlds children meet with shouts and dances.

They build their houses with sand and they play with empty shells. With withered leaves they weave their boats and smilingly float them on the vast deep. Children have their play on the seashore of worlds.

They know not how to swim, they know not how to cast nets. Pearl fishers dive for pearls, merchants sail in their ships, while children gather pebbles and scatter them again. They seek not for hidden treasures, they know not how to cast nets.

The sea surges up with laughter and pale gleams the smile of the sea beach. Death-dealing waves sing meaningless ballads to the children, even like a mother while rocking her baby's cradle. The sea plays with children, and pale gleams the smile of the sea beach.

On the seashore of endless worlds children meet. Tempest roams in the pathless sky, ships get wrecked in the trackless water, death is abroad and children play. On the seashore of endless worlds is the great meeting of children.

61

THE sleep that flits on baby's eyes—does anybody know from where it comes? Yes, there is a rumour that it has its dwelling where, in the fairy village among shadows of the forest dimly lit with glow-worms, there hang two timid buds of enchantment. From there it comes to kiss baby's eyes.

The smile that flickers on baby's lips when he sleeps—does anybody know where it was born? Yes, there is a rumour that a young pale beam of a crescent moon touched the edge of a vanishing autumn cloud, and there the smile was first born in the dream of a dew-washed morning—

the smile that flickers on baby's lips when he sleeps.

The sweet, soft freshness that blooms on baby's limbs—does anybody know where it was hidden so long? Yes, when the mother was a young girl it lay pervading her heart in tender and silent mystery of love—the sweet, soft freshness that has bloomed on baby's limbs.

62

WHEN I bring to you coloured toys, my child, I understand why there is such a play of colours on clouds, on water, and why flowers are painted in tints—when I give coloured toys to you, my child.

When I sing to make you dance I truly know why there is music in leaves, and why waves send their chorus of voices to the heart of the listening earth—when I sing to make you dance.

When I bring sweet things to your greedy hands I know why there is honey in the cup of the flower and why fruits are secretly filled with sweet juice—when I bring sweet things to your greedy hands.

When I kiss your face to make you smile, my darling, I surely understand what pleasure streams from the sky in morning light, and what delight that is which the summer breeze brings to my body—when I kiss you to make you smile.

63

THOU hast made me known to friend whom I knew not. Thou hast given me seats in homes not my own. Thou hast brought the distant near and made a brother of the stranger.

I am uneasy at heart when I have to leave my accustomed shelter; I forget that there abides the old in the new, and that there also thou abidest.

Through birth and death, in this world or in others,

wherever thou leadest me it is thou, the same, the one companion of my endless life who ever linkest my heart with bonds of joy to the unfamiliar.

When one knows thee, then alien there is none, then no door is shut. Oh, grant me my prayer that I may never lose the bliss of the touch of the one in the play of the many.

64

ON the slope of the desolate river among tall grasses I asked her, *Maiden, where do you go shading your lamp with your mantle? My house is all dark and lonesome lend me your light!' She raised her dark eyes for a moment and looked at my face through the dusk. 'I have come to the river,' she said, 'to float my lamp on the stream. When the daylight wanes in the west; I stood alone among tall grasses and watched the timid flame of her lamp uselessly drifting in the tide.

In the silence of gathering night I asked her, 'Maiden, your lights are all lit—then where do you go with your lamp? My house is all dark and lonesome—lend me your light' She raised her dark eyes on my face and stood for a moment doubtful. 'I have come,' she said at last, 'to dedicate my lamp to the sky.' I stood and watched her light uselessly burning in the void.

In the moonless gloom of midnight I asked her, 'Maiden, what is your quest, holding the lamp near your heart? My house is all dark and lonesome—lend me your light.' She stopped for a minute and thought and gazed at my face in the dark. 'I have brought my light,' she said, 'to join the carnival of lamps.' I stood and watched her little lamp uselessly lost among lights.

65

WHAT divine drink wouldst thou have, my God, from this overflowing cup of life?

My poet, is it thy delight to see thy creation through my eyes and to stand at the portals of my ears silently to listen to thine own eternal harmony?

Thy world is weaving words in my mind and thy joy is adding music to them. Thou givest thyself to me in love and then feelest thine own entire sweetness in me.

66

SHE who ever had remained in the depth of my being, in the twilight of gleams and of glimpses; she who never opened her veils in the morning light, will be my last gift to thee, my God, folded in my final song.

Words have wooed yet failed to win her; persuasion has stretched to her its eager arms in vain.

I have roamed from country to country keeping her in the core of my heart, and around her have risen and fallen the growth and decay of my life.

Over my thoughts and actions, my slumbers and dreams, she reigned yet dwelled alone and apart.

Many a man knocked at my door and asked for her and turned away in despair.

There was none in the world who ever saw her face to face, and she remained in her loneliness waiting for thy recognition.

67

THOU art the sky and thou art the nest as well.

0 thou beautiful, there in the nest it is thy love that encloses the soul with colours and sounds and odours.

There comes the morning with the golden basket in her right hand bearing the wreath of beauty, silently to crown the earth.

And there comes the evening over the lonely meadows deserted by herds, through trackless paths, carrying cool draughts of peace in her golden pitcher from the western ocean of rest.

But there, where spreads the infinite sky for the soul to take her flight in, reigns the stainless white radiance. There is no day nor night, nor form nor colour, and never, never a word.

68

THY sunbeam comes upon this earth of mine with arms outstretched and stands at my door the livelong day to carry back to thy feet clouds made of my tears and sighs and songs.

With fond delight thou wrappest about thy starry breast that mantle of misty cloud, turning it into numberless shapes and folds and colouring it with hues everhanging.

It is so light and so fleeting, tender and tearful and dark, that is why thou lovest it, O thou spotless and serene, and that is why it may cover thy awful white light with its pathetic shadows.

69

THE same steam of life that runs through my veins night and day runs through the world and dances in rhythmic measures.

It is the same life that shoots in joy through the dust of the earth in numberless blades of grass and breaks into tumultuous waves of leaves and flowers.

It is the same life that is rocked in the ocean cradle of birth and of death, in ebb and in flow.

I feel my limbs are made glorious by the touch of this world of life. And my pride is from the life-throb of ages dancing in my blood this moment.

70

Is it beyond thee to be glad with the gladness of this rhythm? To be tossed and lost and broken in the whirl of this fearful joy?

All things rush on, they stop not, they look not behind, no power can hold them back, they rush on.

Keeping steps with that restless, rapid music, seasons come dancing and pass away—colours, tunes, and perfumes pour in endless cascades in the abounding joy that scatters and gives up and dies every moment.

71

THAT I should make much of myself and turn it on all sides, thus casting coloured shadows on thy radiance—such is thy maya.

Thou settest a barrier in thine own being and then callest thy severed self in myriad notes. This thy self-separation has taken body in me.

The poignant song is echoed through all the sky in many-coloured tears and smiles, alarms and hopes; waves rise up and sink again, dreams break and form. In me is thy own defeat of self.

This screen that thou hast raised is painted with innumerable figures with the brush of the night and the day. Behind it thy seat is woven in wondrous mysteries of curves, casting away all barren lines of straightness.

The great pageant of thee and me has overspread the sky. With the tune of thee and me all the air is vibrant, and all ages pass with the hiding and seeking of thee and me.

72

HE it is, the innermost one, who awakens my being with his deep hidden touches.

He it is who puts his enchantment upon these eyes and joyfully plays on the chords of my heart in varied cadence of pleasure and pain.

He it is who weaves the web of this maya in evanescent hues of gold and silver, blue and green, and lets peep out through the folds his feet, at whose touch I forget myself.

Days come and ages pass, and it is ever he who moves my heart in many a name, in many a guise, in many a rapture of joy and of sorrow.

73

DELIVERANCE is not for me in renunciation. I feel the embrace of freedom in a thousand bonds of delight.

Thou ever pourest for me the fresh draught of thy wine of various colours and fragrance, filling this earthen vessel to the brim.

My world will light its hundred different lamps with thy flame and place them before the altar of thy temple.

No, I will never shut the doors of my senses. The delights of sight and hearing and touch will bear thy delight.

Yes, all my illusions will burn into illumination of joy, and all my desires ripen into fruits of love.

74

THE day is no more, the shadow is upon the earth. It is time that I go to the stream to fill my pitcher.

The evening air is eager with the sad music of the water. Ah, it calls me out into the dusk. In the lonely lane there is no passer-by, the wind is up, the ripples are rampant in the river.

I know not if I shall come back home. I know not whom I shall chance to meet. There at the fording in the little boat the unknown man plays upon his lute.

75

THY gifts to us mortals fulfil all our needs and yet run back to thee undiminished.

The river has its everyday work to do and hastens through fields and hamlets; yet its incessant stream winds towards the washing of thy feet.

The flower sweetens the air with its perfume; yet its last service is to offer itself to thee.

Thy worship does not impoverish the world.

From the words of the poet men take what meanings please them; yet their last meaning points to thee.

76

DAY after day, 0 lord of my life, shall I stand before thee face to face. With folded hands, O lord of all worlds, shall I stand before thee face to face.

Under the great sky in solitude and silence, with humble heart shall I stand before thee face to face.

In this laborious world of thine, tumultuous with toil and with struggle, among hurrying crowds shall I stand before thee face to face.

And when my work shall be done in this world, O King of kings, alone and speechless shall I stand before thee face to face.

77

I KNOW thee as my God and stand apart—I do not know thee as my own and come closer. I know thee as my father and bow before thy feet—I do not grasp thy hand as my friend's.

I stand not where thou comest down and ownest thyself as mine, there to clasp thee to my heart and take thee as my comrade.

Thou art the Brother amongst my brothers, but I heed them not, I divide not my earnings with them, thus sharing my all with thee.

In pleasure and in pain I stand not by the side of men, and thus stand by thee. I shrink to give up my life, and thus do not plunge into the great waters of life.

78

WHEN the creation was new and all the stars shone in their first splendour, the gods held their assembly in the sky and sang 'Oh, the picture of perfection! the joy unalloyed!'

But one cried of a sudden—'It seems that somewhere there is a break in the chain of light and one of the stars has been lost.'

The golden string of their harp snapped, their song stopped, and they cried in dismay—'Yes, that lost star was the best, she was the glory of all heavens!'

From that day the search is unceasing for her, and the cry goes on from one to the other that in her the world has lost its one joy?

Only in the deepest silence of night the stars smile and whisper among themselves—'Vain is this seeking? Unbroken perfection is overall!'

79

IF it is not my portion to meet thee in this my life then let me ever feel that I have missed thy sight— let me not forget for a moment, let me carry the pangs of this sorrow in my dreams and in my wakeful hours.

As my days pass in the crowded market of this world and my hands grow full with the daily profits, let me ever feel that I have gained nothing—let me not forget for a moment, let me carry the pangs of this sorrow in my dreams and in my wakeful hours.

When I sit by the roadside, tired and panting, when I spread my bed low in the dust, let me ever feel that the long journey is still before me—let me not forget for a moment, let me carry the pangs of this sorrow in my dreams and in my wakeful hours.

When my rooms have been decked out and the flutes sound and the laughter there is loud, let me ever feel that I have not invited thee to my house— let me not forget for a moment, let me carry the pangs of this sorrow in my dreams and in my wakeful hours.

80

I AM like a remnant of a cloud of autumn uselessly roaming in the sky, 0 my sun ever-glorious! Thy touch has not yet melted my vapour, making me one with thy light, and thus I count months and years separated from thee.

If this be thy wish and if this be thy play, then take this fleeting emptiness of mine, paint it with colours, gild it with gold, float it on the wanton wind and spread it in varied wonders.

And again when it shall be thy wish to end this play at night, I shall melt and vanish away in the dark, or it may be in a smile of the white morning, in a coolness of purity transparent.

81

ON many an idle day have I grieved over lost time. But it is never lost, my lord. Thou hast taken every moment of my life in thine own hands.

Hidden in the heart of things thou art nourishing seeds into sprouts, buds into blossoms, and ripening flowers into fruitfulness.

I was tired and sleeping on my idle bed and imagined all work had ceased. In the morning I woke up and found my garden full with wonders of flowers.

82

TIME is endless in thy hands, my lord. There is none to count thy minutes.

Days and nights pass and ages bloom and fade like flowers. Thou knowest how to wait.

Thy centuries follow each other perfecting a small wild flower.

We have no time to lose, and having no time we must scramble for our chances.

We are too poor to be late.

And thus it is that time goes by while I give it to every querulous man who claims it, and thine altar is empty of all offerings to the last.

At the end of the day I hasten in fear lest thy gate be shut; but I find that yet there is time.

83

MOTHER, I shall weave a chain of pearls for thy neck with my tears of sorrow.

The stars have wrought their anklets of light to deck thy feet, but mine will hang upon thy breast.

Wealth and fame come from thee and it is for thee to give or to withhold them. But this my sorrow is absolutely mine own, and when I bring it to thee as my offering thou rewardest me with the grace.

84

IT is the pang of separation that spread throughout the world and gives birth to shapes innumerable in the infinite sky.

It is this sorrow of separation that gazes in silence all night from star to star and becomes lyric among rustling leaves in the rainy darkness of July.

It is this overspreading pain that deepens into loves and desires, into sufferings and joys in human homes; and this it is that ever melts and flows in songs through my poet's heart.

85

WHEN the warriors came out first from their master's hall, where had they hid their power? Where were their armour and their arms?

They looked poor and helpless, and the arrows were showered upon them on the day they came out from their master's hall.

When the warriors marched back again to their master's hall where did they hide their power?

They had dropped the sword and dropped the bow and the arrow; peace was on their foreheads, and they had left the fruits of their life behind them on the day they marched back again to their master's hall.

86

DEATH, thy servant, is at my door. He has crossed the unknown sea and brought thy call to my home.

The night is dark and my heart is fearful—yet I will take up the lamp, open my gates and bow to him my welcome. It is thy messenger who stands at my door.

I will worship him with folded hands, and with tears. I will worship him placing at his feet the treasure of my heart.

He will go back with his errand done, leaving a dark shadow on my morning; and in my desolate home only my forlorn self will remain as my last offering to thee.

87

IN desperate hope I go and search for her in all the corners of my room; I find her not.

My house is small and what once has gone from it can never be regained.

But infinite is thy mansion, my lord, and seeking her I have come to thy door.

I stand under the golden canopy on thine evening sky and I lift my eager eyes to thy face.

I have come to the brink of eternity from which nothing can vanish—no hope, no happiness, no vision of a face seen through tears.

Oh, dip my emptied life into that ocean, plunge it into the deepest fullness. Let me for once feel that lost sweet touch in the allness of the universe.

88

DEITY of the ruined temple! The broken strings of *Vina* sing no more your praise. The bells in the evening proclaim not your time of worship. The air is still and silent about you.

In your desolate dwelling comes the vagrant spring breeze. It brings the tidings of flowers—the flowers that

for your worship are offered no more.

Your worshipper of old wanders ever longing for favour still refused. In the eventide, when fires and shadows mingle with the gloom of dust, he wearily comes back to the ruined temple with hunger in his heart.

Many a festival day comes to you in silence, deity of the ruined temple. Many a night of worship goes away with lamp unlit.

Many new images are built by masters of cunning art and carried to the holy stream of oblivion when their time is come.

Only the deity of the ruined temple remains unworshipped in deathless neglect.

89

NO more noisy, loud words from me—such is my master's will. Henceforth I deal in whispers. The speech of my heart will be carried on in murmurings of a song.

Men hasten to the King's market. All the buyers and sellers are there. But I have my untimely leave in the middle of the day, in the thick of work.

Let then the flowers come out in my garden, though it is not their time; and let the midday bees strike up their lazy hum.

Full many an hour have I spent in the strife of the good and the evil, but now it is the pleasure of my playmate of the empty days to draw my heart on to him; and I know not why is this sudden call to what useless inconsequence!

90

ON the day when death will knock at thy door what wilt thou offer to him?

Oh, I will set before my guest the full vessel of my life—I will never let him go with empty hands.

All the sweet vintage of all my autumn days and summer nights, all the earnings and gleanings of my busy

life will I place before him at the close of my days when death will knock at my door.

91

0 THOU the last fulfilment of life, Death, my death, come and whisper to me?

Day after day have I kept watch for thee; for thee have I borne the joys and pangs of life.

All that I am, that I have, that I hope and all my love have ever flowed towards thee in depth of secrecy. One final glance from thine eyes and my life will be ever thine own.

The flowers have been woven and the garland is ready for the bridegroom. After the wedding the bride shall leave her home and meet her lord alone in the solitude of night.

92

I KNOW that the day will come when my sight of this earth shall be lost, and life will take its leave in silence, drawing the last curtain over my eyes.

Yet stars will watch at night, and morning rise as before, and hours heave like sea waves casting up pleasures and pains.

When I think of this end of my moments, the barrier of the moments breaks and I see by the light of death thy world with its careless treasures. Rare is its lowliest seat, rare is its meanest of lives.

Things that I longed for in vain and things that I got—let them pass. Let me but truly possess the things that I ever spurned and overlooked.

93

I HAVE got my leave. Bid me farewell, my brothers! I bow to you all and take my departure.

Here I give back the keys of my door—and I give up all claims to my house. I only ask for last kind words from you.

We were neighbours for long, but I received more than

I could give. Now the day has dawned and the lamp that lit my dark corner is out. A summon has come and I am ready for my journey.

94

AT this time of my parting, wish me good luck, my friends! The sky is flushed with the dawn and my path lies beautiful.

Ask not what I have with me to take there. I start on my journey with empty hands and expectant heart.

I shall put on my wedding garland. Mine is not the red-brown dress of the traveller, and though there are dangers on the way I have no fear in my mind.

The evening star will come out when my voyage is done and the plaintive notes of the twilight melodies be struck up from the King's gateway.

95

I WAS not aware of the moment when I first crossed the threshold of this life.

What was the power that made me open out into this vast mystery like a bud in the forest at midnight!

When in the morning I looked upon the light I felt in a moment that I was no stranger in this world, that the inscrutable without name and form had taken me in its arms in the form of my own mother.

Even so, in death the same unknown will appear as ever known to me. And because I love this life, I know I shall love death as well.

The child cries out when from the right breast the mother takes it away, in the very next moment to find in the left one its consolation.

96

WHEN I go from hence let this be my parting word, that what I have seen is unsurpassable.

I have tasted of the hidden honey of this lotus that expands on the ocean of light, and thus am I blessed—let this be my parting word.

In this playhouse of infinite forms I have had my play and here have I caught sight of him that is formless.

My whole body and my limbs have thrilled with his touch who is beyond touch; and if the end comes here, let it come—let this be my parting word.

97

WHEN my play was with thee I never questioned who thou wert. I knew nor shyness nor fear, my life was boisterous.

In the early morning thou wouldst call me from my sleep like my own comrade and lead me running from glade to glade.

On those days I never cared to know the meaning of songs thou sangest to me. Only my voice took up the tunes, and my heart danced in their cadence.

Now, when the playtime is over, what is this sudden sight that is come upon me? The world with eyes bent upon thy feet stands in awe with all its silent stars.

98

I WILL deck thee with trophies, garlands of my defeat. It is never in my power to escape unconquered.

I surely know my pride will go to the wall, my life will burst its bonds in exceeding pain, and my empty heart will sob out in music like a hollow reed, and the stone will melt in tears.

I surely know the hundred petals of a lotus will not remain closed for ever and the secret recess of its honey will be bared.

From the blue sky an eye shall gaze upon me and summon me in silence. Nothing will be left for me, nothing whatever, and utter death shall I receive at thy feet.

99

WHEN I give up the helm I know that the time has come for thee to take it. What there is to do will be instantly done. Vain is this struggle.

Then take away your hands and silently put up with your defeat, my heart, and think it your good fortune to sit perfectly still where you are placed.

These my lamps are blown out at every little puff of wind, and trying to light them I forget all else again and again.

But I shall be wise this time and wait in the dark, spreading my mat on the floor; and whenever it is thy pleasure, my lord, come silently and take thy seat here.

100

I DIVE down into the depth of the ocean of forms, hoping to gain the perfect pearl of the formless.

No more sailing from harbour to harbour with this my weather-beaten boat. The days are long passed when my sport was to be tossed on waves.

And now 1 am eager to die into the deathless.

Into the audience hall by the fathomless abyss where swells up the music of toneless strings 1 shall take this harp of my life.

I shall tune it to the notes of forever, and when it has sobbed out its last utterance, lay down my silent harp at the feet of the silent.

101

EVER in my life have I sought thee with my songs. It was they who led me from door to door, and with them have 1 felt about me, searching and touching my world.

It was my songs that taught me all the lessons I ever learnt; they showed me secret paths, they brought before my sight many a star on the horizon of my heart.

They guided me all the day long to the mysteries of

the country of pleasure and pain, and, at last, to what palace gate have they brought me in the evening at the end of my journey?

102

I BOASTED among men that I had known you. They see your pictures in all works of mine. They come and ask me, 'Who is he?' I know not how to answer them. I say, 'Indeed, I cannot tell.' They blame me and they go away in scorn. And you sit there smiling.

I put my tales of you into lasting songs. The secret gushes out from my heart. They come and ask me, 'Tell me all your meanings.' I know not how to answer them. I say, 'Ah, who knows what they mean!' They smile and go away in utter scorn. And you sit there smiling.

103

IN one salutation to thee, my God, let all my senses spread out and touch this world at thy feet.

Like a rain-cloud of July hung low with its burden of unshed showers let all my mind bend down at thy door in one salutation to thee.

Let all my songs gather together their diverse strains into a single current and flow to a sea of silence in one salutation to thee.

Like a flock of homesick cranes flying night and day back to their mountain nests let all my life take its voyage to its eternal home in one salution to thee.

Bird's Eye-view

of a Widespread Banyan Tree

1

Versatile Genius

Humayun Kabir

Perhaps no one other than Rabindranath Tagore has so fully represented Indian culture in all its richness and diversity and few have worked so devotedly for integrating its values with the demands of the modern world of science and technology. He was fortunate in both the time and the place of his birth. The advent of the West had disturbed the placid waters of Indian life and a new awakening was seeping throughout the land. Its initial impact had dazzled the Indian mind and so impressed some of the early reformers that they at times seemed to be blind imitators of the West. By the time Tagore was born, the first uncritical admiration for the West had worn off and there was a more balanced appraisal of the values of the West. Simultaneously, there was increased knowledge of and regard for the values of the East.

The place of his birth was equally opportune. Bengal had felt the impact of the West earlier and more vividly than perhaps any other part of India, and in Bengal the stirrings of new life were most marked in Calcutta. The meeting of East and West on India's shores was thus for Tagore both a fact and an ideal. The circumstances of his family also helped in the flowering of Tagore's genius. Originally from East Bengal, the family became rich and prosperous during the later Mughal days. The prosperity became even greater after the advent of the British. Co-operation with the ruling powers brought it status, wealth and culture but also attracted the disapproval of the orthodox. Interdining with Tagore family invited social disapproval, inter-marriage ostracism.

Conscious of its wealth and talents, it had already produced three generations of exceptionally able men. When Tagore was born, the family reacted by a proud unconcern with many of the social taboos of the day. The family had, however, for generations been moved by the deeper values of Indian life. Tagore's grandfather was one of the pioneers of Western education and a friend of Raja Rammohan Roy. His father, a deep student of Indian philosophy and Islamic mysticism, began his day with recitations from the Upanishads and Hafiz. Tagore was thus born in a family which was steeped in the traditions of ancient and medieval India and yet responsive to the currents of the modern West. **A deeply religious atmosphere free from adherence to forms and rituals created an ideal background for the flowering of his universal mind.**

We can only hint at his many-splendoured genius in this brief account. The world rightly honours Rabindranath Tagore as **one of the greatest literary figures in history. His writings include more than one thousand poems and two thousand songs in addition to a large number of short stories, novels, dramatic works and essays on diverse topics.** As a writer of lyrics and songs, he has rarely been equalled and perhaps never surpassed. As a short story writer, his rank is among the first three or four masters of the craft. As a novelist and playwright, he has achieved for himself an honoured place in the world of letters. As a literary critic, he has given evidence of rare insight and deep sympathy with the work of men who differed from him widely in tradition and temperament. It is thus not surprising that his works should be translated into all the major languages of the world and bring joy, solace and strength to countless millions.

The diversity of his literary work is amazing but literature in its widest sense could not exhaust his energies. **He was a musician of the highest order and not only composed songs but set them to music.** He started as a traditionalist but very soon the range of his musical compositions expanded till it incorporated elements from Western music and fused them with his Eastern background. With **more than two thousand songs that express every nuance of human feeling and every mood of nature in her infinite variety**, he is undoubtedly one of the greatest song-writers and musicians that the world has known.

Tagore **took to painting when he was almost 70 and yet produced within ten years almost 3000 pictures.** They broke sharply from prevailing Indian styles and explored the unconscious and subconscious levels of the people's mind. Some regard his work as a complete breach with the Indian tradition and yet **many competent critics have described him as one of the most significant and creative painters of modern India.** His affiliation with primitive art on the one hand and with some of the *avant garde* on the other, is only one indication of the sweep and range of his genius.

Tagore was an artist *par excellence* and in addition, he **made notable contributions to religious and educational thought, to politics and social reforms, to moral regeneration and economic reconstruction of India and the world.** He not only thought deeply and creatively on all these topics but he also set his hand to realise in practice what he preached. The educational ideas which inspired his school at Santiniketan have deeply influenced all modern educational thought in India. His programmes of economic, social and political reconstruction of the village through the co-operation and self help of villagers have set the pattern for programmes of reconstruction of national life in contemporary India. **He travelled far and wide to restore India's contacts with the outside world and laid the foundation on which free India**

has based her policy of friendly relations with all peoples of the world.

Tagore's deep feeling for the unity of man made him realise that interdependence of peoples and countries rather than their independence must be the principle of life and progress today and tomorrow if the world is to survive the challenge of modern science and technology. **He was one of the first to recognise and proclaim that the old divisions of nation and race had become outmoded in the modern age.** Today the world is one and our sympathies and loyalties must be expanded to recognise this fact. Steeped in the age-old traditions of the East, an inheritor of the rich cultural heritage of ancient and medieval India, he was simultaneously a modernist who welcomed the values proclaimed by the West.

Perhaps Tagore's greatest contribution to India and the modern world is his recognition that men can unite only on the basis of their deepest spiritual insight. He was a great believer in the dignity of the individual and was one of the strongest champions of cultural autonomy that the modern world has known. He believed that universality can be attained not by suppressing the cultural autonomy of any constituent unit but by finding a place for all of them in a universal approach. He respected his own heritage and was at the same time a great admirer of the intellectual energy and scientific spirit of the West. **He held that the Indian attitude of submission to fate was inimical to man's full development and the popularly accepted Indian concept of salvation as the submergence of the individual in the infinite created a lethargy of spirit.** He welcomed the West's exaltation of the individual, but since Western overemphasis on individuality often leads to aggressiveness and pride, he sought to rediscover a basis of spiritual energy in India's own heritage.

By his emphasis on the universality of law, Tagore provided the Indian renaissance with its intellectual basis of dynamism and optimism. Renaissance and revivalism are the two forces that are still contending for the soul of re-awakened India. Tagore had the greatest admiration for the ancient Indian values of faith, excellence and spirituality but threw the enormous weight of his personality and achievement on the side of science, democracy and humanism. He proclaimed that the attainment of salvation is possible not only for a selected few but for every person that is willing to accept a happy and active way of life on earth. Every individual is a participant in the cosmic endeavour towards greater perfection. In this endeavour, the claims of the whole must never be denied but neither must that claim submerge the identity of the individual. For Tagore, mutual acknowledgment of differences is the basis of real unity.

Tagore restated the basic principles of India's philosophy by his emphasis on the unity of mankind. He gave to it a new orientation by his recognition of the concept of development as intrinsic to the nature of reality. If one takes the doctrine of *maya* seriously, there is hardly any room for change and development. Similarly, the law of *karma* and transmigration imposes restrictions on the individual's freedom of action. Tagore's special distinction is that he advocated vigorous fulfilment of work with a selfless detachment but without any explicit reference to the doctrine of *maya* or *karma*. To recognise the individual means to recognise the restrictions which each imposes on others and Tagore was never tired of insisting that it is only through the reconciliation of the ego and the environment that man can strive towards perfection.

The emphasis on individuality in the context of society implies an acceptance of lawful limitations that is of dynamic significance to Indian thought. Tagore's demand for self-realisation within recognised limits provides a basis for reorientation of the prevailing Indian attitude to the real. For Tagore, the Absolute is not opposed to but already in the process of realisation in that which exists and guarantees human faith in development and progress.

2

Tagore and Indian Renaissance

Mulk Raj Anand

If a generalisation be permitted, the intellectual history of India during the last hundred and fifty years may be regarded as the history of a prolonged frustration. The impact of Western machine civilisation broke up the flaccid, parochial life of our old, self-inclosed villages, rail and road connected mud-huts to the brick-built towns, and the towns to the enormous metropolises of the world. And there began a new ferment, the excitement of a time of rapid change, the stirrings of a transitional age.

But because the transformation was initiated by alien authority without much thought of clearing the debris or of repairing some of the dilapidated ruins, which had not been erased in the process, the world that emerged was a hotch potch of several surviving cultures persisting side by side with the new 'civilisation', without the emergence of a distinctive pattern. The will of the people to relate their traditional modes to the new situation was thwarted from the start. Indian society thus fell into the welter of a mental confusion in which the outworn customs of the darkest feudal past rubbed shoulders with the most modern impulses.

The fact that both at home and abroad English isolationism began to dam the floodgates which had opened, made the confusion worse confounded. For instance, Lord

Macaulay's attempt to make Indians talk English was on a par with Alexander III's forcible imposition of Russian on his Polish, Finnish and German subjects. And the new education scheme which Bentinck sanctioned in 1835 was deliberately calculated to bring into contempt the ancient culture of India and to introduce a counterfeit of the English system in order to provide clerks for the various government departments. To add to all the other inhibitions came the vigilant guard on 'dangerous thoughts'.

Under the circumstances the continuous mental effort necessary to diagnose the ills of society, which is the harbinger of a creative age, became difficult; while experiments in replacement and renewal were doomed to take place in the vicious circle of a society which frowned upon all radical talk.

I do not mean to suggest that there is any exact correspondence between the outer social life of an epoch and the art of that epoch. Otherwise how could the great writers in our language have produced their work in the modern era at all? The dialectic of art in subtler. The inventive artist is, for instance, much more concerned with processes than with the beginnings and the ends of these processes. And social activity, concerning itself as it does with the outer forms of life, does not necessarily approximate, in time to the personal and psychological curves of an age. But, in so far as social action ultimately seeks to recreate the institutions with its attacks, its interconnection with cultural change may be taken for granted.

The French Revolution, for instance, owed not a little to the prognostications of the 18th century encyclopaedists, from Voltaire and Diderot to Condorcet, who were themselves led to destroy on paper all the established institutions, from the divine right of king and church to bad education, by the reaction under which they grew up. And the same is true of the Russian Revolution, which came after the thorough-going criticism of society by Lenin, as well as the great Russian writers from Pushkin to Tolstoy and Gorky.

The lack of much free and uninhibited thinking during the Edwardian and Georgian eras in India, the failure to map the sun-soaked horizons, as well as the deliberate prolongation of old customs and the suppression of new knowledge, all this engendered the frustration of the intelligentsia and the sidetracking of much heroic effort in our renaissance.

I believe that **Rabindranath Tagore was a unique phenomenon, in so far as he was one of the few great writers of modern India who consciously fought against this frustration and made a sustained effort at creating an art at high pressure.**

Of course, it is possible for a sentimentalist to see into Homer more than Homer wrote. And I am not unconscious of the turgidity, the vapidity and the repetitiveness of much of his writings. It is said that throughout his writing career Shakespeare never blotted out a line; and several people, including myself, have often wished that he had cut out the jingoism in his historical plays. Rabindranath Tagore lived to eighty years, and it is believed that each day he wrote a poem, a play or a story. Naturally, therefore, at times he overwrote and critics like D.P. Mukerjee and Amiya Chakravarti are doing great service by sifting the gold from the dross. But I am not fulfilling the functions of a critic here when I draw attention to his unique position as the source of much of our culture. I want rather to bring out three salient characteristics of his genius which inspite of all the multifarious strains of his work, are in my opinion, his chief contributions to our renaissance, facets of his creative activity from which we can take inspiration at this moment.

The first great contribution of Rabindranath Tagore to our renaissance itself, was to make us conscious that we are involved in the process of rebirth as a whole people. I mean by this that, at a very early stage in his literary career, he began to concentrate on those essentially human emotions and ideas which are at the base of all external institutions, which continually well up in the hearts and minds of people and have to be renewed in times of stress, so that when analysed they can supply the basis of the actual life of a changing community, which form the source of the values by which society lives, the poetic or philosophic content, or the principle of life of a new civilisation.

The son of a noble family, growing up in the tradition of the Bengal revival of the 19th century, Tagore was favourably placed to receive both the poetic and literary influence of the classical tradition and Western learning. But it is for the pertinacity of instinct which he soaked himself in the folk culture of Bengal and while imbibing the genuine impulses of the West, escaped from 'the grooves of imitative English forms' which were current among the intelligentsia of his time, that he is of value for us. For it shows that the real synthesis can be achieved in our time only by going back for inspiration to the rich arts and literatures of our village tradition, at the same time as we drink at the fountains of European culture. In this sense **Tagore bridged the gulf between the old world and the new, and in this way he came to be for us a symbol of real modernism in India.**

Apart from his juvenilia, and the early poems written under the influence of his Sanskrit studies, every one has heard of the effect on his sensibility of the Vaishnava lyrics. But few have realised how intimate was his debt to the folk songs of these animistic and totemistic people who lived in the self-enclosed congeries of hamlets cut off from all contacts with the town life. Among these communities the age-old culture of the country had filtered and thoroughly absorbed, and it had developed into an indigenous culture, vital enough to resist all attacks from outside and to tinge strongly anyone who came into contact with it. Rabindranath has often recorded the joy with which he entered into the wonderland of this heritage of folk tales and lyrics, and how he drank the ecstacy of these simple songs of the village-poems addressed to the powers of nature, the air, the water, the trees, the rivers and the hills richly sensuous as they are deep, humorous as they are tragic. And it was not only from folk song or legend and story but from that popular versions of Buddhism and Hinduism current in Bengal that Tagore evolved a pantheon to symbolise his own mental struggles.

The wedding of folk culture with the technique he had learnt from the West is a remarkable transformation. He took his poetry to the earth. He gave back the songs he took from the people, as highly finished lyrics to the people, so that they have made the local dialect of Bengal into one of the great modern languages of the world. Unique enough in translation, the difficulties of transposing the sentiments of one poetry with another have prevented the range of his experimentations and innovations, as well as the spirit which informs his work, from being reflected in the foreign versions of his books, but if any single writer taught his countrymen how to know nature, it was Rabindranath Tagore. For he inspired the people with the belief that men can conquer nature, possess it and reap the rich fruits that it can yield. Always he was where the tiller is tilling the hard ground and where the pathmaker is breaking stones, as he says in the *Gitanjali.* And already before the turn of the century, on the strength of that alliance between his genius and the genius of the men of the soil through which he ushered the renaissance in our century, **he had become to our land what Pushkin had been to Russia, Whitman to America and Wordsworth and Coleridge to England.**

I have deliberately emphasised the fact that Tagore went to the people for inspiration, because the intelligentsia of his time, as well as of our own, shows a tendency to despise the only integral tradition of culture which has survived among us to any extent, the culture of our primitive, closely knit communities, on the basis of which alone a renaissance can be built up. Tagore realised, as Tolstoy did in Russia, that most of the life-giving qualities: simplicity, sincerity, sensibility, remain among the people, while the false, imitative, pretentious gestures of the middle sections lead to vulgarity.

If the attempt at a new religion of man was the first great contribution which Tagore made to our renascent effort, **his second significant contribution was to incarnate some of the chief types of the emerging middle section of Bengal in his writing and to re-integrate the arts of poetry, drama, story, and particularly the novel, in our country.** And in this he showed an even greater courage than any other Indian of his generation. For he was not afraid to present his own people to themselves, and the whole world, as they really were, without the fear of being abused and condemned for revealing them as saints and sinners, free spirits and chauvinists, parochial, slave-minded mendicants and devotees, great peoples as well as small peoples, as great as any in the world and very small. But in this respect also he did more than merely reflect the life of the region of Bengal. He caught it in the grip of that peculiar moral tension which had risen among us, through the clash of the two dominating traditions: the incoming hedonism of the West and the various strands of religion and custom of our own society.

That is to say he showed how the individual in the modern sense began to rise in our society. And more than his subject matter, he took the technique of prose fiction forward. The nature of his contribution of the making of an emotive prose style, by the amalgamation of the literary language and common speech, has often been ignored because he was known in Europe primarily as a mystic poet. But, on the strength of his early novels alone, I will make so bold as to claim that **Tagore was, in the 'formal' sense, the first novelist of India.**

Some people may wonder why, in view of the fact that so many novels were written in ancient India, why, inspite of the fact that before him Bankim Chandra Chatterji had written copious fiction, I have chosen to call him 'the first novelist of India.' So before I come to mention the names of some of the fascinating individuals he created in his novels, let me explain what I mean by 'the novels.' In a word I want to differentiate between the old novel, or 'recital' as

I should like to call it, from the new novel in the contemporary sense.

The novel as an art form, with its own integral laws, arose in Western Europe through the growth of an industrial society which needed a highly finished mirror to reflect its complex problems. It is far in advance of the early mythical and poetic narratives, or even of the prose narrative born of the printing press, where whole chunks of narrative are strung together without much respect of the laws of balance and proportion.

Now, if we remember that the novel form has an inner coherence and sensitive logic of its own, we may roughly say that it has tended to be an ever more skilful representation of events in time, seeking the illusion of life through the dramatic sequence based on development of character. As such it is distinct from what, for want of a better word, may be called a report or a recital, which is the presentation of past events, as crudely as when an Arabian story-teller recounts a tale or as subtly as when a narrator regulates the reproduction in the light of his own, or someone else's external opinion.

This is a somewhat tentative definition. But one can see that the long or short romantic narratives in the Indian epics, or the Kavyas, court stories which developed from them, are still myth and legend, while Tagore's *Broken Ties* is a novelette; one can see that the *Adventures of Ten Princes* by Dandin, who lived in the latter half of the 7th century, is prose recital, whereas *The Home and the World* by Tagore is an essay in the novel form; one can even see that *Anandamath* by Bankim is an historical recital while *Gora* by Tagore is an attempt at an historical novel.

The parallel with Europe really makes the point I am making more obvious. For it was not until the break up of the collective life of the Middle Ages that poetry had begun to be personal and individualistic in the West; it was not until the rise of the scientific spirit and the empirical outlook later that prose narratives had prospered there; and it needed a whole series of commercial and cultural developments, the breakdown of feudalism, the expansion of trade and the rise of a highly developed industrial society, to make the transition from Chaucer's *Canterbury Tales* to Defoe's *Robinson Crusoe* and the flood of 18th and 19th centuries' fiction. Much of this fiction remained mere recital, though with the emerging self-awareness of the middle classes in Europe, the novel in its dramatic sense was already beginning to take shape.

If, however, we ask why the novel form was not achieved in India before the time of Tagore, the answer lies in the changes which took place in India at the end of the 19th century. But, as soon as Indian society began to break up under the impact of Europe, the old narratives remained only as survivals, and the modernist Tagore began to attempt more complex patterns to present the psychological relationship of individual men and women in the newly arising society of Bengal. And the time was ripe for the emergence of the novel in India as an integral form.

It is in this sense that I choose to regard Tagore as the first novelist of India. For although Bankim has the vitality of experience and a grasp of life frequently absent in Tagore, he is mainly a romancer who is extending the old myth and legend of India, and the recital element survives in his work almost as in the lay of an ancient bard, minstrel of troubador. It is true that Bankim displays intense feeling, and even attempts to create character, as in *Rajani* or *Krishnakanta's Will*. But even at his best he remains a storyteller, like that awful obtuse feudalist, Sir Walter Scott, on whom he modelled himself. In fact, he does not seem to have bothered much about technique, and is content to tell us of things as they are, or have taken place, rather than of how and why they took place. Apart from this, due to his fanaticism, his work cannot be considered as a great advance on the older fiction, except in so far as it was written in the 19th century and was cast in the form loosely called 'the novel.'

I will not say that Tagore is altogether free from all or at least some of the surviving traces of recitalism, but all the same, he is a self-conscious artist in the novel form. And if there is a certain redundancy and a lack of vigour in his fiction as compared to Bankim's, it is more than compensated for by his lyricism and his sensitiveness. Alone among our nineteenth century writers, he shows a sense of homour in the midst of tragedy. And he has an uncanny gift for penetrating into the hearts, especially of his female characters. For who among us has created that eternal type of the Indian mother as Anandamoyi in *Gora* or that self-sacrificing, devoted girl who tame the priggish Gaur Mohan in the same novel? Even Bimala, the sincere but muddled wife of the liberal landlord Nikhil, in *The Home and the World,* is relieved in her blind and foolish worship of the manoeuvering firebrand Sandip by the gentle and constant devotion she gives to an ideal. And the village girl in the *Wreck* shines like a flame inspite of all the oppression of society, forcing the hedonist lover, Ramesh, to respect her even as he longs for his beloved girl-graduate from Calcutta. To the end this kind of woman recurs in Tagore's novels, the typical Indian woman whom we so often meet in life, whom Tagore brings before us, sometimes shrill, sometimes gentle and devoted and always saying 'I want,' 'I want,' but challenging us, almost accusing us with the words: 'I constitute one half of Indian civilisation, the suppressed half.'

Then there are the old men of Tagore's novels, Pares Babu, the patriarch in *Gora,* who is more or less the same figure with a new name as Anand Babu in the *Wreck,* or the rationalist uncle in *Broken Ties,* the wise old men, who are always the guides, philosophers and mentors of all and sundry, consulting physicians of an old bedridden society, who have diagnosed the age in which they live and who pass on the knowledge and help the young to usher in the new life. In this type too Tagore has delineated perhaps an idealised version of the cultured old gentlemen whom we knew so well a quarter of a century ago, the liberal commonsensical spirits who recommended 'sweet reasonableness' even as they compromised on the golden mean and whom we ignored or despised because we thought they lived in a kind of 'no man's land'. Tagore's portrayal of them teaches us that we must beware of adopting the cheap manner of the European young in regard to old men, that we must not consider them as only fit for the rubbish bin, even though we do not share many things in common with them.

And then there are Tagore's young heroes, a whole galaxy of contemporary Indian portraits, from the lovers who have learnt through modern education not to regard woman as a mere landscape, the friends Gora and Benoy, and Amulya, the young student, devoted unto death, and the tough Europeanised share-pushers and go-getters, Haran, Sandip, Amrit Roy and Co. Representatives of our age, they do not offer much hope; bitter, disillusioned, impetuous, mostly concerned to make romantic gestures, they are only relieved by the fact that Rabindranath shows very skilfully how much more they are sinned against their sinning. Victims of Moloch they lapse for lack of opportunities, leaving their ideals behind them. But in the lovable and human qualities which cling even to the most vicious of them, they remain in our memory as the poignant symbols of fighters who fell in the all-embracing, manifold struggle of our generation to find a new way of life.

And this brings me to **the third aspect of Tagore's genius, his search for a new way of life.** For throughout his work this one fact dominates the atmosphere, that the struggle for a new way of life is eternal, perennial and on many different planes, and that it is primarily always the struggle for new values, the struggle to be human, to be individual.

What is to be done? he continually asks. How are we to live between Asia and Europe? What are to be the fundamental values of our civilisation? So intense and honest is his search for values that I believe **this third contribution of Rabindranath is probably the most significant for us because of the wide variety of thoughtful suggestions he**

has made as to which institutions we should accept in the historic transition in which we are involved and which way of life we should choose to live by.

From the beginning of his career as a writer, Rabindranath was not only a poet but also a philosopher. The early influence of his father, Maharshi Debendranath Tagore, the mystic founder of the Brahmo Samaja, brought him into contact with ancient Hindu thoughts. 'To me,' he wrote in the *Sadhana,* 'the verses of the Upanishad and the teaching of the Buddha have ever been things of the spirit, and therefore, endowed with boundless vital growth and I have used them both in my own life, and in my preaching as instinct with individual meaning for me as for others, and awaiting their confirmation my own special testimony must have its value because of its individuality.'

But this was no mere pedantic, parrot-like repetition of holy incantations and spiritual formulas. Rather it was an attempt to define a new set of spiritual values which could contribute something genuine to the solution of the intellectual crisis which was spreading from the West through the impact of 19th century science and rationalism. 'The mantram which gives our spiritual vision its right entrance into the soul of all things is the mantram of India' he said, 'the mantram of peace, of goodness and unity—*Shantam, Shivam, Advaitam.* The distracted mind of the West is knocking at the gates of India for this. And is it to be met with a hoarse spout of exclusions?'

In thus seizing upon the fundamental conflict of Asia and of Europe, roughly representing the conflict between Belief and Unbelief, he showed the same insight as Goethe did in the Germany of his time. And like Goethe, he incidentally sought to seek for the meaning and purpose of life, away from the dogma of an authoritarian church and mere academism, and thus helped us to live a richer life.

His definition of 'spiritual experience' was, indeed, completely unconventional. For instance, **he regarded much of the materialism of Russian socialism as essentially**

spiritual in character. And he may be said to be the first modern Indian who inclined to the view that a new faith, based on man's creative potentialities in art and literature, music, philosophy and science, may rise, and through that a new world may be build up, far greater and higher in accomplishment than that which has been going down before our own eyes.

I must confess that I do not share his belief in some of the sanctions which he felt impelled to invoke from time to time. He was a pilgrim who carried a great deal of luggage on his back, souvenirs from our long past, mementos, charms, and tokens etc. We who are young prefer to travel a little lighter. But I would be ungrateful if I did not record here the immense debt which our generation owe him for showing us that there are other ways of living than those thickly encrusted doxies, castes and creeds, which often choking venal greed, selfishness and love of power, have fought each other in history and brought so much misery, bitterness and frustration to generations of men, including our own.

If after lifting the weight of dogma off our minds he left us all free to find our own individual beliefs, this is not to say that he did not recommend a number of ways in which we could tackle the most pressing problems of our age.

For instance, **in regard to science he realised fairly early, what we have come to see much later, that it should be regarded as a means and not as an end.** He saw, even during the heyday of the scientific endeavour of the 19th century, that in limiting their field of enquiry to inductive experiment under laboratory conditions, and despising philosophers for pronouncing judgments on reality, the scientists were assuming a pontifical solemnity which would soon yield to a fit of humility in the face of unanswerable questions. True to the tradition of the old Indian sages he assimilated the reports of the laboratory but never forgot that the beauty of falling water is not in the formula H_2O but in the colour, the sheen and the movement of water. In effect he was a poet of science. He hailed Darwinism and the Spencerian philosophy as great achievement of the observing mind, and he showed the deepest sympathy for Huxley's attempt to show the radical difference between men and the lower animals, but he never succumbed to the specialism of the 19th century European intellectuals. To the end he remained a whole man, actively interested in the aesthetic, social, moral and political life of his time. And, through all experience, the inner flame, in the light of which he contemplated the world, was more important to him than the mere sensationalism which registers impressions: 'I am praying to be lighted from within', he said, 'and not simply to hold a light in my hand.'

The tendency of his thoughts was, therefore, mainly modern and humanist. And he believed that, given courage and vision, man could subdue nature and himself sufficiently to his higher ends.

But what are the more concrete proposals he made to cure this sorry sick world of ours? I think that, **by and large, he believed with d'Eolbach that until social thinking revolutionises ideas and transforms institutions, the common life of society cannot advance.**

And, as he apprehended the nature of the change in the catastrophic upheavals of our age yet saw that this change was not integral but mostly mechanical and superficial and at the most of much that he himself valued in the past, **he crusaded for exchange of knowledge among the nations through a new kind of universalism.** This ideal, a noble precursor of the dreams of our own day, is peculiarly Indian in feeling. It is an aspect of the tolerance which has characterised our history inspite of all our conflicts, a kind of sympathy or compassion which was the basis of our old humanism. Being a vast collection of peoples and nationalities ourselves, a kind of miniature cosmos of our own, with ten distinct major languages, and yet knit together for two thousand years by a common culture, we in India can claim to have been possessed by a strong passion for universalism for a very long time. The universalism of the old Buddhist ideal was proved when it travelled across the frontiers and took roots in ancient China and Japan. Similarly, the influence of the philosophy of the Vedanta on modern German thought, especially through Hegel and Schopenhauer, and on recent British thinkers, shows that the tendency of our thought has been mainly universalist. **But it was through Rabindranath Tagore that Indian Universalism became known to the modern world.**

I think that he had vaguely foreseen, even before the World War, how a country organised as a military force and integrated in its own selfish economy, was potentially an aggressive force. And he felt that the older forms of nationalism, the King state, as well as the middle class state which followed the French Revolution, were already passing away yielding to the state in which a new kind of man was emerging. And with a world vision, far in advance of his time, he tried to shift the emphasis from national rights to individual rights, and from political to economic rights, at a time when national rights were being secured, a local struggle being waged in the bulk of the world with an aggressive intensity. And he stood for a rough and ready functional association of nations across frontiers, so that the claims of nationality should not became too exclusive. **He was, therefore, our first real internationalist.**

The final and decisive power to hold the peoples of the world together should be felt, be left to the way tolerance that the new type of man might practise. And he had in mind the tradition which had united the multi-national populations of India in a common civilisation for long periods, inspite of their disparities.

But though he was a visionary who believed that, in sentiment a mutli-national civilisation was on the way through which individuals and nations might surrender their powers, he knew as an Indian, that in actual fact, several of the potentially freedom-loving nations were handicapped by the numerous aggressive nations, built on greed and plunder.

So he struggled against the imperialists of his day with a resilience that lends to his political thought a peculiar realism as well as a visionary quality.

Nor was he merely concerned to make paper pleas. He took active stepes to put his ideas into practice. **Despising the 'mendicancy' of our own politics on the one hand, and the exclusive cult of the nation in Europe on the other, he believed that a new kind of education alone could restore the balance and create real international understanding.**

That was the kind of feeling which actuated him to open the world-famous school at Santiniketan in Bolpur, that later developed into the nucleus of an international university, the Vishva-Bharati. Here young men from all parts of the world were brought up in harmony with nature and each other, and allowed to absorb, in an atmosphere of creative activity, as much and what they liked of book knowledge, and to cultivate their sensibilities, so that they could grow up to be healthy individuals, independent, capable of taking initiative, happy and free from racial and national bias.

Also, he travelled widely in Europe, America and the Far East to promote world unity. And with a fearlessness of spirit rare in intellectuals, he continued to utter warning after warning of the nemesis that would overtake civilisation if the nations of the West continued to flout all scruples in their lust for economic exploitation and political supremacy.

When, however, after the betrayals of their plighted word by the great powers in China, Abyssinia, Spain and Czechoslovakia against which he had vehemently protested, the Second World War at last came, he delivered one of the most personal addresses to the students of his international university on his eightieth birthday. It was a kind of reckoning in view of the judgement day, and he spoke from his heart, a bitter and dissappointed man, but one who had not yet lost his faith in man:

'It is now no longer possible for us to retain any respect

for that mockery of civilisation which believes in ruling by force and has no faith in freedom at all!...

'And yet my good fortune has brought me into close contact with really large-hearted Englishmen. Without the slightest hesitation, I may say that the nobility of their character was without parallel. Had I not met them, not even the faintest hope would mitigate my despair with regard to the Western nations...

'Today my one last hope is that the deliverer will be born in this poverty-stricken country...'

3

The Poet-Philosopher

Louis Renou

In France, we appreciate Rabindranath as a novelist, a dramatist and, above all, as a poet who has expressed with felicity the sentiments of Indian spirit and of his own time; the uniform and sweet flow of his poetry in delicate lyrical accents, which off and on give rise to forte and deep notes, has made impression on the Western readers, a little surfeited with the excess of the symbolist poetry and its esoteric refinements. Finally, one breathes pure air; one finds, without illusion, the abundant and fresh spring, out of which, it appears, poetic inspiration had gushed forth to the depth of the ages.

To tell the truth, the rhythmic and sound-value (if one is permitted to say so) of Tagorean poetry is totally missed in the translations; it required all the talent of one of our great writers, Andre Gide, for translating one of the most famous works of the Indian Poet, *Gitanjali*, without compromising its spirit.

For those among us who hardly know what Indian culture stands for, who know not the spiritual tradition of India, the personality of Tagore has possibly appeared as emerging from obscurity, as an erratic block emanating from the unknown literature, It was imagined indeed that he had been a writer permeated by religiosity, it was felt vaguely that he had allowed himself to be lulled by this sort of pantheism in which some see the very sign of all Oriental poetry.

Actually things are much more precise. Tagore has been, without possibly wishing it, one of the leading men of a file which is commonly known as Renaissance of Hinduism.

Properly speaking, they are not reformers; much less, again, founders of sects as have been in the religious history of India; they are the chosen few who wished to inject new vitality in the tradition, by raising ethical values, social and purely human, which were latent.

Tagore has been, from his early youth, strongly attracted by the Upanishads. Later, he published a few works on these ancient texts and thus he nurtured his Vedantic thought. Then the ecstatic theism of medieval Vaisnavas, the songs of Bauls, the Brahmo thought inherited from his family—these have enriched his profound culture, have paved the way for the synthesis which characterises his tendency, a synthesis in which Hinduism gets wedded harmoniously to Humanism nurtured by Western values. Of all the spiritual masters, whom contemporary India has known, none was more tolerant than he; his non-violence possibly had not the acuteness of that Gandhi; that is to say, it was with him not a weapon, but only a creed; he wanted to unite, to open the approaches (to bring about the rapprochement), he did not want to separate nor to oppose.

Still he was not at all the image of a writer who had withdrawn himself to an ivory tower. He pursued and felt keenly the struggles and the sentiments of his age; he was not indifferent to the afflictions and sorrows of the people. **It is for realising his desire of unity and synthesis that he became a poet, philosopher, essayist, educationist, that he founded the school at Santiniketan, transformed subsequently into a university, to which he dedicated a part of his fortune.**

The dominant trait of his philosophy is that it is precisely the philosophy of a poet. If one goes through the spiritual works of ancient and modern India, certain pages of those books are so beautiful and of such gripping grandeur, one finds that this is not the beauty which their authors have pretended to attain, it is the efficacy, the investigation of intimate experience or the translation of a religious conviction.

To Tagore, on the contrary, beauty comes first, the idea presents itself before any precise feature has perhaps been traced on paper. It is in this particularly that he distinguishes himself and that his work has chances of enduring. He has discovered beauty in the faces and the hearts, but initially in nature. Undoubtedly, nature has been described by Indian poets since Kalidasa's time, but Tagore has given to his vision a matchless relief, because he has nurtured and exhaled nature through permanent communion with the Divine. In a poem addressed to the Earth (and which is remotely related to the famous hymn of Atharva Veda), he says:

> 'O mother of clay, I wish I could spread myself on the earth and scatter myself in all senses as the joy of spring. I wish I could smash this cage of my bosom, demolish the barriers of stone, impervious wall, dark and dismal prison of mine, and let myself be carried from one end to the other by the tide of the universe, like the waves dancing, murmuring, rustling, stumbling, fluttering and then discovering myself suddenly with an ecstacy, in the light.'
>
> (*Sonar Tari*)

But adoration of nature, of mysteries of life and of splendours of creation is in itself but an approach to what must be the end of our life: "To be conscious of the fact that one is absolutely enveloped by Brahman," it echoes back the initial words of the Isa Upanishad: "Know that all that is there in the Universe is enveloped by Isa."

A Sampler of Tagore's Paintings

Selections: Harshvardhan

'I strongly urge our artists to deny vehemently their obligation to produce carefully something that can be labelled as Indian art according to old world mannerism. Let them proudly refuse to be herded into a pen like branded beasts that are treated as cattle and not as cows.'

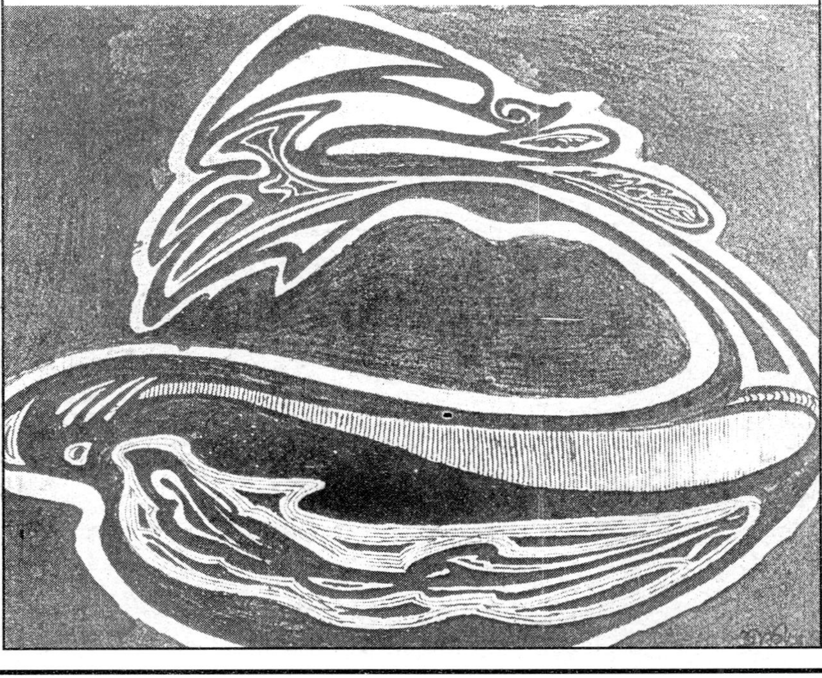

Erasures, Shapes, Birds, Faces, Masks, Moods, Anguish, Melancholy, Females, Life in its true colours

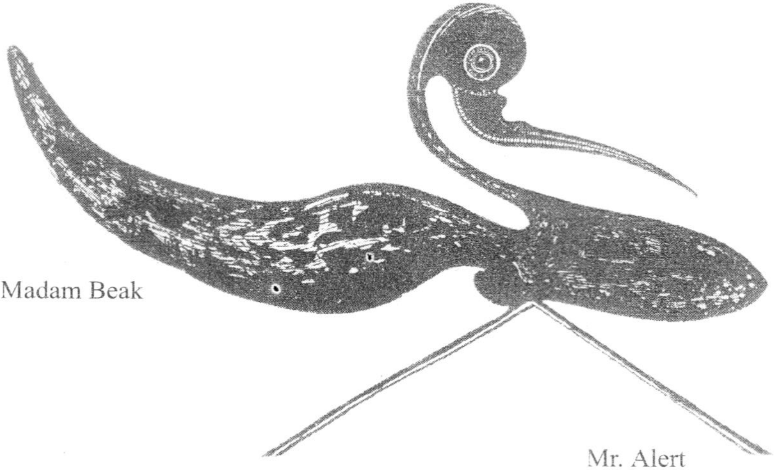

Madam Beak

Mr. Alert

Wow...!

'In his paintings Tagore is more contemporary than he is in his poems.'

—Timothy Hyman

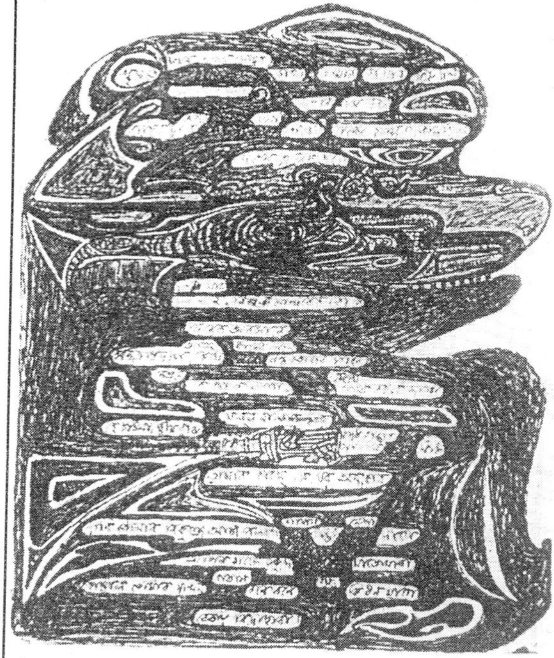

Erase and design

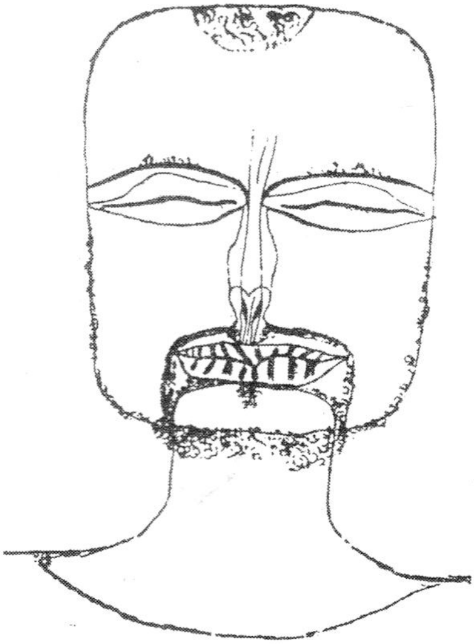

'Art is an expression of the inner, subconscious, purposeless...words are aware, lines are not.'

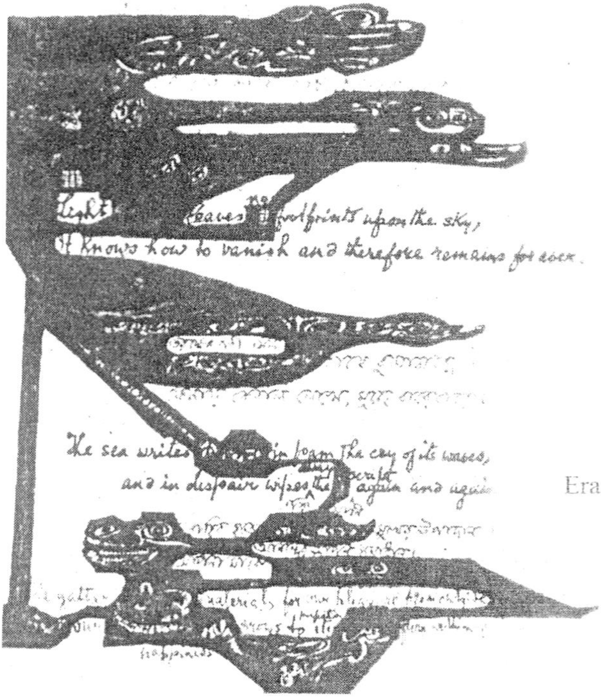

Erasure Birds

'I am intoxicated with the game of inventing forms.'

Mr. Strong

Let us quarrel...

My Real Self

'He was a prophet like Goethe, as Malreaux said of him, and like him he did not know of what.'

—Timothy Hyman

Angst

India ?

'All traditional structures of art must have a sufficient degree of elasticity to allow it to respond to varied impulses of life, delicate or virile, to grow with its growth, to dance with its rhythm.'

Growl

In the sky

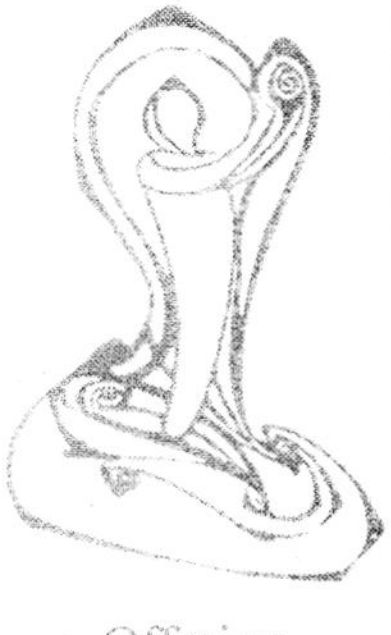

Offering

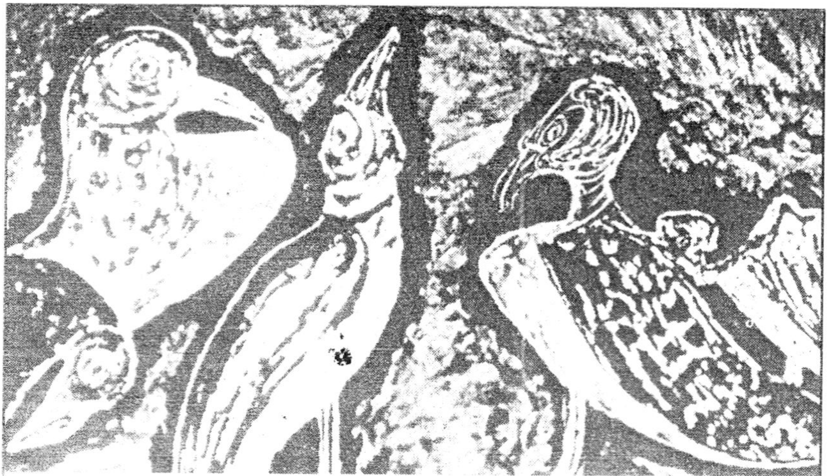

Vultures

Looking straight

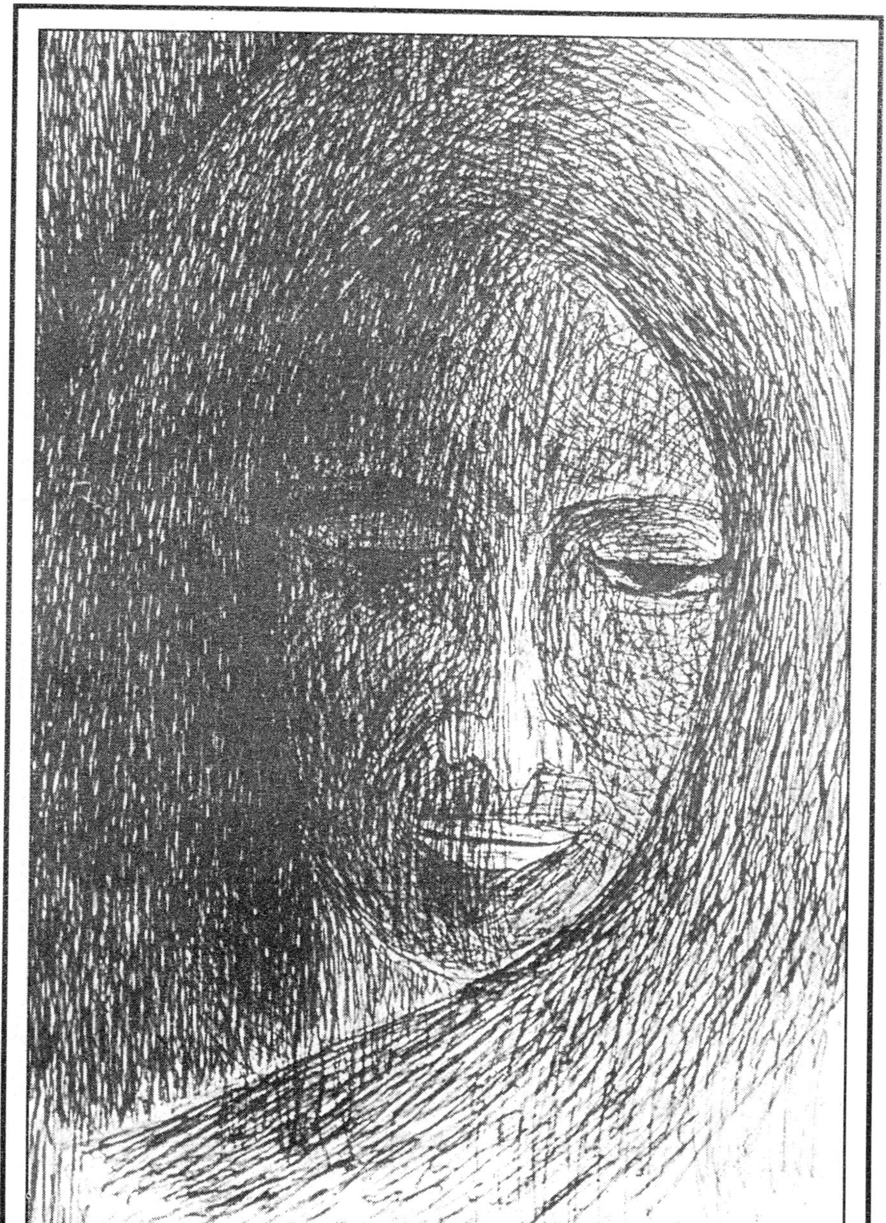

Friends

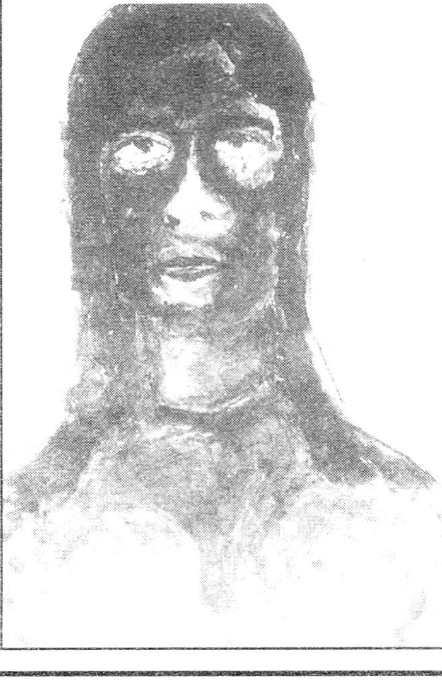

Grim

A little smile
(but more than Mona Lisa's)

Lady Bengal

The slab put up by the University of Calcutta expresses well what Tagore gave to the modern world: 'Through him India has delivered her message to humanity; his extraordinary achievements in the domains of literature, philosophy, education and art have won for him imperishable glory and have raised the status of India in the eyes of mankind.'

(Translated from the French)

4

The Poetry of Tagore

Sri Aurobindo

ONE of the most remarkable peculiarities of Rabindranath's genius is the happiness and originality with which he has absorbed the whole spirit of Vaishnava poetry and turned it into something essentially the same and yet new and modern. He has given the old sweet spirit of emotional and passionate religion an expression of more delicate and complex richness voiceful of subtler and more penetratingly spiritual shades of feeling than the deep-hearted but simple early age of Bengal could know. The old Vaishnava *bhava*—there is no English word for it—was easily seizable, broad and strong. The *bhava* of these poems is not translatable in any other language than that the poet has used,—a striking proof is the unsatisfactory attempt of the poet himself, to explain in prose his own poem, *Sonar Tari.* But while the intellect tries in vain to find other intellectual symbols for the poet's meaning, the poetry seizes on the heart and convinces the imagination. These poems are of the essence of poetry and refuse to be rendered in any prose; equivalent poetry is not created from the intellect or the outer imagination, but comes from a deeper source within to which men have no means of access except when the divine part within seizes on the brain and makes it a passive instrument for utterance of the full meaning of which the brain is unable at the moment to grasp. This is the divine mania and enthusiasm which the subtle spiritual discernment of Plato discovered to be the real meaning of what we call inspiration. And of this unattainable force the best lyrics of Rabindranath are full to overflowing.

The first condition of the complete emergence of this new poetic inspiration and this vaster and deeper significance of poetic speech must be the completion of an as yet only initially spiritualised turn of our general human feelings and intelligence. At present the human mind is occupied in passing the borders of two kingdoms. It is emerging out of a period of active and almost materialistic intellectualism towards a primary intuitive seeking to which the straining of the intellect after truth has been brought in the very drive of its own impulse by a sort of slipping over unexpected borders. There is therefore an uncertain groping in many directions, some of which are only valuable as transitional effort and, if they could be the end and final movement, might lead only to a brilliant corruption and decadence. There is vitalistic intuitivism, sometimes taking a more subjective, sometimes a more objective form, that lingers amid dubious lights on the border and cannot get through its own rather thick and often violent lustres and colours to finer and truer spiritual vision. There is an emotional and sensational psychical intuitivism half emerging from and half entangled in the vitalistic motive, that has often a strange beauty and brilliance, sometimes stained with morbid hues, sometimes floating in a vague mist, sometimes (and this is a common tendency) strained to an exaggeration of half vital, half psychic motive.

There is a purer and more delicate psychic intuition with a spiritual issue, that which has been brought by the Irish poets into English literature. The poetry of Whitman and his successors has been that of life, but of life broadened, raised and illumined by a strong intellectual intuition of the self of man and the large soul of humanity. **And, at the subtlest elevation of all that has yet been reached, stands or rather wings and floats in a high intermediate region**

the poetry of Tagore, not in the complete spiritual light, but amid an air shot with its seeking and glimpses, a sight and cadence found in a psycho-spiritual heaven of subtle and delicate soul-experience transmuting the earth tones by the touch of its radiance. The wide success and appeal of his poetry is indeed one of the most significant signs of the tendency of the mind of the age. At the same time one feels that none of these things are at all the whole of what we are seeking or the definite outcome and issue. That can only be assured when a supreme light of the spirit, a perfect joy and satisfaction of the subtlety and complexity of a finer psychic experience and a wide strength and amplitude of the life-soul, sure of the earth and open to the heavens have met, found each other and fused together in the sovereign unity of some great poetic discovery and utterance.

The most considerable representatives of this new and free form of poetic rhythm are English and American, Carpenter and Whitman. Tagore's translation of his lyrics have come in as a powerful adventitious aid, but are not really to the point in the question at issue; for these translations are nothing but a rhythmically poetic prose and that kind of writing, cadenced prose-poetry, a well recognised form, cannot and does not try to compete with the established principle of measure; it is an indulgence, a minor variation which has met its definite place and serves certain purposes which could not otherwise be fulfilled with any adequacy. It is perhaps the only method for the work. Tagore intends a poetic translation of poetry reproductive of the exact thought and spiritual intention of the original; for a version in the fixed measures of another language not only substitutes another mould for the original movement, but by the substitution gives it almost another soul, so powerful, distinct and creative a thing is poetic rhythm; but the more flexible, less insistent cadence of poetic prose does not so seize on and recast the spirit of the original movement; it may even give a far-off minimised shadow, echo, illusion of it, may have some echo of a similar suggestion. When for instance Tagore writes in English:

> Thou settest a barrier in thine own being and Thou callest thy severed self in myriad notes. This thy self-separation has taken body in me. The great pageant of thee and me has overspread the sky. With the tune of thee and me all the air is vibrant, and all the ages pass with the hiding and seeking of thee and me.

We have a very beautiful, delicately cadenced poetic prose and nothing more. **Tagore is what some of the French writers of *vers libre* and Whitman and Carpenter are not, a delicate and subtle craftsman, and he has done his work with a perfect grace and spiritual fineness**; but there is no attempt to do anything more than the work just in hand, no intention of displacing the old way of poetry, in which he has done in his own language such wonderful things, by a new principle of poetic movement. If there were any such intention, it would have to be pronounced a failure. One has only to compare this English prose, beautiful as it is, with the original poetry to see how much has gone out with the change; something is successfully substituted which may satisfy the English reader, but can never satisfy the ear or the mind that has once listened to the singer's own native and magical melodies. And this is so, even though the intellectual substance, the intellectual precision and distinctness of the thought are often more effective, carry home more quickly in the translation, because in the original the intellectual element, the thought limits are being constantly overborne and are sometimes almost swallowed up by the waves of suggestion that come stealing in with the music; so much more is heard than is said that **the soul listening goes floating into that infinity and counts the definite contribution of the intelligence as of a lesser value.** Precisely there lies the greatest power of poetic rhythm for the very highest work that the new age has to do, and that it can be done by a new use of the poetic method without breaking the whole form of poetry, Tagore's own lyrical work in his mother tongue is the best evidence.

The spirit gives us not only a greater light of truth and vision, but the breath of a greater living; for the spirit is not only the self of our consciousness and knowledge, but the larger self of life. To find our self and the self of things is not to go through a rarefied ether of thought into Nirvana, but to discover the whole greatest integral power of our complex existence.

This need is the sufficient reason for attaching the greatest importance to those poets in whom there is the double seeking of this twofold power, the truth of things and the insistence of life. All the most significant and the vital work in recent poetry has borne this stamp; the rest is of the hour but this is of the future. The poetry of Tagore owes its sudden and universal success to this advantage that **he gives us more of this discovery and fusion for which the mind of our age is in quest than any other creative writer of the time.** His work is a constant music of the overpassing of the borders, a chant-filled realm in which the subtle sounds and lights of the truth of the spirit give new meanings to the finer subtleties of life.

The objection has been made that this poetry is too subtle and remote and goes away from the broad, near, present and vital actualities of existence. But this is to mistake the work of this poetry and to mistake too in a great measure the sense of life as it must reveal itself to the greatening mind of humanity now that mind is growing in world-knowledge and towards self-knowledge.

The future poetry has not to stay in their achievement; it has yet to step from these first fields into new and yet greater ranges, to fathom all the depths yet unplumbed, to complete what has been left half done, to bring all it can of the power of man's greater self and the universal spirit into a broadened and even the broadest possible call of life. That cannot and will not be achieved in its fullness all at once; but to make a foundation of this new infinite range of poetic vision and creation is work enough to give greatness to a whole age.

5

Aesthetics and Tagore's Thought

Agehananda Bharati
(Dr. Leopold Fischer)
Washington University

There is one thing which has to be borne in mind when we try to analyses Rabindranath's thought: he was not a systematic thinker. More than that, he would have resented being called a systematic thinker, or a school-philosopher. Dr. Radhakrishnan, who is always at pains to trace philosophical thought and speculative ideas in the world's great authors, stated that he could not find 'a systematic exposition of Rabindranath's philosophy' in the works of the poet—presumably not only in his poetic works, but neither in his philosophising essays.

Be that as it may, there is no doubt that a modern critic who has had philosophical training in any school—analytic or otherwise—would be pressed hard to assign any aesthetical nomenclature to Tagore's philosophical views, yet it would be presumptuous to deny that his *Weltanschauung* was not a philosophical one. It was not systematic by any means, but we must not identify systematic reasoning with philosophy—philosophy is wider than that, despite the analysts' invectives. To be more exact, this is a matter of definition—if Tagore's thought does not figure as philosophy (and all anti-metaphysical thinkers of our day would deny the epithet 'philosopher' to Tagore), then neither do Bradley, Bosanquet, or even Bergson. Nor, for that, any of the Indian scholastics, Brahmin, Buddhist, or Jaina. Tagore uses sentences, he does not analyse them; and so do the Indian thinkers—their dicta were meant to persuade their votaries to a course of meditation or to a course of action, or to convince them of the validity and the supremacy of their particular doctrine. Now this might be readily admitted where the doctrines concerned are of a religious or spiritual type. It is less obvious, though equally valid, in an area which is closer to Tagore's own interests and methods—i.e., in the Indian traditional philosophy of poetics, *rasavada*. Let me adduce an example:

A medieval Brahmin theorist in poetics, Vamana, differing from most of his predecessors, averred that aesthetical sentiment (*rasa*) was not an ornament or a rhetorical device of poetry (*alamkara*), but that it was a poetical quality proper (vd. his *Kavyalamkarasutra, III., ii. 14*). But the entire *alamkara*-tradition of India—and that includes Vamana's theses as well—regards both qualities and ornaments (*guna* and *alamkara*) as attributes of poetry, as equally essential factors, and that the aesthetical sentiment (*rasa*) subsists in all the constituent factors; *rasa* must therefore be the basis or the receptacle of poetical ornament (*alamkarya, gunin*), and neither an ornament nor a quality (vd. *Dhvanyaloka*),

"श्रलंकार्यातिरिक्तश्चालंकारः श्रभ्युपगन्तव्यः लोके तथा सिद्धत्वात्"

In other words, *rasa* is its foundation, not its content. This is corroborated by the *sruti* which has *'raso vai sah'*, although scholars like Prof. Raghavan would probably deny the semantical identity of the poetic '*rasa*' and the '*rasa*' of the Upanishadic dictum.

From this example it seems to follow that even apparently analytical arguments or statements are persuasive in the final analysis. And it is for this reason that I cannot admit that Tagore stands outside the Indian tradition of poetics and of philosophy. He is an innovator of style rather than of content; his dislike for system is stronger than with the classics, and his antisystemicity is codified, as it were, in his theoretical essays, esp. *Sadhana,* the only opus, incidentally, from which some sort of philosophical system might be construed *post mortem.*

The parallel might not seem too obvious at first sight. Let me elaborate: the idea that eventually everything is the matrix, the Self, *atman* or *Brahman,* is an axiom with much of the Indian tradition, and there is hardly any branch of orthodox learning which would not pay homage to the axiom by making its own specific research subservient to the redemptive frame. Even during the first stages of commentative speculation there was a split into two fundamentally different attitudes: should statements of revealed literature be taken to define or should they be taken to enjoin a course of action or contemplation (*vidhi*). The balance was to be in favour of the latter: whatever text, whatever research, *shruti* or *smriti* alike, there has been, and there remains up to this day, the notion of *vidhi*—either overtly or implied—is the predominant notion.

It is this fact—and I don't think this has been said before—which may account for the reluctance of the traditional scholar in India, as well as of the poet who has preserved, to whatever meagre degree, his traditional roots, to define his position. And this holds for Tagore just as much as for the author of the *Dhvanyaloka*, irrespective of the fact that the two are diametrically opposed to each other in their attitude toward poetics: Tagore dislikes theorising, and scoffs at system; the Brahmin poetics-philosopher theorises, albeit in verse, and propounds system. But in spite of this seemingly important difference, there is a common denominator between the two: there is injunction, *vidhi* at the basis of their philosophy. For even if you 'be something' (a sentiment shared by all who participate in the mystic idiom of India) rather than 'do something', the imperative remains. There never is anything like pure description for description's sake as we find in the West's philosophers. All Indian thought, however abstract and recondite, enjoins something on its votaries; and though that sounds paradoxical again, the avowedly contemplative East, in its Indian paradigm at least, is intensely pragmatical in the sense of non-descriptive; 'action' may be transferred onto the mental plane, but there is no mere description anywhere.

Tagore stands, then, deeply in the Indian scholastic and poeticist tradition, and he extends the axiom of action, or affection, to all realms of philosophical speculation. With the modern philosophical analysts—of the Viennese and the British-American schools in particular—ethics and aesthetics are purely descriptive, they are no longer normative; the normative portion of ethics, or what used to be thought of as ethics, as well as the normative portion of aesthetics being relegated to the pulpit, to the preacher, the sermonist; they no longer are deemed worthy of the academical philosopher's attention. Modern analytical philosophy gives a wide berth to the 'great' and 'interesting' issues which classical philosophy in the West used to concern itself with, and which are the topic of all Indian philosophy up to this day; in India, the separation of philosophy from theology has not been accomplished, and its promulgators reject the suggestion that such a separation is either necessary or desirable.[1] Tagore stands with the Indian philosopher, from Yajnavalkya and Bhamaha to Radhakrishnan, and also with the system-building philosophers of the European philosophical tradition, before it forswore Aristotle and the 'interesting' issues. "Like ethics, aesthetics aims chiefly at influencing life," said Tagore. This is an eminently traditional view, both Indian and Occidental, and it is precisely what contemporary philosophy denies.

Now though Tagore shuns systematisation—both of the orthodox Indian traditional sort and of the Occidental philosophical sort (though the latter must be inferred—he was never exposed to modern analytical philosophy—like for most Indian thinkers up to this very day, Western philosophy ends with Bradley and Bosanquet)—there is no doubt that

1. *The Philosophy of S. Radhakrishnan*, New York, 1952.

his work and his personality correspond in every point to the postulates of the *kavya* and *alamkara shastras;* he has, in an eminent degree, what the texts call *sadyah paranirvriti,* the bestowing of aesthetical delight, and *priti* which is downright pleasure in the most refined hedonistic sense. The scholar-preceptors who coined these terms were rigid speculators, aestheticians of the rigour of a Collingwood or a Croce; Tagore was profoundly averse to rigour. But this is precisely how he fits into the pattern; for the *kavya*-theoreticians presribed the delight, the empathy, the warmth for the poet and they probably felt that they themselves should not own these emotional assets themselves; or if they had them, they would keep them private, very much as modern analytical ethicists and aestheticians may well be personally affected by aesthetical warmth and by ethical appeal.

In India and in the modern West alike—strange how ancient India and the modern West should be at one in an important way—the literary scholar and his object are separate persons, and if (this holds especially for the modern West) a scholar of literature chances to be himself affected by poetical sentiment, is likely to be viewed with suspicion—particularly here in America, people quickly use the term 'fake' for a scholar who dares identify himself with the object of his research. On this count, Tagore was of course not a philosopher; he lived his philosophy too much. But then there are the existentialists in Europe today, especially Jaspers, for whom philosophy is identical with 'being affected'. Far from claiming that Tagore would have had anything to do with existentialist thought as conceived by the professional thinkers of that school, it yet remains to be seen whether Tagore's work—or part of it—could not be viewed under an angle similar to that of the existentialists.

I am thinking of his novels—take such masterpieces as his early *The Wreck* and then again his most perfect novel *The Home and the World,*—the characters are not in any sense un-Indian, but there is an implied identification of moral value with the rebel against convention; for the first time in Indian literature, it appears that Tagore brought characters to the fore that tried to be themselves, and not what was expected from them. The novel is a new genre and has no precursor in the *kavya* tradition; it is therefore not possible to judge it by traditional Indian standards.

The instrument of aesthetical analysis, diametrically opposed to traditional Indian critique of literature and thought, is contemporary Occidental analytical philosophy, especially of the linguistic type: authors like C. L. Stevenson or R. Hare, and all those who have been probing normative problems through the analysis of the language that constitutes them. None of them, to my knowledge, has so far analysed Tagore's philosophy, or his poetical statements with a philosophical reference. This has to be done some day. But in conclusion of this paper, I might adumbrate what I would think to be the main points of study, were Tagore's thought—especially his aesthetical views—subjected to linguistically oriented philosophical analysis; Tagore used persuasive definitions in his theoretical work (as *Sadhana* etc.); like most traditional ethicists and aestheticians he used indicative propositions to convey imperatives, or hortatives (for he was a mild man).

His *Weltanschauung* was universal, no doubt, but not devoid of a large backlog of ideological indoctrination; the Brahmo worldview, insistence on a bulk universe, which was an outcome of the eclectic atmosphere of his home—his ancestors' interest in the Upanishads and in the Sufis alike, with no specific predilection of the one or the other—the wealth and general somatic well-being of his parental environment, and the fact that he was a pioneer, and prolific—all these made him a bit pompous as a person, so much so that in his late years it was hard for anyone to communicate with him, because Rabindranath never came down from his high cloud. The Bengali language is eminently apt as a medium of emotive impression and in a way he created that medium afresh. But his philosophy was limited by his language: the emphasis on universal oneness, on what

Levy Bruhl would have subsumed under his 'participation mystique', the axiomatic notion of a personal god, not quite as atrociously fatherlike as the orthodox Islamic or Christian godfather, and the postulate of a monistic universe where differences were both negligible and irksome—all this makes Tagore a bit tedious to the critical analyst.

All Bengalis hold Tagore to be the greatest that ever lived in the letters, *nabhuta na bhavishyati*, and no literary critic in the world would dispute the greatness and his uniqueness. But then the analyst has to pose the question: if all that has been said about him (or any other great man) was good and tremendous and incomparably excellent, *what was wrong*? There is no such thing as perfection in the world, a fact even the pathological optimist grudgingly admits—so what was wrong with Tagore? The answer would have to be sought somewhere along the lines which I have hinted above: emotional oversimplification —the universe is not necessarily one, one can see it as manifold without oneness; many philosophers and poets have seen it that way, and some of them have even rejoiced in diversity *without* any underlying oneness (the Buddhists, for instance, and many modern empiricists); if we are all children of God, some of these children are nice and tolerable, others stink—Tagore's pompousness may well be the result of what the psychologists call 'overcompensation': his 'all is basically good, true, and beautiful' and his implied 'all bad, untrue, ugly things are eventually unimportant and must be poetically overlooked'—quite apart from going on some people's nerves—may have been his defence-mechanism, built up against the philosophical and empirical fact that the universe can well be seen as pure misery (with the Buddhist, Jaina, many Hindu schools, and many western skeptics), or as a mixture of misery and beauty, in various degrees.

6

Tagore's Concept of Beauty

K. Krishnamoorthy

There is no one who does not eat or drink,
but few there are, who know the flavour.

—*Confucius*

If Tagore has been known to the English-speaking world more as a poet than as an aesthetic philosopher, it is because most of his essays on art and literature have not yet appeared in English translations. Tagore, of course, laid no claims to be considered as an academic philosopher. Yet he was an original thinker and his essays and studies reveal how he had arrived at his own philosophy of beauty, a philosophy which combines ancient Indian wisdom with a modern spirit of enquiry.

It may be said of Tagore that his poetry was his philosophy, for there were no separate compartments in his personality. **His whole personality was permeated by the joy of beauty, beauty within and beauty without.** He was not only a high-priest of Nature, but a mystic who felt the glory of universal man everywhere. Tagore's approach is integral and touches the very essence of art-creation. His philosophy of beauty derives directly from his all-embracing humanism which was a religion with him and is more universal than individual. It is more or less a modern commentary of the basic Upanishadic text—*raso vai sah.*

The cardinal tenet of Tagore's philosophy is contained in the following passage which forms the peroration of a lecture delivered by him in America on the question 'What is Art?':

> What is it in man that asserts its immortality in spite of the obvious fact of death? It is not his physical body or his mental organisation. It is that deeper unity, the ultimate mystery in him, which, from the centre of his world, radiates towards its circumference; which is in his body, yet transcends his body; which is in his mind, yet grows beyond his mind; which through the things belonging to him, expresses something that is not in them; which, while occupying his present, overflows its banks of the past and of the future. It is the personality of man, conscious of its inexhaustible abundance; ... And this consciousness of the infinite, in the personal man, ever strives to make its expression immortal and to make the whole world its own. In Art the person in us is sending its answers to the Supreme Person, who reveals Himself to us in a world of endless beauty across the lightless world of facts.

The insistence throughout in on the creative personality of the poet which is akin to that of the divine Creator of the universe itself in deriving and diffusing joy by the work of creation. Man's inner spirit is said to be most free when it is creating beauty, not when it is acquiring knowledge in the study or when it is applying that knowledge to acquire some power or pelf.

> Man has a fund of emotional energy which is not all occupied with his self-preservation. This surplus seeks its outlet in the creation of Art, for man's civilisation is built upon his surplus.

Tagore's ideal, naturally, may be described as 'Art for Art's sake' in an infinitely extended sense than the one we are familiar with in English criticism.

Tagore does not agree that the world of art is remote from reality. On the other hand, it is more real to him than science and metaphysics. As he observes in a lecture:

> Abstract truth may belong to science and metaphysics, but the world of reality belongs to Art.[1]

> Art is *maya* in a positive sense:

> Art has the magic wand which gives undying reality to all things it touches, and relates them to the personal being in us.[2]

Tagore's is a kind of pantheism in whose infinite glow the creative spirit can see nothing but infinite even in things seemingly plain, because **beauty is the very 'soul' of things,** giving rise to bliss (*ananda*) in the universe:

> I believe that the vision of Paradise is to be seen in the sunlight and the green of the earth, in the beauty of the human race, and the wealth of human life, even in objects that are seemingly insignificant and unprepossessing.[3]

It is only the refined sensibility of an artist that can capture this all-pervading *rasa* in the universe and immortalise it in a creative work of art:

> I say that a poet's mission is to attract the voice which is yet inaudible in the air; to inspire faith in the dream which is unfulfilled; to bring the earliest tidings of the unborn flower to a skeptic world.[4]

In the philosophy of Tagore, the three values, Truth, Goodness and Beauty, shed their rivalry, and even their difference, and emerge as different facets of the same reality.

---

1. *The Religion of an Artist,* Visvabharati, 1953.
2. *Ibid.*
3. *Ibid.*
4. *Talks in China,* Vishvabharati, 1925.

Artists are regarded as revealing the good through the medium of beauty, the good which is veritably felt as true.

The highest joy of the inner self is felt neither in the achievements of the intellect nor in the feverish economic activities, but in the feelings and the emotions of the heart. The feeling for beauty is deeply embedded in the very nature of man and Art answers to this instinct. **A society's culture or a country's civilisation is to be measured through its creative works of art and not through scientific or technical achievements. Tagore was convinced that ancient Greece and India were the most civilised of countries in so far as they could leave immortal epics like the *Iliad* and the *Ramayana* to posterity.** Such classics are the highest assets of man and the most permanent moments, for they transcend Time and Space, unlike man's activities in other fields.

The chief obstacle in the way of man's realising beauty is said to lie in his self-centredness or egoism. True beauty is that which, in one sweep, embraces the universal man; and the walls of egoism that rise between man and man only serve to shut out the glimpses of the all-pervading beauty in Man and Nature. Sensual beauty is thus to be distinguished clearly from spiritual beauty which is the law of life. The latter cannot to appreciated by one whose life is unrestrained. Sensual restraint, then, is the first and foremost requirement in the appreciation of genuine beauty. Tagore takes great pains to show the hollowness of the popular notion that licence and creativity can coexist.

We find the aesthetic theory of Tagore very well illustrated in his illuminating appreciation of Valmiki and Kalidasa. In the vast epic of Valmiki, what strikes Tagore is the essential "humanness" or *rasa* informing the whole work. Rama is a great hero for Tagore not because he is a god come to earth for the redress of suffering humanity, but because he embodies in himself the highest human values. He is an ideal son and an ideal brother, an ideal husband and an ideal friend. The

Ramayana itself appears more as an epic of family-life than as a saga of heroic warfare. The *Kumarasambhava* of Kalidasa assumes new significance as the saga of an ideal Indian housewife, whose beauty of heart outshines her beauty of person; the former alone leading to the cherished goal while the latter is foredoomed to failure despite the assistance of the god of physical love. This contrast of physical passion with what Tagore calls spiritual love is most prominently brought out in his study of Kalidasa's masterpiece, the *Shakuntala.* Physical love whose concern is the joy of the hour proves a moral lapse bringing down upon itself a curse; and what saves it ultimately is suffering and sacrifice.

Tagore thus bridges the gulf between the life-affirming and life-denying philosophies of ancient India, the one rankly materialistic and the other severely monastical. Kalidasa's greatness, according to Tagore, precisely lies in this synthesis which he poetically achieved when Indian poetry had not yet lost its youth. Even the dark rain-cloud in Kalidasa's *Meghaduta* appears to be symbolic to Tagore of sublime and fertilising phenomenon in the inmost heart of man. These studies by Tagore of our Sanskrit classics are masterly examples of aesthetic analyses in which are retraced the various stages of artistic creation with a sympathy unknown in the critics of today.

Perception of beauty according to Tagore is directly dependent on the degree of sensibility cultivated by man towards fellowmen and nature. The sensibility can be cultivated to embrace even the whole of humanity; and therein lies the highest privilege of man, compared to other animals. The present crisis in civilisation due to a lopsided growth of reason and manipulating power can be averted, and joy found for all, only by the cultivation by everyone of the aesthetic outlook whose essence is love and whose realm is infinity.

Poetry, in the opinion of Tagore, is a subtly organised,

synthetical product and not just "some natural sorrow, loss or pain," harmonising into a unity the most disparate experiences of the poet. The technical and formal excellences are inseparably associated with the material he handles and the underlying wholeness of the work is what merits the attention of the cultured critic. Thus Tagore avoids the controversies that have been raging about the relative importance of Form and Matter in Western aesthetics. Tagore has strikingly shown how the aesthetic life of man is embedded in his total life, and how the internal standard is the best of the many standards by which it may be judged, and how the internal standard, when fully cultivated, helps in breaking down the walls between the morally good and the beautiful and the true.

Tagore, who inherited the best in ancient Sanskrit classics and later Bengali Vaishnavite poetic tradition, tried to give an aesthetics which was at once Indian and universal. He was something of a revolutionary in his own way when he gave a new meaning altogether to the schoolmen's concepts of *Rasa* and *Alamkara* and invested them with new significance. A creative writer that Tagore was, he could illustrate his points with homely and poetic metaphors; and the influence of his aesthetics is felt even in the works of great poets like Kuvempu in other languages (like Kannada) in remote provinces like Karnataka.

7

Tagore's Philosophy of Literature

Sachin Sen

Man has his physical needs which have to be satisfied. But he has his mind also which seeks its own food. According to Tagore, there is the physical man, and there is the personal man. The physical man lives in the world of necessity; the personal man establishes relations with the world through his love, through his emotions, through the expression of his personality. Literature is concerned with the world of personality.

Then there is the distinction between the animal and man. The animal is bound by its necessities; its activities are found in self-preservation and the perpetuation of race. **But man is not satisfied with mere living. He has a surplus which is not exhausted in mere living. It is upon this fund of surplus that man's creations, science and philosophy thrive.** Tagore intensely believed that literature had its origin 'in this region of the superfluous'. To quote his words: 'Man has a fund of emotional energy which is not all occupied with his self-preservation. This surplus seeks its outlet in the creation of Art, for **man's civilisation is built on this surplus'.**

In the analysis of Tagore, man is not an isolated individual. He is 'the organic man' who not only lives in his surroundings but eternally creates himself. He selects things from his surroundings 'in order to make them his own'. Man creates himself by his emotional forces. Man expresses his personal world, not the abstract world of physics or metaphysics. Man has love and hatred, pain and pleasure, fear and wonder. He develops his own emotions, his own sentiments. The outer world has its own juices, exciting the emotional activities of man. But the outer juices must be integrated with the inner juices of man's emotions. Thus, information of facts is not literature. But when facts have their relations with the personal world of the writer, we get literature which is 'the object of perennial interest'.

Literature must arouse our emotions; it must intensify our consciousness; it must have the tunes of the personal man. In literature, information and explanation are not the basic things. Facts and suggestions which reveal the personality of the writer and move the hearts of readers have their importance in literature. In short, literature is concerned with 'personal facts', conjuring up pictures and songs in other minds. Self-expression is important, but Tagore valued the self-expression which has no relation to the claims of necessity.

Tagore was a millionaire in similies. **He compares the function of an artist to that of a woman. A woman has to be picturesque and musical to make manifest what she truly is. She is to be judged not by her usefulness but by her delightfulness. She, therefore, takes infinite care in expressing her personality. The artist similarly has to express his personality; creations of art to be judged by their delightfulness.** In art, the matter and the manner are important. They are to be united.

If the artist has known the inner man, he is a true artist. The true artist must find out 'the unique, the individual, which yet is in the heart of the universal'. Man has soul; it is not enough. The universe has a soul. Man must express the universal soul. That is the solemn task before the writer. Thus, he is interested in truth, beauty and joy. He has to take note of the life which is of the mind "with its one side in the dark and the other in the light."

In true literature, man expresses his infinite side. To quote Tagore: "Man is true where he feels his infinity, where he is divine, and the divine is the creator in him.." The infinite side of man has to be revealed in symbols which have the elements of immortality. It refuses all that is flimsy and feeble and incongruous. It is in this view of things that Tagore had never been weary of proclaiming that men were the children of light and delight. The function of literature is to build the world of truth and beauty. Tagore believed that "the real is not that which is merely seen and wealth is not that which is stored." The person who is infinite is revealed when there is the joy of living and love of fellow-creatures.

When facts are mere facts, they are rejected by the true artist. Tagore accepts the position that "our world of expression does not accurately coincide with the world of facts, because personality surpasses facts on every side. It is conscious of its infinity and creates from its abundance. This consciousness of the infinite, in the personal man, ever strives to make its expressions immortal and to make the whole world its own." According to Tagore, "The variety of creation is due to the mind seeing different phenomena in different foci of time and space."

Tagore's philosophy of literature cannot be understood if his basic proposition is not accepted that **the artist is concerned not with the scientific world, which is our world of reasoning, but with the world of personality, which is our world of emotion and intuition.** "The reality of the world belongs to the personality of man and not to reasoning." In a game the personality of the player counts much. The techniques of the game are changed by different players. Similarly, different artists behave differently, because their personalities differ.

Here two things are to be noted. First, the artist has its own forms and techniques, but he must try to express more than what they contain. Form is necessary, but **the artist must express something which transcends the form.**

Second, the artist as a creator must contribute his own voice to the concert of the world-music. He is to produce harmony, not discord. Hence, the Tagore thesis is this: "Let us express our infinity in everything around us, in works we do, in things we use, in men with whom we deal, in the enjoyment of the world with which we are surrounded. Let our soul permeate our surroundings and create itself in all things, and show its fullness by fulfilling needs of all times."

Life must move on; there must be perpetual giving up. The movement, the consciousness of the infinite in man, the form of perpetual giving out of abundance, all these are the marks of great literature. The eternal in us cannot be expressed if there is not the joy of living. The true joy of life comes when the individual pours himself out in his own creation. A person who does not express does not feel the abundance of joy. Life is to be lived for the expression of our personality through love, through work, through songs, through devotion, through art, or through writings. **He who does not express, kills his soul. "We must not slay our soul."** Isa Upanishad says: "He who sees all things in the soul and the soul in all things is never more hidden."

Tagore's postulate is this. There is the world of nature and the world of humanity. In the natural world, man deals with science. In the moral world, man is concerned with the world of sympathy and understanding. For all other creatures, nature is final. But man wants to move further; he has his own career of creative life. He is not satisfied with the world that is given to him; he is bent upon making it his own. He is restless; he wants to create; he wants to express himself in the creation of his moral world. Man may be foolish, but he does not fully trust the world he lives in. In this view of things, literature is great when it is concerned with the life of soul, with the world of humanity.

According to Tagore, **the eternal man is a thinker and a lover.** The world of necessity has urged him to make various experiments in physical science, but the world of emotions drive him to create art and literature. There are two forms of expression: through the conquest of nature, and through the world of emotions. Man is to be fully known through the recognition of both forms of expression. But literature knows the essential man, the eternal man, the emotional man. Tagore is not indifferent to the unity of thought and action. Through action man wants to maintain and preserve his material existence; through thought man wants to reveal himself to realise his kinship with the world. We cannot afford to be indifferent to the technique of preservation of self, but the task of self-realisation drives man to carve new paths, to make experiments, to find union in the hearts of people.

There is the world of facts and the world of truths. Facts are scattered, limited. Truths are found when facts are harmonised. Literature looks to the harmony in facts. Facts are diverse, they have different facets, they are studied differently by different persons. But facts are important in literature when they seek to interpret the eternal man and the universal. It is true that the true end of literature is to present life. **But much of life is off the point; much of it is unessential and unrelated. Literature, when it deals with the unessential and unrelated facts of life, is not good. Literature is to eliminate the unessential.**

T.S. Eliot emphasised the point that "the great poet, in writing himself, writes his time." It means that every good poet starts from his own emotions. But there is the struggle in the poet "to transmute his personal and private agonies into something rich and strange, something universal and impersonal." It was Tagore's dream that he was the poet of the world whose varied voices and tunes would find response in his flute. According to Tagore, the true end of literature is to interpret the writer's emotions and impulses through language, to make personal joys and pains impersonal, and to invest the spirit of universality with the matters of the moment. There must be profound realisation and deep penetration so that the writer and the reader become united.

There are two fundamental traits of good literature:

(1) Literature takes note of the various tunes of man's flute,

(2) It has to give distinctive form and direction so that an imperishable impression is created on the reader. The true artist has his own angle; he can find out the essential from the so-called non-essentials.

Man has a cage to live in, the road to travel on. He needs both. The cage without the road creates bonds; the road without the cage brings punishment. The two worlds must meet in the artist. Man must be on the move. Tagore hates those who refuse to move. **But roads are not straight. They have their turns and twists. In every turn and twist, new tempers, new urges, new tests appear.** Every age has its own temper, its own form and style of expression. New forms of expression and new urges are inevitable. **Thus, literature which treats man as an eternal wayfarer has a message for all times.** Tagore's literature is instinct with the message for all men of all times.

The Marxist is critical of Tagore's philosophy of literature. With him the emphasis is not on the interpretation of the world, but on the methods of changing the course of history. **According to Tagore, the purpose of literature is not to express any particular point of view. The writer is not to be the broker of any political party. When man in his agony is dumb, the writer has to give expression to his sufferings. The writer is to deal with man, not with the class.**

The personal world in which the writer lives is being circumscribed by the ascendancy of State power and of machine civilisation. It will be a bad day for the writer when the individual loses his soul and is submerged by the State and the machine power. Hence, Tagore had been critical of the machine civilisation and the totalitarian system which throttles the individual and the diverse means of expression. He does not offer any definite solution, nor does he line up openly on any particular side. He is influenced by the ideals of the complete man, the higher purposes of society through human morality.

8

Tagore and English Romantics

Bani Chaudhuri

Tagore is indeed a vast phenomenon to the modern readers, who, though separated from him hardly by a few decades, live in an age of specialisation and dilletantism rather than largeness and versatility of purpose.

Tagore includes all possible forms of literature beginning with poetry to the literary essay—poetry being the most ancient and literary essay the most modern of the forms of literature, so to say. In comprehending such a vast range of artistic experiences, he has been subject to different trends of thought belonging to varied types of mind and culture. But these by no means have been the building principles in his works. They have come, fallen, mixed and finally been lost to create a chemical compound, as it were, in the oceanic vastness and suppleness of his mind. Thus, the essence of the Upanishad and Kalidasa are woven into the very fabrics of his mental texture—the one expressing itself in his conception of God and life, as a whole, and the other, especially in his quick and deep response to beauty.

His relations with the English Romantics, however, is not as fundamental as that. But, there is a peculiar sense of affinity that makes one believe that Tagore in one combines all the imports of romanticism, but in a maturer and more oriental way.

Wordsworth, Keats and Shelley, the three symbols of the Romantic Revival, have come down to us as the theorists of three different trends of idealism. Although the division is slightly overlapping, to be short, Wordsworth idealised nature, Shelley—love, and Keats—beauty. Tagore, in his turn, conceives of a *Manasasundari,* who is more than the spirit of beauty loved and adored, as she expresses herself in the changing marvels of nature and distils through art into poetry.

The vision of nature that Wordsworth had, was essentially pantheistic. He felt the spirit of God in the details of nature and therefore its significance to him was manifold; as the abode of God, it was endowed with the moral principle that guides the universe, and as the eternal companion of mankind, its influence on him was not only maternal but also that of a guide and a friend. It was the moral teacher, guide, and soul's companion to his Lucy, who represents the ideal creature that may be born through constant intercourse with nature.

Tagore goes one step further, and that essentially because he is an Indian. An Indian sees God in the manifestation of the self and vice versa. Tagore feels with nature a kinship of generation and traces himself through the labyrinth of a birth cycle, to the pre-historic flowers and trees. It is the universal self that he discovers dormant in nature as the transmuted expression of God. This feeling comes to him not once, but in the different stages of *Manasi, Valaka* and even in *Shyamali* or *Punashca.* He does not anywhere in his poetry expressly indicate nature as the moral guide or friend of mankind, but his faith in this respect is evident in his choice of Santiniketan as the university of learning of his students.

But whatever resemblance lies between Wordsworth and Tagore, it is never vital. There is a fundamental difference between the two both on the temperamental and the philosophical level. In Wordsworth, mysticism reigned for ever and reigned supreme. But **Tagore, although he is known**

to the world mainly as a mystic poet, is adorable equally, if not more, for his hymns to beauty and to love and it is here that we discover his more significant and more pronounced relations with the English romantics like Keats and Shelley.

Keats' world of beauty lay mainly in perceptible and tangible forms and his enjoyment was keenly and deeply sensuous. The frail poet, pining and despairing for ever could never follow the wild dynamism of a Byron or a Shelley and sought truth in static but lively forms of beauty—the flowers, the moon, the Grecian urn or the fascinating figures like those of Endymion or Hyperion fossilised in the hollow of time itself. Tagore perceives through senses but transcends them as well. He visualises beauty as distant, omnipresent and indifferent, as in *Urvashi* he pays homage to this eternal beauty and interprets her as one of her own kind for ever alluring man into impossible dreams and yet retaining her divine chastity from their aspiring hands. She comes nearer, as in *Niruddeshya Yatra,* but confounds and baffles man as before.

This sense of confusion, however, is never able to wear out the poet's patience and stir his habitual tranquillity, as it does in Shelley. **Shelley cries, falls and faints while Tagore inquires, waits and overcomes.** Shelley is one of those unfortunate philanthropists whose tragedy lies in the very sincerity of their faith which is based on a total misunderstanding of human nature. For all the complications of his nature, Shelley had the innocence of a romantic which led him to an illusory identification between appearance and reality. For, the noble principle of love he believes in, is impossible unless in a millenium. The dreams of a millenium might seem possible to the poet who witnessed the French Revolution, but the hope of its realisation naturally seemed more and more fantastic to one who witnessed its results as well. Therefore, the poet goes on weaving a chain of dreams and decides to unbound all the Prometheuses, but starts at moments, when the consciousness of the utter difference of the situation dawns on him. Then he writes in pain and bleeds upon the thorns of life,—Shelley's philanthropism is essentially Christian and its centrifugal forces distract him from thoughts of himself to a diffused consideration of universal neighbourhood.

But Tagore's philanthropism is profoundly influenced by Buddhism, which sees universal well-being in directing one's full concentration to one's own self and thus by a simpler process seeks to correct and elevate the whole humanity. It is for this simple philosophical reason that Tagore succeeds in his quest of love which ends in the centre of his own soul, while Shelley sees it vain and fleeting, choosing 'the frailest of cradles' for its home. It is also for this reason that Shelley for all his noble ideals had to live a life of distraction and disintegration, while Tagore turned every stumbling block of sorrow to decide stepping stones towards spiritual progress.

Tagore's is indeed, a long history of steady triumph over life. Shelley realised that

Life, like a dome of many-coloured glass,
Stains the white radiance of Eternity,
Until Death tramples it to fragments.

This vision, however inspired, never brought him any spiritual consolation, and he saw death here and there and everywhere, with but a melancholy and bleak prospect of total oblivion. Tagore realises this too, but he proceeds nevertheless, to see it whole. In the final realisation, the bleakness changes into an ethereal promise of joy and life itself, with its enormous store of sufferings, stands transfigured in the supreme bliss of reunion with death.

9

Tagore on Spirituality, East and West

Charles A. Moore
Hawaii University

One of the most important aspects of Tagore's philosophy is his broadmindedness and liberalism with respect to the meaning of spirituality in East and West. It is almost customary to distinguish the spiritual East from the materialistic West. Tagore has put an end to this falsifying contrast—and without even mentioning Judaism or Christianity, jointly the near-universal basis of the West's strictly religious spirituality. He recognises many facets, and forms, and expressions of the spiritual. Also, although he recognises such differences of expression, he is convinced that there is "a spiritual kinship which is universal among the peoples of mankind" (*The Religion of Man*), and does not believe that material values have been the driving force of any great civilisation.

He establishes the spirituality of the West on three counts.

(1) First, he finds specifically that the West is significantly spiritual. He cites the spiritual significance of the typically Western activity of fighting against evils and for ideals and spiritual values. **He specifically praises (Western) science**

and reason as spiritual, lifting man above appearances in search of truth, lifting him above the material, and also serving mankind, although, of course, science is great, as is the machine also, only when it is working in these directions, but not, of course, when used for other purposes. More specifically, and as a very revealing specific example, he says, **"When the aeroplane rises into the sky, we may marvel at it as the acme of mechanical perfection but it is more than this: it is a victory of the spirit. For it was not until, in the West, man had overcome the fear of death that he could master the art of flying—the art of the Gods!"**

It is pertinent and significant that, in his story of the beggar woman in a Bengal village who found the infinite in the stale flowers that were about to be thrown away, he says, "But in spite of it all she lacked that energy of worship, that Western form of direct divine service, the service of man, which helps the earth to bring out her flowers and spread the reign of beauty on the desolate dust."

(2) Second, he approvingly describes many aspects of the spiritual which are recognised as such by Westerners—although there are many in Asia, perhaps especially in India, who ignore such spirituality.

Tagore is universally considered a "humanist par excellence." In essence, he says that true humanism is, or at least involves, genuine spirituality. He seems to be saying quite clearly that the West is spiritual, even if—or because—it is humanistic, or as often alleged, "merely humanistic" or "merely ethical." He cites in this connection many specific activities and attitudes of the West which qualify as spiritual. In such a short paper it must suffice simply to mention these items, one by one, without elaboration:

Religions, he says, arise from human need and for human good. Further, that "the humanity of God, or the divinity of Man" is the topic of his chief concern. Also, "Humanity is the dharma [religion] of human beings." He speaks of religion as the development or fulfilment of personality.

In perhaps the most pointed and enlightening passage in this connection, he says. "It [man's developed consciousness] inspires these creations of his that reveal the divinity in him—which is his humanity—in the varied manifestations of truth, goodness and beauty, in the freedom of activity which is not for his use but for his ultimate expression. **The individual man must exist for Man the great, and must express him in his disinterested works, in science and philosophy, in literature and arts, in service and worship.** This is his religion, which is working in the heart of all his religions in various names and forms."

Furthermore, he speaks of human perfection as the criterion even of truth, as well as the test of true spirituality. He raises to the height of spirituality the life of activity—whether it be in accordance with the teaching of the Buddha or the West's looking for and fighting against evil, or in accordance with the *Bhagavad Gita*, the ordinary activity of social duty for social welfare. He praises the love of man which "gives us the testing of the great whole, which is the complete and final truth of Man." As personal confirmation, he cities his own case of rejecting the ivory tower of literary activity and forcing himself out of seclusion and into practical affairs, even though this seemed to violate his traditional Indian point of view. He says, "I vaguely felt that my need was spiritual self-realisation in the life of Man through some disinterested service."

He pays respect to leisure, which is obtainable only after material fulfilment has been achieved. **He feels that prosperity is a boon to mankind unless it is gained by evil means or used for evil purposes** or takes one's mind away from the spiritual. Also, he says, **"I refuse to imagine any special value in poverty when it is a mere negation ...."** He feels quite clearly that "our material poverty in the East" is a barrier to "the meeting of East and West in full spirituality."

He quotes a Chinese sage as saying, "To increase life

is called a blessing." He praises the dignity of man as man. **He repeatedly refers to art as spiritual, especially music, and painting and literature.** Morality is also praised as a spiritual activity. He also speaks of "our consciousness of an ideal—in every sense—as spiritual.

(3) Third, he challenges the sole or adequate spirituality of the extreme form of the spiritual found in India (which constantly serves as the basis of the charge that the West is not spiritual). The extreme spirituality of India is not a true criterion of spirituality. For Tagore, the only significant infinite is the infinite in its human aspect. He rejects what he calls the Indian "ideal of the utter extinction of the individual separateness." **He strongly criticises the interpretation of the Vedanta doctrine that "Brahman is the absolute Truth, the impersonal It, in which there can be no distinction of this or that, the good and the evil, the beautiful and its opposite, having no other quality except its ineffable blissfulness** in the eternal solitude of its consciousness utterly devoid of all things and all thoughts." Instead, he seeks for "a Being who comprehends in himself all things that are human in knowledge, will and action."

Tagore never abandons the high spirituality of his Indian tradition, but seems to recommend a more human content for it, and thus prepares the way for his very telling remark: "When the streams of ideals that flow from the East and from the West mingle their murmur in some profound harmony of meaning it delights my soul." This is Tagore's comprehensive—and profound—vision. He explains further: "And I had intently wished that the introspective vision of the universal soul, which an Eastern devotee realises in the solitude of his mind, could be united with this spirit of his outward expression in service, the exercise of will in unfolding the wealth of beauty and well-being from its shy obscurity to the light." Here is the basis of East-West understanding and the way to mutual respect.

10

The Religion of Tagore

P. Nagaraja Rao

Gandhiji and Tagore have been the two outstanding personalities that put India on the map of the world by spreading her message to the world and by awakening Indian humanity to the awareness of their precious spiritual heritage. Both the savants, each in his unique way, dominated the cultural and political life of the country in the first half of the twentieth century. Tagore represents the true spiritual religion of the Upanishads and the *Gita.* The Upanishads have been the chief unfailing source of his inspiration, his outlook on life and religion. He writes: "To me the verses of the Upanishads and the teachings of the Buddha have ever been the things of the Spirit and therefore endowed with boundless vital growth and I have used them in my preaching as being instinct with individual meaning for me."

He did not look upon the Upanishads as theological scriptures, expounding closed systems of thought. They represented to him the "Himalayas of the Soul." He was essentially a poet. He writes: "My religion is essentially a poet's religion. Its touch comes to me through the same unseen and trackless channels as does the inspiration and music of my poetry. All that I feel about it is from vision and not from knowledge." Tagore in another context writes: "It is evident that my religion is a poet's religion and is neither that of an orthodox man of piety, not that of a theologian. Its touch comes to me through the same unseen trackless channels as does the inspiration of my songs. My religious life has followed the mysterious line of growth as has my poetical life. Somehow they are wedded to each other and, though their betrothal had a long period of ceremony, it was kept secret to me." (*The Religion of Man*)

Tagore's approach to the Upanishads is unique. It is that of a *rishi,* i.e., a *religious poet.* The Upanishads embody the spiritual experience of the sages and seers of ancient India. Mere scholarship and the knowledge of the critical categories of metaphysics are not enough. One has to understand them by a flicker of wisdom and insight which is singularly free from prejudice and partisanship, and which has the capacity to look beneath appearances. Tagore had this intuitive capacity and by this he saw the colourful unity of existence in the spirit along with its varied manifestation. He sings with the Upanishadic seer: "He who in one, and who dispenses the inherent needs of all peoples and all times, who is in the beginning and the end of all things, may He unite us with the bond of Truth, of common fellowship, of righteousness."

Tagore realised the fundamental oneness of Reality. He saw the one in the many. He did not deny the many in order to affirm the one. He asks God: "Grant me my prayer that I may never lose the bliss of the touch of the one on the play of the many." The infinite for Tagore is a rich reality. It is not the denial of the finite. The spirit is a rich personality. It is not an abstract Absolute deprived of all *gunas* and activities. It is not a bare homogeneous, non-composite substance. He was opposed to an impersonal Absolute. His philosophy is not an Absolute Idealism, but it is more a concrete Idealism. His system has great affinity to the philosophy of Hegel. The spirit has given itself existence on earth. It has manifested itself in His sport in different phases, in nature and man. The manifestations do not militate against the unity of the Spirit. Manifestation is of the Real and is illumined by the Real. They are dependent on the Real and subserve His purposes and are sustained by Him. He is the *Jivana Devata.*

Tagore's religion is warm, human and emotional. Besides the Upanishads, the *Gita,* the songs of the Bauls of Bengal and the Vaishnava lyrics of Vidyapati and Chandidas have influenced Tagore. Tagore's poetical approach to Reality and the resultant religion is not a hodge podge statement of ideas. It is one definite way of arriving at Truth. It is as serious and as earnest as the scientific or the logical approach. Hence, it is not fair to state as E. Thompson does that 'there is a certain mental laziness about him. We often feel that there is a slackness somewhere probably at the very spring of his thought and conception.'

Tagore's vision is his reality. Religion for Tagore is the man's realisation of the fellowship with God, through service, through devotion and through contemplation. To achieve this unitive experience is the goal of spiritual religion. Religion is the experimental affirmation of the unity of existence and the fundamental oneness of Reality. From this realisation follows the fellowship of human beings.

To Tagore religion is essentially a matter of spiritual experience. There are two main kinds of religion: (1) the religion of immediate experience and (2) the religion of the cult and the dogmas. Tagore belongs to the first type. He is a mystic par excellence. His art-experience is his spiritual realisation. His awareness is direct, non-discursive and trans-personal in the sense that he surrenders his ego to the divine. Tagore's love of God has no restraints, no fears and no reserves. On an occasion he said: "I am able to love my God for He gives me freedom to deny Him." Tagore like all seers of Vedanta believes that spiritual experience is gained through intuition and not through the logical staircase. Tagore's religion and philosophy is the result of his direct experience and not dialectical knowledge. It is not the result of fancy or faint imagination. It is a vivid experience born of the fact of immediate comprehension.

Tagore's conception of the Supreme Reality as the one in the many has influenced his world-view. He looks upon life as the glorious ground for the opportunity offered to the soul of man of realising his fellowship with the Lord. His conception of the world of humanity and man's life on earth is optimistic and positive. He looks upon nature as the manifestation of God and hence asks us not to erect an antithesis between nature and man. He is against all dualisms that hide Reality from us, e.g., life and nature, God and man, art and life, theory and practice.

Tagore was not pantheist in the cheap sense of the term. He has stressed a number of times the transcendent and the immanent aspects of the Lord and it is unfair to describe such a system as pantheistic. Coleridge observes that according to pantheism God minus the world is zero, and according to theism God minus the world is still God. I leave it to the reader to judge Tagore in the light of the above equation.

Tagore looks upon creation as the sportive manifestation of the Lord arising from the abundance of His grace or *rasa.* "Joy is at the root of all creation." Creation is the result of *ananda,* bliss. It is not a veil that hides the Lord. It is not the distortion of Brahman or God. Tagore's conception of the universe and human life has a positive element in it. The world of nature is akin to us if we can shed our egoism.

Tagore regards the human life as lived by the average man in this world as not sensitive enough. **He makes a distinction between the 'ego' of a man and his 'true self'.** The ego, i.e., *ahamkara* or *avidya* is responsible for our unregenerate activities. Egotism tears us away from our real context and views us in an abstraction. It is this wrong way of plucking out ourselves from our intimate relation to the Lord that is the cause of our fall. It is this false separatist view that makes us see things as evil. Evil is imperfection. It is not absolute, it is relative, and its existence alone can make man's 'freedom of will' meaningful. If there is no evil to avoid or fall a victim to, moral activity becomes automatic and its essential element, choice, is undermined. Tagore is not afraid of the problem of evil. He finds its pragmatic function in man's art of self-realisation. But evil is not ultimate.

The individual finite soul has to learn the art of becoming a real personality. As he is, he is only an ego, torn from his interrelation to Lord. He is a truncated statue. He is a strangulated consciousness. He has to get rid of this limited nature of his consciousness by growing into nature, deepening and widening the scope of his consciousness. Man has to intensify awarness and grow into a larger consciousness.

Of all categories in creation, man is considered by Tagore as the profoundest and the highest. Man is made in the image of God. The interrelation between man and God is inseparable and intimate. It is a reciprocal relation and involves a two-sided functioning. Tagore, unlike ordinary theists, lays stress not only on the 'divinity of man' but also on the 'humanity of God.' God fulfils Himself and expresses His best through His chief agency, man. God needs man as much as man needs God. The human being is the centre of God's activity. Tagore was the greatest humanist of our age. **He forced men out of their narrow grooves. His religion is the religion of man.** He writes: "I have found my religion at last, the religion of man in which the infinite became defined in humanity and has come close to me so as to need my love and cooperation.' (*The Religion of Man*) 'Man, as a creation, represents the Creator and that is why of all creatures it has been possible for him to comprehend this world in his knowledge and feeling and in his imagination to realise in his individual spirit a union with a spirit that is everywhere."

The pathway outlined by Tagore for the individual to realise the union with the Infinite is not the *via negativa*. It is not asceticism nor hedonism. It is the method of joyful acceptance of life and "a reverence for life," in the celebrated phrase of Schweitzer. Tagore looks upon himself as a perfect instrument for the great musician the Lord to sing His songs. Unreserved, total surrender to the Lord is what he should do to achieve God-union.

This is done not by renunciation, but by an active dedication of our spirit to the Lord. To feel His glory and touch in nature and in all our activities is real *upasana* or worship. He writes: 'Deliverance is not for me in renunciation. I feel the embrace of freedom in a thousand bonds of delight. No, I will never shut the doors of my senses. The delights of sight and hearing and touch will bear thy delight.' (*Gitanjali*)

Tagore often dwells at great length about the intimate relation between man and God and describes the different moods experienced by the devotee in his person. He looks upon the Lord as the giver of plenty unasked. He also describes God's love for man in choosing man to spread His message. He loves human life for the opportunity it gives to experience the play of the divine in all its aspects. He writes: 'I have had my invitation to this world's festival, and thus my life has been blessed.' 'Day by day thou art making me worthy of the simple, great gifts that thou gavest to me unasked—this sky and the light, this body and the life and the mind—saving me from perils of overmuch desire.' (*Gitanjali*)

Tagore is not slow to realise the utter weakness and the depravity of man and he is not afraid of it, because the Lord is not squeamish about it in His abundant grace. He writes: 'My debts are large, my failures great, my shame secret and heavy.' 'I am certain of the priceless wealth in thee and thou art my friend, but I have not the heart to sweep away the tinsel that fills my room.'

Tagore has the firm faith that the Lord has the most tender concern for man and that Lord and man are tied together in an inseparable bond. To realise that intimate relationship is the goal of man's life and the source of his strength. 'To realise one's life in the infinite is to live in perfect goodness.' 'Thou feelest thine own entire sweetness in me.' Religion for Tagore is not a weak whimpering resignation and self abnegation but a vital self assertion of the unity of all existence. The doctrine of *bhakti,* at the hands of Tagore, has assumed a new beauty and a profound significance. His Lord is not the sectarian personal God of either Vaishnavas or Saivaites. He is universal love and joy. *Bhakti* or self-surrender does not result in the annihilation of the individual in the infinite, but it transmutes man into a perfect personality from his unregenerate ego-state. Tagore respects man's personality. He is a spiritual humanist. His religion is the religion of man. He often writes: 'We must know with absolute certainty that essentially we are Spirit.'

Tagore practised the living presence of God in all the things of the world and delighted at the touch of the infinite in human life. He did not believe that the Lord only took on the human form in times of crises, in the form of *avataras*, he believed that the Lord was ever with us. He writes: 'He comes, He comes. He ever comes, every moment, every day, every night. He comes, comes, ever comes.'

Tagore believed in the sanctity of human life and regarded that spirit-realisation must be experienced here and now in the mortal body. To lose that opportunity is to experience great loss. He writes: 'Where can I meet the Lord, unless in this home made thine. Where can I join thee unless in this my work transformed into thy work. If I leave my home, I shall not reach thy home. If I cease my work, I can never join thee in thy work. For thou dwellest in me and I in thee. Thou without me or I without thee are nothing.'

Tagore was a radical reformer. He wanted each to follow his *svadharma*, but extricated *svadharma* from the conservative *varna-dharma* based on birth. He coordinated the three disciplines, *karma, bhakti* and *jnana* into a synthesis and gave them a deep humanitarian touch. He fought all social injustice in the face, boldly, and stood firm by his cause. He achieved all this by the enormous range of his work, which comprises more than two thousand poems and two thousand songs in addition to a large number of short stories, novels, dramas, essays on religion, education, politics and literature. The extraordinary quality of his works holds our loyalty to him. His spiritual earnestness, his robust resistance, his universality have all given him an undying place in our hearts. **Tagore represents the true positive culture of India in all its beauty and correct proportions.**

11

Western Influences on Tagore

Buddhadeva Bose

Rabindranath's works are European literature written in the Bengali language, and they are the first of their kind."

This remark, made by a Bengali poet of today, is of course an exaggeration, but it is exaggerations of this sort that reveal the truth in a flash and make us cogitate on its implications. Orthodox Tagorites may be offended at this, and so may the generation of beatniks who regard the West as an arid area where all things worth doing have been done before and there is nothing left but to enliven poetry with acrobatics. And then, Tagore's vogue in Europe was as an Oriental sage, the opponent of Western turmoil and the devotee of *Shanti*—'the peace that passeth understanding'—of Truth and Beauty and Good. And Tagore himself, we must admit, contributed to this idea of himself, both before and after he was acclaimed in the West. Nevertheless, any perceptive reader of Bengali poetry must acknowledge that he was very much of a European.

In academic circles the word 'influence' is understood in a rather mechanical sense: Shaw reads Ibsen's *Ghosts* and writes *Widowers' House,* Eliot paraphrases the *Bhagavad Gita,* and so on. But the deepest and abiding influences often remain concealed; either they do not appear on the surface, or, when they do, elude the grasp of the most assiduous seekers of the doctoral degree. **In Rabindranath's case the difficulty is augmented by the extreme scantiness of biographical material. We do not even know how much he had read and on which subjects;** which were the books he had skimmed through, which enjoyed, and which he had studied with devotion. Rarely does he mention other people's books in his own; and when he does, he scarcely ever gets beyond the Sanskrit scriptures, Kalidasa and the Vaishnavas, and exactly three of the English romantics—Wordsworth, Shelly and Keats. The poems where he directly borrows from one of them are well known: *Varshashesha* (The End of the Year) has often been compared with *Ode to the Western Wind* and *Manasasundari* (To My Muse) with *Hymn to Intellectual Beauty,* and indeed there is substance in these comparisons. But direct borrowings are a different matter from influence, and we have yet to discover where Tagore's real acknowledgments are due. In the books of his old age there are references to Ibsen and John Donne, but that was probably a concession to the rising generation. The only line of European verse he quotes repeatedly and with a constancy of admiration which is rather surprising, is Keats' 'Beauty is Truth and Truth Beauty'—and this not as poetry, but an efficacious formula for aesthetic theory.

It is inconceivable, however, that Rabindranath's reading was limited to half-a-dozen volumes. He must have consumed an incalculable number, and of all sorts, but unlike modern Western authors, he has kept the story of his development hidden from the curious eye. His letters, voluminous as they are, tell us little about the sources of his inspiration. We learn he was interested in astronomy, entomology and books on racial questions, that he respected the author of *Amiel's Journal* and dismissed *Modemoiselle de Maupin* as heartless—although he did not altogether despise the social novel of Victorian England. In late life he praised Sturge Moore—at the cost of Amy Lowell and Ezra Pound. Judging by the evidence left by himself, we cannot even be sure of his taste. Not once does he mention the new and authentic poets who were his contemporaries and near predecessors: Baudelaire or Swinburne, Verlaine or Mallarme, Valery or Rilke. Not once does he mention the fiction of Russia or the painting of France or the music of Germany. His slight sketch of W.B. Yeats shows little understanding of the stature of the Irish poet. And he was a man ever in personal touch with the West, befriended by some of the greatest European writers of his time.

Strange paradox, this apparent indifference of one of the most receptive of poets to the main modes of poetry of his time! But can we be sure that it was really indifference? Tagore's attitude to the West was ambivalent, to say the least; **we suspect his admiration of the West was warmer than he felt it to be compatible with the political status of his nation; and that was why he strove hard to conceal or disguise it in his writings.** Sometimes it becomes impossible for him not to applaud the solid achievements of Europe after the French Revolution: its ideals of humanism, religious tolerance and parliamentary government; and yet, repeatedly during his travels, he wearies of the hustle of Western life and longs for the quiet of his Bengali home. There is a curious passage in which he goes to the extent of wishing that foreigners had never discovered India; but if they had not, the poet Rabindranath could not have blazed forth in glory. And he knew it too.

One can detect an insidious war going on in Rabindranath's mind; between the poet and the Indian nationalist, the artist and the religious and social reformer, the lover of beauty and the avowed enemy of imperialism. Historically placed as he was, this conflict was inevitable, and by this we can explain—or at any rate understand—many of the paradoxes we encounter in his life and literary works. One result of this was that he developed two soul sides: one to face the world with and the other to be expressed only in his deepest and most mysterious poems. The aspect presented to the world conformed literally to the popular conception of him: it was the face of a benevolent sage, nourished on Upanishadic traditions, a tranquil and meditative Hindu who regarded peace as the supreme value of human existence. And the other aspect—revealed only in a body of deceptively simple verse—was that of a romantic in the best nineteenth century tradition, dark and turbulent and passionate—in short, a modern European.

In a passage he wrote or dictated for a ceremonial occasion, Rabindranath gave an outline of his encounters with European literature. He tried Dante and Goethe, but being averse to translated poetry and not gifted in learning languages, he dropped both. He read some Heine with the help of a German lady staying at Santiniketan, but then too his patience wore out. **Shakespeare he knew, but did not quite approve of.** 'In our time,' he says—meaning the eighteen-eighties—'we Indians got more intoxication than nourishment out of English literature.' What impressed us,' he continues (I am translating freely from his *Reminiscences*), 'was the demented fury of a Lear or the flaming jealousy of an Othello. It is the mire of human nature that comes to the surface in these works'. After this Tagore blames his countrymen for not knowing those specimens of Western literature which express what he calls the *shanta rasa*—the mood of peace.

Theoretically, Rabindranath declared himself to be an opponent of what is most characteristic of Western art—namely, romanticism. But what about practice? He said he gave up Goethe and knew Heine only scantily, but he published an essay on Goethe and the women he loved, and Heine is the only non-British European poet whose direct influence is palpable in him: the best pieces in *Kshanika* (Poems of Transience) are no doubt the outcome of a happy encounter between the Hindu sage and the Frenchified German Jew. He officially disliked Shakespeare, but his two delightful comedies employ Shakespearian devices, and the blank verse of his tragedies are reminiscent of Shakespeare rather than the Miltonic-Madhusudanesque tradition. Again, in a little portrait of Dante which he painted in old age, the lean Italian face reveals the poet of *Inferno* rather than *Paradiso.* **Most revealing of all are Tagore's self-portraits in which he is seen as a man who suffered—and that, we recall, is what Goethe declared himself to be.**

But it is scarcely necessary to refer to his paintings in order to adduce evidence: there is enough in what he wrote. His official, ceremonial verse may be different, but in his authentic poems—not excepting the celebrated *Gitanjali*—there runs a streak of dark turmoil, of conflict, struggle and even anguish. I am by no means suggesting that he knew the European masters more intensively than he said was the case. The point I want to make is that he did not have to know those poets thoroughly, in the manner of student or professor. Romanticism was in the air, and his genius imbibed it down to the roots of his poetic being. For a poet to be influenced by another intimate or even first-hand knowledge is scarcely necessary. Shakespeare digested the whole of the Western antiquities and Renaissance merely through hearsay. Why should not that have happened with Tagore?

We have no right to assume that the poets he never mentions or the schools he disapproves, had no share in his making. We can never be sure that he did not know those poets of France who in his youth were recreating European poetry. Scantily perhaps, scrappily perhaps, perhaps through quotations or reviews in magazines—but a single spark is enough to ignite the mind of a genius. His poem *Niruddesha Yatra* (The Aimless Voyage) bears a strange resemblance to Baudelaire's *The Voyage* and *The Drunken Boat* of Rimbaud. Let us also hope that the mysterious woman in it is a foreigner and the golden boat is journeying westward. Is not that a veiled confession of Tagore's debt to the West?

12

The First Modern Novels

R. P. Bhaskar

Tagore has written a large number of short stories, novels and plays which rank among the best works in these fields produced by Indians. **But in the glare of his international fame as a poet, his achievements in these spheres have not been seen properly and appreciated.**

The first Tagore novel to appear in English was *The Home and the World* (1919). I was followed by *Gora* (1924) and an original novel in English, *The Wreck* (1925). *Farewell My Friend,* was published a few years after the author's death.

The Home and the World is Tagore's most important novel, though *Gora* has been more popular with readers. It tells the story of a temptation from three different angles—the entire story being unfolded through the accounts of the principal protagonists, Nikhil, the husband, Bimala, the wife, and Sandip, a friend of the family. A cultured young man, Nikhil gives his wife a good private English education by engaging a governess, contrary to the general practice of denying girls higher education. His troubles start when the ambitious young politician, Sandip, comes to stay with them. Nikhil realises for the first time, after nine years of married life, that his wife has only come into his home, not his life. He sees that there is a despotism in his desire to mould his relations with her in a hard, clear-cut, perfect form; that her life, not finding its true level by reason of his pressure from above, is seeking an outlet by undermining its banks. Bimala too realises before it is too late that she has been drifting away from her husband. After a painful ordeal, husband and wife come closer to each other and Sandip goes out of their lives as abruptly as he entered.

Dovetailed into this social theme of the problems of a woman who comes out from the home into the world is the deepening crisis of the political drama of the time. Nikhil and Sandip are both nationalists, and have their visions of a strong and free motherland. Yet they are poles apart. To Sandip means are of no consequence as long as they lead to the goal in view, while to Nikhil it is inconceivable that foul means can lead to noble ends. Hatred of the foreigners and blind worship of the country are justified in Sandip's eyes as they are powerful aids in attaining the objective; Nikhil, on the other hand, disapproves of such hypnotic tests of patriotism. Sandip believes in meeting force with force, but Nikhil holds the use of force in any form as a sign of weakness—for only the weak dare not be just and try to get at results through the shortcuts of injustice. Bimala is carried away by Sandip's arguments for a time, until a succession of events reveals to her the inherent strength of Nikhil's position.

The Home and the World **is clearly an allegorical novel. Bimala represents India, which in poetic fancy has always taken the feminine form. Nikhil symbolises all that is good and vital in the Indian tradition, and Sandip personifies aggressive, Western-type nationalism, which Tagore feared was beginning to take shape in India.** Sandip openly advocates the "Western military style" as a substitute to the traditional system. Nevertheless, he is compelled to acknowledge the strength of the Indian tradition. "I was born in India," he says, "and the poison of its spirituality runs in my blood. However loudly I may proclaim the madness of walking in the path of self-abnegation, I cannot avoid it altogether." Nikhil is the true inheritor of this tradition.

He cannot think of gaining success at the cost of the soul, for, to him, the soul is greater than everything else, including success.

In *Gora* the story centres round the love affairs of two young men, Gora and Binoy, who cross the social barriers erected by the caste system to marry the Brahmo Samaja girls, Sucharita and Lolita, respectively. Narrow-minded sectarianism presents many hurdles but these are overcome, thanks to the broad outlook and understanding of two elders, Paresh Babu, the Brahmo Samajist, and Anandamoyi, the Hindu lady.

Gora, however, is no novel of romance. **The love affairs are mere devices to provide an occasion for discussing the contemporary social situation,** just as the temptation in *The Home and the World* is a mere aid to deliberate upon the political situation. Haran, who aspires for Sucharita's hand, is a typical representative of that section of the youth of 19th century Bengal, which through an English education, had come to know of the evils of Hindu society and condemned the entire Hindu teaching on that score. Gora is an example of another section of the youth, which, reacting sharply against the above mentality, sought to stick tenaciously to the orthodox ways, motivated solely by a spirit of defiance. The hostilities of these two groups created an atmosphere in which religion became a wedge between man and man instead of being a unifying force.

Most of the characters of *Gora* are so deeply immersed in this controversy that they do not see the absurdity of their positions. The ridiculousness of the situation is obvious to Lolita, the spirited young girl who dares to challenge the whole of society. "I have come to the conclusion, after much thought," she says, "that it can never be necessary for a man to cut off all connections with his religion, his beliefs, or his society, no matter of what nature they may be, in order to be united with other men. If that were necessary then no friendship could exist between a Hindu and a Christian, and we ought to raise high walls round each sect and keep them each within its own fence."

Gora **portrays the predicament of the caste-ridden Indian society after the flow of Western liberal ideas and shows a way out of the tangle.** Gora, who constantly strives to realise the Indian nation and finds it impossible to free himself from the fetters of tradition and those of his own making, secures relief from his oppressive thoughts at last when he learns that he is not the full-blooded Hindu Brahmin that he imagined himself to be, but an Irish boy orphaned during the Mutiny of 1857 (First War of Indian Independence) and brought up by a Hindu family. Ironically, this overwhelming sense of relief enables him to declare in the end, "Today I am really an Indian, Muslim and Christian. Today every caste in India is my caste, the food of all is my food."

In a sense *Gora* and *The Home and the World* are complimentary to each other. In one there is repudiation of the idea of a nation-state in India—a negative approach—while in the other India is defined—the approach here being positive—as a cultural unit, transcending the limits set by caste and religion, and creating the true Indian as the inheritor of a composite culture in the making of which many religions and cultures played their part.

Gora contains many incidents typical of the time—imprisonment for political offences, police repression, etc. The hero's wanderings in the villages in search of the "real India" are significant; they are manifestations of a new socio-political trend which was growing stronger day by day. The divided, narrow, weak, rural India of *Gora,* supinely unconscious of its own power, is the India into which Gandhi came, and out of which he created a nation. Like *The Home and The world, Gora* too was a prophetic novel.

The Wreck has an unusual theme. Two marriage parties

are proceeding in separate boats along a river, when a whirlwind descends on them and blots the flotilla out of existence. One of the bridegrooms goes home with the other's bride, mistaking her to be his spouse, who in fact has died in the accident. He realises his mistake, searches for the girl's groom and ultimately restores her to him.

Plot gets precedence over theme in *The Wreck*. The intricacy of its plot is in fact unrivalled. Unlike other Tagore novels, here is a total abandonment of socio-political content which may be accounted for by the fact that **it was written directly in English with non-Indian readers in view.** The novelist who felt it necessary to explain the Puja holidays, a period of festivity in India, as corresponding to the English Christmas, may well have thought that an intimate treatment of the Indian scene, such as is to be found in the other novels, will not prove popular with his foreign readers, thus making a grievous error which others were to repeat later.

Farewell, My Friend, which, stripped of all embellishments, is a futile romance, actually a pungent satire on the educated classes. Amrit Rai, fastidious, with intellectual pretentions, spent seven whole years in Oxford, flirting with examinations. Though he is "too intelligent to be studious", his native wit hides his deficiencies. Pitted against him in the story is Labanya, whose only passion is learning, who looks down on love as a weakness. Their brief infatuation is brought to a speedy end by the return of two old flames. The playful mood of the author makes the novel eminently enjoyable reading. Tagore's humour is at its liveliest in this work.

Tagore's chief asset as a novelist is his skill in character delineation. Nikhil, soft and strong, and Gora, vigorous, ebullient and youthful, stand before the reader's eye as men of flesh and blood in spite of the rare fineness and abstraction of the ideas they represent. The ill-tempered fanatical Haran and the good-humoured, amusing pseudo-intellectual Amrit Rai are lively characters rather than grotesque caricatures. The scheming, vicious Sandip, in whom there is much of the stuff with which an Iago is made, is perhaps the most charming villain in Indian fiction. The older characters in all novels are generally persons with the practical wisdom of a life-time of experience.

The women in Tagore's novels are just as genuine as the men, Sucharita and Lolita, Kamala and Bimala represent the many faces of Indian womanhood. Classical standards have been followed to a large extent in their characterisation, and they truly belong to the long line of heroines which include Sita and Savitri and Sakuntala, though they have undergone the changes dictated by a lapse of centuries. The older women are generally orthodox types, and yet are not mere reproductions of a common prototype, for they differ widely among themselves.

The actions and interactions of characters revel the deep psychological insight of the novelist. The subtle handling of the Nikhil-Bimala-Sandip affair is perhaps the best evidence of the novelist's understanding of the organic relations between individuals and society, and between individuals and their past of which there are ample manifestations in all the novels.

The main features of Tagore's narratives are a lyrical beauty and a mild humour. In *Farewell, My Friend,* the novelist departs from his standard practice to provide a frolicsome narrative with bubbling humour.

Tagore is often explicit in the advocacy of the ideas with which his novels are impregnated. However, the aesthetic qualities are not sacrificed in the anxiety to deliver the message. Indeed he devotes great attention to the literary qualities since he realises that a damaged container may spoil the content. His novels are the literary expressions of his thoughts.

13

Delightful Plays

Balwant Gargi

Rabindranath Tagore stands as a unique figure in the history of Indian theatre. A talented actor, producer and composer, he had an inborn feeling for the stage. At the time when the commercial companies were burdened with unwieldy sets and ornate productions, Tagore discovered the vitality and freshness of the folk theatre and taught his contemporaries simplicity of form and depth of theme. Steeped in the classics of Hindu dramaturgy and alive to the European technique of production and indigenous folk forms, he evolved a dramatic form which influenced the Bengali theatre at the beginning of this century.

His dramas are more suitable for the open-air than for closed theatre. He invoked the spirit of Yatra (folk opera) which had been hounded out of Calcutta by the professional stage. As time passed, he was more and more drawn to this form. In his later plays he often introduces street pageants humming with life, and characters cross the stage speaking, singing, commenting—a kaleidoscope of dancing thoughts.

Nature's Revenge (Sanyasi), one of his earlier (1884) plays, tells the story of an ascetic who has broken all bonds with the world, and after having conquered Time, sits in a cave and mockingly views the trivialities of the finite and the narrow existence of the household which is oblivious of anything beyond. The first seventy lines of the ascetic, a philosophical soliloquy, captures the atmosphere of the cold and bleak Himalayan cave where 'a naked spirit' dwells 'amidst a naked world of winds and icicles.' The ancient frogs croak and water drips from the crevices making the silence more eloquent. The ascetic boasts of a joy which like Shiva he has found in being alone in the heart of the infinite. Light seems to him shut up in a cage of darkness; he sits beyond Time and Space. It is poetry touched with the sublimity of the ascetic's soul. But his self-evolved infinity proves empty when a girl brings him back to the bondage of human love and leads him to the little joys of days and nights.

Tagore's plays—vehicles for the expression of his ideas—are not filled with action which is the generic of drama. His search for the infinite in the finite, of the limitless in the limited, of cosmic energy in a speck of dust, continued throughout his work and he led his characters down the path of love to the final comprehension of the infinite.

During the years 1895 to 1905 Tagore wrote a series of tragedies in verse. In *Bisarjan* (*Sacrifice*), Raghupati, the high priest, a staunch devotee of Kali, the Goddess of War, strongly believes in human sacrifice and persuades his pupil Jai Singh to his philosophy of life. Jai Singh, torn between the inner voice of his conscience and the dominating philosophy of his teacher, sacrifices his own life at the altar of Kali—to Raghupati's horror whose belief is so shaken that from that day he denounces the Goddess and throws away her statue.

The passionate speeches in Raghupati's mouth which voice forth his philosophy about the universal Mind calling for an orgy of butchery are brilliant. They overawe the audience which feels aghast when the horrible truth dawns upon it that Raghupati was a victim of his own philosophy which fed on murder and butchery. **Raghupati's last words, 'Look how she stands there, the silly stone—dead, dumb, blind!' show the terrible realisation of one who learns with bitterness and agony the futility of his worship of Kali.**

There is excessive declamation in *Sacrifice.* Tagore himself acted as Raghupati and the character lived through the poet's inspired acting.

Tagore's greatest success as an actor was when he played Raghupati on the Calcutta stage. He staged the play at Jorasanko, the family home to which theatre enthusiasts, family friends, foreign guests and the elite of Calcutta flocked. Later on, he shifted to Santiniketan, the cultural centre which he had founded in 1901 and where amongst his pupils, the family nieces, nephews and cousins also acted. The players understood the psychological and philosophical strains of the poet and brought depth and lyricism to his productions.

King and Queen, written in the same period, is full of great potentialities, but Tagore filled it with too many irrelevant details. If the characters were more concentrated it would be his greatest work. His scorn of Governments and their lust for power and glory—a theme that recurs again and again in his subsequent plays—is vividly and powerfully portrayed. *Dak Ghar* (The Post Office), written during 1912, is the story of Amal, the sick child who, forbidden to go out by his uncle and the physician, watches the outside world from his small window and talks to everybody—the watchman, the curd-seller and Sudha, the flower girl,—eternally waiting for a letter from the King's post office. Ultimately in the dead of night the King's personal messenger comes with a letter and Amal is quietened. Sleep settles on his tired nerves and he is beyond Time and the care of the physician. The play could have easily degenerated into a sentimental tragedy at the death of Amal but for the absolute simplicity of Tagore's handling of the child's character.

The play was staged at Santiniketan where Tagore played Thakur Dada, the irresponsible old man whose prattle is packed with wit and wisdom. Tagore's fondness for the character grew with age and Dada appears in the form of a *fakir,* a minstrel or a blind bard in most of his subsequent plays.

Tagore's fight against oppression, stupidity and violence continued in most of his later plays, where characters with the same problems and features appear again and again. Tagore was recreating the same images but dressing them in different costumes. *Muktadhara* (The Free Current), *King and Queen, Natir Puja* (The Worship of the Dancing Girl), *The King of Dark Chambers* and *Red Oleanders,* all have a king who in his lust for glory and power makes the people his slaves. There is either a flower girl symbolising beauty or a young man who defiantly leads the people to freedom.

In *The Free Current*, the young hero defies the royal architect who has dammed the springs and deprived the villagers of water, the free gift of nature. In *Natir Puja*, the dancing girl defies the order of the king who has banned the worship of Buddha. The dancing girl, a Buddhist nun at heart, dances before the image of Buddha and is murdered by the lieutenants of the king. The supreme sacrifice shocks the king and queen and converts them to Buddhism. In *Red Oleanders,* Nandini, the flower girl, is not afraid of the king; Ranjan, her lover, raises the flag of revolt and lays down his life. The monolithic kingly order cracks from guilt and inner tension. All these plays have philosophical overtones, social and political messages and a high lyrical quality.

Most of Tagore's characters are hazy, seen through the mist of his poetry. Shakespeare's Ariel and Caliban are robust. The gambler, the monk and the executioners in *The Little Clay-Cart* are full-blooded. But Tagore's characters are the citizens of an imaginary world. Students, villagers, travellers, men and women in *Nature's Revenge* go back and forth across the stage like phantoms while the ascetic watches them from his cave. Even the more human and vivid characters of the watchman, the curdseller and Gaffar in *Post Office* are shadows. Amal, the child, the sick spirit of humanity, watches them from his window and somehow reminds us of the ascetic. In *Post Office* the voices of the street are the voices of Life calling us; in *Nature's Revenge* it is the infinite darkness that tempts us to the charm of the unknown.

There is expectancy, waiting for something to happen that does not happen in Tagore's plays. The king in *Natir Puja* is expected every moment but he never comes. The king of the *Dark Chambers* talks from behind the palace walls. The dark, cruel power of repression cannot see the light of the day. The king in *Red Oleanders* is hidden from view. The viewlessness lends occult charm and tension.

Though Tagore did not create characters that have the earthy, lusty realism of Bertolt Brecht, or the passion of Lorca, he invested drama with poetry and employed it for a larger function. He mixed reality with fantasy, songs with prose, and brought purity and lyricism to the theatre. His decor was simple and mellow in order to give characters full scope. He invested theatre with imagination and broke the chain of shoddy realism. A silver crescent scrawled on the wall would be the new moon, patches of white and black the clouds, a clay toy, the living bird, and mountains, jungles, groves and stormy winds were created by the enchantment of descriptive poetry and evocative songs. In the beginning of the *Cycle of Spring*, he says, 'We don't need any scenery. The only background we need is the background of the mind—on it we are going to paint a picture by passing the brush of music over it?'

Tagore's language is as starred with imagery as a village pond with lotus flowers. It breaks into poetic flights, and songs are an integral part of the action. While the singer comments on the play in song, the action is carried on without words at times. The songs often come at the climax of a scene when intensity of emotion seems to burst the bonds of the spoken word. Like a fast-spinning colour wheel which blends into white light, the emotions converge into song. The singer's function as Tagore uses him is to generalise on the particular scene being enacted and this adds another dimension to the characters and the situation. The blind bard in his plays, like the Greek Chorus, sings and commends on the events of the play. The commentator's blindness adds to his detachment. He philosophises and prophesies about the action but stands outside it.

Tagore's social comedies, an aspect of his dramas generally neglected by critics, have bubbling mirth and lashing satire. In his inimitable style he captures the middle class morality and petty values of life and makes fun of them. The idiom of his comedies defies translation. *Shesha Raksha* (The Last Cause), light comedy on the absurdities of young people, moves with speed in a series of hilarious incidents. Out of his many satirical comedies, ***The Bachelors' Club* is a rib-splitting farce about some young men who form a club and take a vow to remain celibate all their lives. The well-guarded fortress of celibacy cracks at the first touch of a woman.** There is amazing realism both in language and character-drawing. These comedies were not only the expression of Tagore's youth, but found expression periodically up to his last days.

Tagore's contribution as a producer has not yet been fully realised and assessed. His range as an actor can be judged from the fact that when he was twenty-two years old, he played Raghupati and at the age of sixty-two at the Empire Theatre in Calcutta he acted Jai Singh, the young pupil. When his plays were produced on the stage under his direction, the minutest detail was worked out with imagination and they throbbed with life. **His plays must be judged in terms of production and not by their written texts** which are like dead butterflies pinned to a blank paper.

In 1936 I saw Tagore at Lahore performing *Chitrangada,* a dance drama. He was sitting on the stage in his velvet toga and streaming silver beard, chanting bits of commentary while his pupils danced the play. But the Lahore audiences—corrupted by the cinema and Western naturalism—looked at the poet aghast and wondered why the old man did not sing from behind the wings and why he was bent upon breaking the illusion of reality.

When we talk of an Indian theatre, national in form,

we look around vaguely and wonder what it is. Is it the folk theatre? Or the mummified Sanskrit drama which some purists are trying to resurrect? Or the Western-influenced professional stage? Nobody can lay a finger on it definitely, as for example one can in the case of Peking Opera or the Kabuki theatre. But one could say with certainty that Tagore's plays are Indian through and through.

14

Enchanting Music

G.D. Hiya

Rabindranath was always very proud of his songs. Once he said to an English friend: 'There can be no question that I have conquered my people by my songs. I have heard even drivers of bullock-carts singing my latest and most up-to-date songs. In fact, many vendors of patent medicines use them to advertise their wares.'

Indeed this is no small achievement for one born in a big zamindar family known for culture, position, learning and wealth to have so completely assimilated himself with the joys and sorrows of the common men. As a composer and singer, his success is monumental as the charm of his songs is overwhelming, and their melodies intoxicating.

His three thousand odd songs differ in length—from two, three or four lines to fifty or sixty—and their themes are equally varied. He sings of the spring, autumn and other seasons, of earth, sky, rain and other aspects of mother nature, of love, laughter, patriotism, sorrow, devotion and death. Every phase of human and natural life is depicted in them, thus creating a complete whole of experience. Words and tunes are wedded in such a manner that 'sometimes it is hard to say if the song is popular for the words or the tune; or it can be sung without any meaning, the tune itself bringing the meaning.'

As is well known, the Bauls and the Vaishnavas—with their Kirtana type of folk music—had a great influence on Tagore. The Baul mendicants and singers are a special feature of the basic culture of Bengal and they are to be found in all villages singing their soulful songs. Tagore drank deep at their fount and composed a large number of songs after them. One popular song is as follows:

O amar sonar Bangla
Ami tomay bhalo bashi,
Tomar akash, tomar batash
Amar prane bajay banshi.

The Kirtana songs are a variety of mass recitals full of love and devotion, popularised by Chaitanya. Their subject is the love of Krishna and Radha and other *gopis* of Vrindavana, their accompaniments are simple musical instruments like *khol, khartal, manjir* etc. and dance makes an essential part of them. Gandhiji's *Ramadhun* follows this style and Tagore wrote quite a few such songs which became very popular.

The third influence on Tagore, of folk nature, has been that of the Bhatiali variety of songs. This is a type popular in those districts of Bengal where rivers play a large part in the lives of the people. As their lands are almost always flooded and they have to put up a brave fight against this unconquerable force of nature, they try to find solace in their woeful songs. The circumstance has infused in them the rhythmic quality of the waves of the river and their playfulness. Their songs of sorrow, loss and separation reflect it in a most pathetic manner. Whenever Tagore heard them, he was deeply moved and it was natural that he used these tunes to his utmost benefit. Other musicians of Bengal have also copied these tunes and popularised them among the urban people.

So Tagore adapted this whole rich tradition of Bengal and presented it to the masses in a reedited version. He grafted it to the classical music and created a most wonderful variety of his own, known as Rabindra Sangita, which immensely influenced the contemporary trends in Bengali music. And Bengal being a volatile country, after a period of high adoration, he was equally criticised and condemned. But this proves his success in being able to shake and provoke the soul of Bengali music which, some say, is now reverting to the love of Tagore. In part, the case seems to be a parallel to the case of his paintings which were not appreciated by the Calcuttans; Tagore had to show them in Paris to win due recognition—more than he and his friends had expected. The tradition-tied Indian consciousness takes its own time to appreciate anything that is fresh and different.

Tagore did not like the tendency of the classical style in which the threads of music are extended to undesirable ends. He was against the frequent repetitions which he considered as the product of a lacking imagination and real artistic sense, to be compromised by pure indulgence. Balance and restraint in the composition of tunes were his ideals. 'He looked upon music as a compact comprehensive art which would be colourful yet unconfessed, charged with sincere emotions without being sentimental, curious and variegated expressions without disorganising the structure.' This may be regarded as his philosophy of true music, the purest of arts.

Inspired by these worthy ideals, his songs have been characterised by beauty, grace and dignity. And because they were so extremely simple and natural, they confused the habitual lovers of complexities. The exponents of the conventional Hindustani style could never understand the depth and technique of his creations. But this does not mean that Tagore himself did not understand this style; he had a very fine grasp of the application of the Hindustani music which he introduced in his songs every now and then, retaining their own essential character and special flavour.

In his songs, Tagore was always very careful about

precision. He could never tolerate any lapse in their framework and the desired effect. His short lyrics are very suggestive and the touches intended to enhance their effect are most subtle. In this regard he was considerably influenced by the composers of Tappa and Dhrupad. *Tappa* songs are short and the subtle touches in them express the desired poignancy. The compactness and the dignity of the Dhrupad songs is a class in itself. Tagore composed a number of songs in these styles and used them in his own way.

The power of his personality tended to make his songs extremely self-centred. But as he was a romantic composer, even in his own estimate, he could not do otherwise. And he was not individualistic in the wrong sense of the term, it was synonymous with the universalism which he propounded, and his attempt was to convey the universal feelings and sentiments, in their best form, to the listeners.

An example of his highly dignified, melodious and meaningful song is our National Anthem:

Jana gana mana adhinayaka jaya he
Bharat bhagyavidhata
jaya he, jaya he
jaya jaya jaya jaya he.

Another is his familiar tuning of Bankim's

Bande mataram
Sujalam suphalam malayaja shitalam
shasya shyamalam mataram
Bande mataram.

But he excelled in his exotic love songs. When youth descends upon a maiden, he sings:

Mama jobane nikunje gahe pakhi, sakhi jago

Similarly, when lovers are separated, the poet sings:

Radana bhara e basanta
Sakhi kakhono ashe ni bujhi age

Mor biraha bedana rangalo
Raktim kim'suka rage

His songs on nature are as varied as they are subtle and beautiful. Addresing the breeze, he says:

Dhire dhire bow, ego utal hawa
Nishit rate bansi baje
shanta hawa
ogo utal hawa

He composed for children also, and as he retained the feelings of his childhood throughout his whole life, he could easily conquer his tiny friends, of whom he also wanted to be a playmate. His devotional songs were very popular with the Brahmo Samaja. In fact, they were an important factor in Brahmo religious life. Ninety per cent of the hymns used by the Sadharana Brahmo Samaja were his. The Adi Brahmo Samaja used hundreds of his songs, including many from *Gitanjali*, essentially a collection of devotional songs. His other collections are *Gitamalya, Gitabitan, Gitali, Naivedya,* etc.

Now witness the atmosphere created by the singing of a Tagore song at Santiniketan. The occasion is the felicitation of an engineer who has provided water-supply to the ashrama, the author of the description being a visitor from South India:

> A song had been composed for the occasion and it was sung by more than half a dozen young men and women to the accompaniment or drums and a *tambura*. It opened with a typical catch—with EY—in three tiers of movement apostrophic of *Akasa bihari, nirada bahana jal* with *jal, tal, sthal, phal, samujjal* as liquid rhymes. Repetition like *arune-hirane, shikhari-shikhari, tutiya-putiya* were there. So were the familiar *Shasya shyamala mati* etc. But it was a remarkable song for lilt and cadence and had a melting melody which only Tagore could bring off. It was clever in meaning as well; again typical

of his mind and manner. The water had once come down from heaven out of love for the earth as gentle rain, but the earth held it prisoner within her dark rocky bowles for long, long. The engineer luckily had now set the prisoner free and made it spring up again to let it join its cloud-riding peers in the sky.

Rabindranath's songs were liked by the peasant and patrician alike. He created his own epoch and closed it; he was himself the culmination of the process.

15

Paintings: Breaking the Tradition

A. S. Raman

It is easy to exaggerate the importance of Tagore as an artist. Easier still is it to underrate him. Coomaraswamy places the paintings and drawings by the poet in their proper perspective when he observes thus: "It would be a great mistake to search in them for hidden spiritual symbolism; they are not meant to be deciphered like puzzles or code messages. It is obvious that the poet must have looked at many pictures in the course of his long life, but there is nothing in his own work to show that he has seen them. This is a genuinely original, genuinely naive expression; extraordinary evidence of eternal youth persistent in a hoary and venerable personage." Indeed it is surprising that the poet's art, which had always remained his private pastime, should have become, in his own lifetime, a subject of serious public discussion all over the world.

Of late, there has been a tendency among our critics to project the poet as one of the pioneers of the modern movement in India. Attempts continue to be made to interpret his work in the context of this *ism* or that. For example, the name of Paul Klee is frequently mentioned as his mentor. A highly intellectual bias is attributed to Tagore's art which is anything but cerebral. The impulse behind his paintings and drawings is best described in his own words: "I have fallen under the enchantment of lines." Thus one who tries to affix a label to the poet's naive, nervous compositions can never understand them. Cubism, Expressionism, Surrealism and many more—these are at best convenient cliches and at worst dangerous dogmas. In either case, these are meaningless in the Indian context, and where Tagore's genuinely primitive art is concerned, they are imprecise and unrealistic. **His paintings exist in their own right independent of all modernist mumbo-jumbo. They are as pure as his poems, and as profound, though they are inevitably different in essentials, such as attitudes, methods and techniques**—poetry being a matter of faith with him and painting, of amusement.

What precisely is the significance of Rabindranath's art? Connoisseurs, as has already been mentioned, differ rather sharply in their assessment of the poet's contribution to Indian painting. All the other modern Indian masters such as Abanindranath Tagore, Nandalal Bose, Jamini Roy and Amrita Shergil have made a deep impact on their younger contemporaries among whom Subho Tagore seems to be the solitary exception. Subho's work suggests the positive imprint of the poet, particularly in its metaphysical undertones. George Keyt mentions Rabindranath among his earlier influences though the Ceylonese master in his own work never attempts to follow anybody, the reason being his faith in his personal vision and in his individual technique. Keyt's line is too definite and dynamic and has nothing in common with the delightful effusiveness of the poet's abracadabra. What has Keyt then inherited from Tagore? Nothing consciously except perhaps his passion for remaining stubbornly original and Oriental in a fast disintegrating world.

Rabindranath's work has a masterly touch about it in spite of his apparent lack of discipline. We must remember that **he took to painting in the evening of his life. He proclaims: "My morning was full of songs. Let sunset days be full of colour."** He was 67 when he realised that "the scratches in my manuscript cried, like sinners, for salvation" and decided to "rescue them into a merciful finality of rhythm." **In 1941, at 80, he died leaving a legacy of over 2,000 drawings and paintings** which revealed a new facet of his genius. Even during his lifetime, he had kept the art critics busy all over the world. They had by turns remained overwhelmed, enchanted, intrigued. They had discovered that Tagore's lines were as eloquent as his words. **His numerous exhibitions in foreign capitals had assured him of a place among the significant painters of our time.**

What strikes one most in a Tagore composition is its **primeval intensity.** Apparently there is no attempt at organisation. But the **inner rhythm** is obvious enough. The drawing and the colour scheme being untutored are inevitably naive. But they have **a plasticity that few professionals achieve** in their work. **Spontaneity, simplicity, serenity**: these are the rare qualities that distinguish the art of Tagore. Other variations of naivete, represented by the work of neoprimitives, such as Klee, are studied, self-conscious and sensuous and there is a highly urbane philosophy behind them. **Tagore's doodlings reveal his sense of bewilderment at the mystery of life and his determination to express himself as honestly and forcefully as possible.** Here his poetry presents a pleasing contrast—restrained, articulate and tender.

Thus Tagore's paintings and drawings have a deeply spiritual basis. They are also significant because of the milieu in which they were produced. The poet chose to become a painter at a time when the prevailing artistic norms and idioms in the country were hardly congenial to a creative genius of his stature. Well-meaning but ill-equipped illustrators, imbued with revivalist zeal, dominated the scene. They found themselves engaged in a crusading mission and

Rabindranath not being a painter by training, could not identify himself with them. Naturally when he decided to express himself through the plastic medium, he would rather depend on his own fertile imagination and feeling for form than go through the cramping academic routine imposed by his contemporaries with the laudable objective of revitalising the Indian traditions and techniques. Tagore's international outlook and his poetic sensibility were responsible for his choosing to remain a silent spectator rather than an active participant where the spirited revivalist movement was concerned. No wonder that his contribution to the development of the modern Indian idiom continues to be nebulous and out of focus. Essentially his work belongs to the whole world and is not to be interpreted in the terms of the Indian renaissance. His sensitive, symbolical painting and drawings are profoundly universal in their appeal, in spite of their Indian themes. They represent the core of the poet's humanism in visual shorthand.

The art of Rabindranath Tagore has a lesson for our present-day painters who find themselves confronted with a serious stylistic dilemma. They cannot go back because they lack faith. Not can they march ahead in the absence of proper guidance. Indeed Tagore's work should be of special import to them for many reasons. Firstly, **it never dates**. Secondly, its strength lies not in other people's convictions, but in the artist's own. Thirdly, **it is not only creative but communicative, despite its abstract look.** Fourthly, it has an inner harmony and rhythm though apparently devoid of design and structure. For there is genuine inspiration behind it, an intense urge to create new forms. Fifthly, it proclaims the artist's sheer joy in his creative endeavour. And finally, **it conveys a message—positive, pleasant and profound—unlike he bulk of Modern Art, which is morbid.**

16

Santiniketan: An Experiment in Universal Education

Franklin Edgerton
Yale University

(Written in 1961)

On January 12 and 13, 1927, I was able to spend two days at Santiniketan, getting superficially acquainted with the Poet (so he was then always called on his homeground) and the institution he had founded. It was an unforgettable, though regrettably brief, experience. What follows is based on notes I took at the time.

I arrived by railroad from Calcutta, about midnight on Tuesday, January 11, at Bolpur station, from which a motor-bus took me the two miles to the Guest House at Santiniketan, where I was expected. Next morning I was roused before 7 with the news that the Poet was about to conduct a service in the Prayer House, which was observed as a sabbath.

I hurried over to the Prayer House, a square hall enclosed by glass doors, most of which were open this morning, though the day was raw and windy. The Poet sat on the floor facing the audience. There were some Bengali hymns, and then Tagore spoke in Bengali on God or Brahma as joy, using Upanishad passages as texts. I could understand nothing except occasional Sanskrit words, but the substance was interpreted for me afterwards. At the end the audience went up and saluted him by bowing and touching the hem of his garment, after which I went up and presented myself. He shook hands and said he would receive me after I had my breakfast, which he did.

I think he was the most beautiful man I ever met. He was well built with a fine head, clear skin, well tended hair and beard, and a beauty of expression that revealed the gentleness of his character. It suggested also strength, strength of a special kind which goes with gentleness. He had a first-rate mind, which produced excellent ideas, one or two of which will be mentioned later. But his methods were not strenuous. He did not lack energy or persistence; his was the energy of steady, gentle pressure, rather than of a whirlwind attack.

I confess that I was never an ardent admirer of his poetry, so far as I knew it (only in English versions). But the brief acquaintance that I got with his institution gave me a quite enthusiastic opinion of him as an educationist and social reformer. I thought at the time that if what he was doing could only be done in a hundred thousand or so other places throughout India, the country would soon be much better off; and that it would be hard to suggest a better plan of action for improving the condition of the Indian masses. It seemed a well thought out, and reasonable scheme, as far as one man, with limited funds, could manage it.

He started with the village as a unit. He criticised all other agencies of that time, governmental or other, for lack of co-ordination. He thought the life of the village must be treated from all points of view at once, not from this, that, or the other separately. Economic, social, religious, educational, intellectual, moral, hygienic—all these sides must be treated together, since these are simultaneous aspects of human life.

In 1961, this point of view may seem less novel than it did in 1927. Others have adopted much or most of his programme; it came to be recognised by many that Indian villages need attention in most if not all of these respects. But he was a pioneer in having "surveys" made of particular villages in his vicinity; and he went to work on that basis. He was operating a model farm, run by several graduates of American agricultural colleges, including his own son. Here they experimented with crops and agricultural methods. There were a poultry farm, a cattle and dairy-husbandry centre, weaving, tanning and other industrial establishments; a medical and hygienic service (which was not entirely free, he wanted to avoid charity); and troops of what Westerners would call Boy Scouts, but he objected to that term. These were called "Brati Balakas", boys under vows, who, after special training, voluntarily and systematically looked after village hygiene, and especially the hygiene and sanitation of popular festivals where crowds of people came and lived together for days at a time or longer. These boys or young men also ran some village schools, including evening schools for children of the Harijans who had to work by day.

All this Rural Development Department was centred at Surul, a couple of miles away from Santiniketan, and covered a considerable number of villages. Their purpose was to get the best-trained people they could in each line, but then to proceed experimentally; only when satisfied with their own results would they try to introduce them widely in the villages. They needed, I was told, some years to gain the confidence of the villages, but they said they had it by 1927. They thought they had been able to improve methods and results in everyone of the industrial lines they had undertaken.

The "School" proper was at Santiniketan itself; though Tagore regarded the two parts of his work as integrally connected. The School itself was part of the "rural improvement" experiment. Further, the older students in it took a large part in the programmes of the rural department. However, the School was 25 years old when I was there, the Surul part only half a dozen years. The Poet regarded the primary school as the most important department of the School. There were in 1927 about 60 children in it; boys and girls together (at that time a radical step in India), of all creeds and castes, all eating together and associating in perfect equality. I asked the Poet if he had any trouble due to caste lines. He said: "At first I did. Some high caste boys would't eat with the low-caste ones. Of course I couldn't force them to, since freedom is the very principle of the School; and then they would have rebelled and been stubborn about it. So I said: 'Very well, if you are high caste Brahmanas and can't eat with the other boys, you may eat at a separate table'. So they did; but they didn't enjoy it. They felt cut off, excluded, as if they were being punished. And it wasn't long before one by one they came and asked to be allowed to eat with the majority. Since then I have had no trouble."

This illustrates Tagore's idea in educational methods, all through; not to use compulsion, but to give the best side of human nature a chance to show itself. There was a minimum of curriculum, hardly any in fact. Everything was left to the initiative of the pupils, though they were always in close touch with their elders. The primary school teacher was a graduate of an English university, in Education, and had also studied in the United States, at Columbia University. "I was afraid this would have spoiled him," said Tagore shrewdly, and I admitted that I too would have been afraid of that. But after I had spent nearly a whole morning with the young man (a Ceylonese), I felt, as did the Poet, that he had not been spoiled. He was a born teacher, and a very fine man.

That morning there were no classes; the weather had been bad, and the children all wanted a holiday. So the teacher said: "Well, what would you like to do?" Some wanted this, some that; none wanted lessons. So the school was dismissed, and they all set about their chosen occupations. Some did carpentering, some masonry, some gardening, some drawing; some just played around. This gave me a chance for a long and valuable talk with the teacher, but no chance to watch classes, unfortunately, as I left that night. The School managed somehow to prepare for university matriculation, and even, in time, for B.A. examinations of the University of Calcutta.

But Tagore didn't quite like this. Of course he didn't forbid it, but he preferred his pupils to have nothing to do with the formal university curriculum. I fully agreed with him in this. I found that curriculum worse than at my home. It seemed to me a feeble imitation of English or American education, which is probably bad enough for Englishmen and Americans, but peculiarly bad for Indians, because so inappropriate for them. It may be less bad now, but in 1927 most English and Indians alike, I found, seemed to agree on the uselessness, for Indians, of most university education in India. But Tagore was nearly the only one with enough vision to try to start something else in its place.

Tagore's school carried on through collegiate work, apparently in humanistic lines only; at least I heard of no laboratory science. Music and art were also cultivated, Sanskrit was taught at higher levels, and occasionally French and German, when there was anybody to teach them. In the Research Department, good scholarly work was already being done, in Sanskrit, Pali, Tibetan, Chinese, and other Oriental fields. This was started by several excellent European Orientialists; Winternitz of Prague, Sten Konow of Norway, and especially Sylvain Levi of Paris, who founded a really important school there. These three great scholars came for various periods of time at the Poet's invitation, though on nominal salaries—not much more than free board and room. There was already a valuable library, consisting largely but not wholly of gifts.

I must mention one who made a greater impression on me than anyone besides Tagore himself. He was a remarkable Bengali named Kshitimohan Sen, who had spent a large part of his life roaming about the countryside and interviewing *sadhus*. He had studied with Sanskrit pundits in his youth, otherwise had little formal education; but he was one of the few people I have ever met that made me feel instantly that I should like to study with him. He was a rare and delightful personality. He read and translated for me some of the sayings he had picked up from (often illiterate) wandering holy men in Bengal—really fine things, comparable with the sayings of the ancient great, and of a kind which could hardly have originated except in such circles. He is worth writing about as an example of the kind of persons who were spontaneously drawn into close personal relations with Rabindranath Tagore.

17

Santiniketan in 1961

Humayun Kabir

Barely three hours' run by a train from Calcutta, there lies Santiniketan, the Abode of Peace, and Vishva-Bharati, India's cosmopolitan University, founded by Rabindranath Tagore. Huddled all around are clusters of Santhal villages, but in Santiniketan itself one finds space and expansiveness, a sense of repose and freedom from restricting bonds. On all sides the open fields stretch far away—bare fields of red earth with deep fissures through which tiny streamlets flow during the rainy months. A few gaunt palms add to the bleakness of the landscape, a landscape that is strangely alien to the soft and monotonous languor of the vast plains of Bengal.

On this barren heath Santiniketan is a little oasis of luxuriant green. "We have planted every one of the trees you see," the Poet told me with a touch of justifiable pride when I had last visited him there. I understood, for I had just been to the festival of *Vriksharopana* or 'Planting of the trees', when the Poet took part in a picturesque ceremony commemorating the enrichment of the earth with the labour of human hands. Boys and girls, students of Santiniketan, formed a colourful procession to carry the young seedlings to the earth and the Poet blessed the saplings at the commencement of this their arboreal life.

This ceremony reveals in a peculiar way the essence of Santiniketan. Like the trees were and are planted one by one and add to the life and richness of the local landscape, the institution has been built up with painstaking care till from humble beginnings it has attained its present status. Started about sixty years ago, with scarcely half a dozen pupils, today it counts almost a thousand members on its rolls. At first only a school where a few small children gathered round the Poet, today it is a University which provides for teaching in many arts and crafts and serves as a cultural centre where people come from distant lands. Vishva-Bharati is itself a later growth, and with Santiniketan, attracts, scholars and pupils, not only from all parts of India, but indeed from all parts of the world.

There is perhaps no other institution in the world which within such a small compass presents such a variety of diverse human specimens. **One of the leading savants of France, two Chinese scholars working on Buddhistic philosophy, a Dutch musician studying Indian music, a young German interested in Indian art, an Iranian poet sent by Reza Shah Pahlavi and an Italian Professor of international fame,**—these are only a few of the many visitors from many countries who have found here their spiritual home. And then one could name Andrews and Pearson and Benoit and Bogdanoff and scores of others who were so deeply welded into its life and gave themselves so fully to its nurture that one can hardly think of them outside the context of Santiniketan.

In other ways also, the *Vriksharopana* ceremony was significant of Santiniketan's life. It seeks to symbolise the close union and interdependence of nature and human life, and remind us that wherever their harmony is disturbed, there follow evil consequences for both of them. Man is often compelled to live a cramped and restricted life, but torn from his natural environment, his inner balance is disturbed and he is restless and ill at ease. He longs to get back to the peace and freedom of the vast open spaces, but this cannot be and he is forced to struggle as best as he may in an environment which is inimical to the secret longings of his soul. Happy is the man who cherishes in his heart Nature's silence and repose, for it is a hidden spring where he can drink when tired with the struggle of life, a secret source of happiness that continually cheers him amidst the vicissitudes of life.

Tagore established Santiniketan to build up for its pupils this sanctuary of the heart. For here, far from the city's madding strife, Nature breathes her presence in every aspect of their lives. The seasons encircle them in a ring of beauty, with silent steps that sink into the conciousness. There is daily communion with nature even though the pupils are often not aware of it, but whether they feel it or not, this constant living in the very presence of nature cannot fail to mould their lives in many imperceptible ways. It gives them a fund of joy which they carry through all their lives, so that one can hardly ever mistake a student who has been through Santiniketan.

Then there is the Kala-Bhavana, or School of Art, for long presided over by Nandalal Bose. Of Nandalal's art there is no need to speak here, for the whole of art-conscious India unites in acknowledging his mastery over line and colour, his firm grasp of reality and yet his power to transmute it in the light of his imagination. A realist in his art, Nandalal's strong sense of reality is evident in his life as well. Unassuming and modest, there is that in him which makes even the casual observer feel that here is one of nature's own aristocrats. Many of the heads of schools and colleges of art in India are pupils of Nandalal, and Tagore, whenever he had occasion to speak of him, referred to him as the very prince of teachers. That is why all Santiniketan unites in still calling him, 'the

Master-moshai'.

Pursuit of scholarship and beauty did not however exhaust Tagore's programme for his cosmopolitan University. He held that educational institutions must be in tune with the social and economic life of the people. For him, there could be no question of the political freedom or the economic regeneration of his country till people in the villages regained their initiative and self-respect. The individual villager may be poor, he said, but if many villagers pool their resources, they can accomplish tasks beyond their individual competence. At Shriniketan, he initiated programmes to bring back dynamism and dignity to the people of rural India by a skilful interweaving of agriculture and industry based on modern techniques.

One thinks of these achievements and then one remembers the opposition and discouragement which the Poet had to face. No doubt there were many mistakes, no doubt more might have been done even with the continual lack of funds from which the institution has all along suffered. But those who speak in that vein are wise after the event and forget that wisdom in criticism does not always imply wisdom in practice. The wonder is that so much has been done in spite of the apathy and passive hostility of the people of the land by a visionary who had to struggle with his own inexperience. In Santiniketan, as in so many other cases, **Tagore proved that he was no mere dreamer or visionary but an idealist with sufficient sense of reality to convert his ideals into facts.**

To my mind Santiniketan's true significance lies in the fact that here we have the makings of a true Indian university. There is no parochialism here, no narrow sectarianism, no arrogance of provincial pride and jealousy. All India is united in the allegiance to a common hero and his ideal. That is how the universities of Europe grew and that is how we hope Santiniketan may continue to grow. Admiration for a great teacher attracted pupils from far and near and they clustered round him to share his life and thought till out of such groups of admirers and students grew the great universities of Europe. Like them, Santiniketan also started with the threefold advantages of nearness to a great city, a healthy and beautiful locality and the presence of a great seer and teacher, but there was for long one great difference between it and the germinal universities of Europe. They centred round a great personality but from the very outset they were impersonal in character, while Santiniketan not only centred round the personality of Tagore but was in the beginning also essentially personal, and therefore to that extent, impermanent in character. For Tagore was Santiniketan and Santiniketan was Tagore. That was its strength when it started but it would have become a source of weakness unless corrected in time.

Shatiniketan owes its all to Tagore, and it was Tagore's greatest gift to Santiniketan when he sought to liberate it from the charm of his own personality. He realised more clearly than any of his contemporaries that his ideal must continue to be the centre of Santiniketan's life and yet Santiniketan must develop a character that is permanent and impersonal and free. After his death, it seemed for a while that the significance of his message might be lost and the future of India's only cosmopolitan university be in jeopardy. Today in the year of his centenary there is again occasion for hope.

18

My Father's Truth

Rathindranath Tagore

It would appear presumptuous on my part to attempt an assessment of my father's genius about which so much has already been written and I dare say more will be written. Father himself has given us his reminiscences and unburdened himself to many friends in his numerous letters. It will be noticed, however, that his reminiscences are not so much a chronicle of events as the story of an inner unfoldment.

Intensely human as he was, **Father's was yet a most complex character. By nature extremely shy and sensitive, there was no knowing how he would react to men and things.** He was extremely capricious in his moods. At times he would throw off all reserve and entertain friends—mostly young admirers—with brilliant sallies of wit and humour; at others he would withdraw within himself, making it impossible for others to fathom his thoughts. In his happiest moods, he could mix with children as though he was one of them.

His ever-changing moods were a constant strain on his closest associates. It has occurred to me that very often Father did not want to admit even to himself his innermost feelings and convictions. It was therefore difficult even for those who were nearest to him, to know the reasons which made him act in a particular way. The delicacy of his own feelings, especially with regard to personal matters, and his solicitude for the feelings of others, often led him to adopt devious means of hiding his real intentions. On many an occasion my wife and I have felt amused when he tried these on us.

My grandfather loved his youngest son and was delighted to discover unusual talent in him while still a boy. Probably for this reason he was very generous to him. Father was given the most convenient and comfortable rooms in the family house, and when even this did not satisfy him, grandfather helped him to build a separate house for himself. Father always liked to change his surroundings. He easily got tired of living in the same room or the same house for long. Santiniketan can boast of more than a score of houses enriched by their association with Father. He, therefore, felt very happy to receive this assistance from Maharshi, and started to build the house. Father suggested that the house should consist of two large upper and lower halls only, so that he would be free to alter the interior arrangements whenever he chose by means of movable partitions. The house was built and then when we wanted to move into it, **we discovered that although there were the two big halls as desired by Father, one on each floor, there was no staircase to connect them.**

Although my grandfather had handed over the management of the estates to Father, he himself controlled the expenditure. He was a strict disciplinarian. On the second of every month the accounts had to be brought and read out to him. He would remember every figure and ask awkward questions whilst the report was being read. Father used to be afraid of this day of trial, like a school-boy going up for his examination. We children would wonder why our father was so afraid of his father.

Father never treated any of his children harshly, nor did he, on the other hand, lavish sentimental affection upon them. I do not remember any occasion when Father subjected any of us to physical punishment. **Temperamentally it was**

impossible for him to use violence. During all the years of my boyhood and youth, only thrice have I seen him get really angry with me. As a child I did not like bathing with its inevitable rubbing and scrubbing as though the body was something meant to be maltreated regularly every day. One day my mother, having altogether failed to make me submit to this ordeal, appealed to Father. He took hold of me, placed me on the top of an almirah, and left me there without any scolding—not even a single harsh word. Mother had no more trouble with me at bathing-time.

Recognition of his genius as a poet and a writer came to Father after he had reached a mature age—but he was much sought after and became a popular social figure while he was still quite young. His extremely handsome appearance coupled with a remarkable voice, probably partly accounted for his popularity. Father liked to dress well. In his youth he always wore the *dhoti* with a silk *kurta* and silk *chaddar* in public. He looked very handsome in his flowing Bengali dress, and people would admire the colour of the *kurta* or the way he wore the *chaddar,* and try to imitate him. At other times, especially when travelling, he liked to wear trousers with a buttoned-up long coat or *achkan* and a small *pugree.* Afterwards at a much later age, he discarded the short *achkan* and took to the long flowing *jhabba* or often a pair of them worn with a soft cap. He was not afraid of colours and his favourite colour was a fawn with a tinge of orange. Most people who have seen him at his advanced age, will associate him with this sober but pleasant colour.

I would like to refer to one interesting thing in this connection. Father and Gandhiji were great friends. Yet, outwardly no two people could be more unlike each other. **Gandhiji in his loin-cloth and Father in his colourful flowing robes, presented a strange contrast.** This could not have failed to attract public notice, and **I have heard people make uncharitable remarks about Father's extravagant tastes.** It may, however, be noted that Father's clothes were not necessarily made of expensive material. He had the peculiar knack of making the simplest thing look beautiful, and the most expensive thing look simple. Austerity as such had little or no appeal for Father. In a land of poverty where life was nothing but a story of systematic deprivation, austerity was not the ideal to be held up before the public.

I think few writers have had to face such severe and unfair criticism as Father, during the greater part of his life. Hardly any of these were literary criticisms—they were acrimonious and sometimes even scurrilous. One obvious reason for the persistence was that the editors had early discovered that slandering Father paid handsomely. There was, however, a more subtle reason behind this. **The public never felt that Rabindranath really belonged to them.** He was born in an aristocratic family, he wrote in a style and language which was too individual and had nothing in common with his predecessors or contemporary writers; moreover, **he belonged to the Brahmo Samaja, a non-conformist movement to reform Hindu orthodoxy and hence a menace to society.** It is perhaps for these reasons that, besides the hack writer, we find even literary coteries presided over by such eminent men as Dwijendralal Roy and Chittaranjan Das trying to undermine the influence of Father over the youth of the country. I cannot say that Father was indifferent to the campaign carried on against him. **It deeply pained him but never did he reply to the attacks made on him,** except once in a poem addressed to the detractor.

All his life he had felt lonely, an intellectual loneliness which is the common experience of a genius of his order. Undoubtedly he had many friends, but they were young admirers, who could not give him the companionship that he craved for. But it did bring considerable cheer to his otherwise lonely life to feel the warmth of their devotion and love.

Very few knew or realized the struggle Father had to carry on his educational experiment at Santiniketan. When the school was established, he had difficulty in getting pupils and those that came were mostly of the difficult type. People looked down upon the institution and ridiculed Father's attempt to introduce new ideas in education. It took years before people began to recognize the Santiniketan school as anything else but reformatory. To this was added the suspicion of the British Government, and the secret circulars that were issued to warn officials from sending their children to Santiniketan. Considered from a worldly point of view, **it was indeed foolhardy of Father to have launched into this misadventure, at a time when he hardly had enough to support himself and his family** and was actually in debt on account of the failure of the Kushtia business. He had to dispose of every thing he possessed including the ornamentals belonging to my mother, in order to start the school. Among other things he had to sell his gold watch and chain—a wedding gift—to a friend. It was a familiar object to us, when we were children. We liked to flick open the lid to look at the monogram engraved on the inside.

Financial difficulties increased with the years, as the school expanded. Father had to go to Sir Taraknath Palit, father of his friend Loken Palit, to borrow money. This debt he was unable to repay during Sir Tarak's lifetime. Among other assets, the amount Father owed him was transferred to the Calcutta University, when Sir Tarak died, leaving all his property to the University. This debt was a constant source of worry.

The lecture-tour in the U.S.A. in 1916-17 was a phenomenal success. It brought enormous returns. But ill luck intervened. The Bureau that was handling his lecture-tour very conveniently went bankrupt towards the end of the tour, and instead of the several lacs due, all that Willie Pearson, who was with Father on that tour, could with difficulty realise, were a few thousand rupees just sufficient to pay off Father's debt to the Calcutta University.

The sale of Father's books in the continental countries of Europe should have brought him a fortune. But his fame reached its height immediately before the first World War, and this effectively prevented the realisation of royalties.

Father had to go constantly on begging missions on behalf of his institution. I was with him in New York in 1920 when an organised effort was made to collect funds in America. With the help of Mrs. Willard Straight and Mr. Morgentheau (Senior), quite a group of Wall Street millionaires had been induced to open the subscription list with handsome donations. He gave a banquet at his house to which about a hundred of his millionaire friends were invited. We were assured that Father would get a few million dollars before he left the shores of America. But not even a few thousands came to him.

Father returned to India bitterly disappointed. It was a bitter trial for me also. I felt I was responsible for encouraging Father to go through this humiliating and painful experience. We afterwards came to know that Wall Street closed its purse-strings at the last moment because of a tip sent through Morgan that financial help to a private institution in India would not be looked upon with favour by the British Government.

Although compelled to seek help for his institution, the idea of begging money from monied men, just the people who were least capable of appreciating him and his work at Santiniketan, was painful to him. Once a friend of ours, a businessman of Bombay, had arranged that Father should meet the Gaekwad of Baroda and ask him for an endowment worthy of him. The friend told me that he had found the Prince, who was living at Lausanne, in a very sympathetic mood and that he had already prepared the ground. Father would only have to invite him to lunch and casually mention the matter. I went over to Lausanne and invited the Maharaja to lunch with Father at our hotel in Geneva. At the lunch-table a very interesting conversation was started and carried on from one topic to another, and so absorbed were they that neither my friend nor myself could find an opening to turn it in the direction we wanted. At last Father noticed the look of alarm in our faces and abruptly told the Maharaja of his mission, and wound up his appeal for funds with the advice that if the Maharaja did decide to give any money to him, he should do it as though he were throwing it into the water. On hearing this my friend gave me a hard kick under the table. The Maharaja kept silent and left without making any promise.

It was left to Mahatma Gandhi to realise the tragedy of circumstances. Once when Mahatmaji met him in Delhi in 1936, and found that Father was trying to raise money through performance of his dance-drama *Chitrangada* by the students of Santiniketan, he asked us what was the amount of deficit which was worrying Father. Before Father left, Mahatmaji gave him a cheque for the amount which he had raised in the meantime and made Father promise that he would never again go out on such a mission. The money thus secured for us by Mahatmaji came like a windfall, and there was great jubilation among those who formed the party.

Father's essentially optimistic and cheerful temperament combined with a sense of humour, helped him to overcome the vicissitudes that pursued him relentlessly throughout his life. **The death of my mother when he was only fortyone, came as the first blow. It left him with five children to manage.** And yet he was not to be spared other greater trials. **One after the other my grandfather, my two married sisters and my young brother died. My two cousins, Balendra and Nitindra, whom Father loved like his own sons, died** in the prime of their youth. The successive deaths of the young poet Satish Roy and of Mohitchandra Sen robbed him of two of his ablest supports in his work for the Santiniketan School. During all these years of anguish and suffering, Father himself was in constant pain, due to a chronic ailment.

Father had an unusual capacity for work. He was gifted with a remarkably strong constitution. One of my uncles had seen to it that Father should improve and develop this natural gift by physical exercises during his boyhood. Besides other exercises, a professional gave him lessons in wrestling. As a result, father looked a picture of robust health in his youth. Even in later years I never saw him suffer from any of the common ailments, except from the chronic trouble he had inherited. He was able to get rid of this in 1912 by an operation, after which he enjoyed perfect health for many years until old age.

Throughout his life he worked all hours of the day. His day began at about 4 a.m., while it was still dark. Before setting down to work at his writing desk, he used to sit in meditation for half an hour or more every morning. At breakfast he liked company. His hour for this meal was so unusually early that very often the people whom he expected could not turn up. He used to send for them and wait till they came. This was the time when he was in his best form—telling humorous stories, cracking jokes and carrying on brilliant conversation.

It is surprising how he could compose poems and songs, write novels and essays—very often all at the same time—and yet receive so many callers. He never liked any visitor, whatever his mission, to be kept waiting. His secretaries had a hard time whenever they tried to shield him from unnecessary intrusion. They would be rebuked by Father for their over-zealousness. Father did not take any rest during the day. **Even during the hottest days of summer, he would sit at his desk and work with the doors and windows wide open, absolutely indifferent to the hot blasts blowing around him.** Most of his reading was done at night. There was plenty of time for this, as he did not go to bed till quite late. Four to five hours of sleep was all that he needed. Nothing seemed to disturb his chain of thoughts. **He could leave a poem unfinished, talked to someone for an hour, and then immediately go back and finish it.** The only form of rest that he allowed himself when he was tired, was to compose songs and set them to music. Latterly, after he had taken to painting, that also became a favourite form of recreation.

No biography, however laboriously written, could ever give an adequate picture of such a complex personality as his. "You cannot find the poet in his biography", he says in one of his poems. Yes, the poet is to be found in his poems. His poems are his best life-story and may I conclude by saying that his greatest poem is the life he has lived.

19

Tagore on Women

Three Significant Selections

Saurovy S. Deka

Comparatively speaking, females are needful to Nature's purpose while males are barely necessary. In the insect world we witness the phenomenon of the females taking it upon themselves to keep down the male population to the bare limit of necessity.

Woman is endowed with the passive qualities of chastity, modesty, devotion and power of self-sacrifice in a greater measure than man is. It is this passive quality in nature which turns its monster forces into perfect creations of beauty. This passive quality has given woman that large and deep placidity which is so necessary for the healing and nourishing and storing of life. Life should be like a lamp where the potentiality of light is far greater in quantity than what appears as the flame. **It is in the depth of passiveness in woman's nature that this potentiality of life in stored.**

Wherever there is something which is concretely personal or human, there is woman's world. The domestic world is the world where every individual finds his worth as an individual, therefore his value is not the market value, but the value of love. This domestic world has been the gift of God to woman.

The ideal of stability is deeply cherished in woman's nature. She is never in love with merely going on, shooting wanton arrows of curiosity into the heart of darkness. All her forces instinctively work to bring things to some shape of fullness,—for that is the law of life.

Woman should use her power to break through the surface and go to the centre of things, where in the mystery of life dwells an eternal source of interest.

The masculine creations of intellectual civilisation are towers of Babel, they dare to defy their foundations and therefore topple down over and over again. Thus human history is growing up over layers of ruins; it is not a continuous life-growth. **At the present stage of history, civilisation is almost exclusively masculine, in which woman has been thrust aside in the shade. Therefore it has lost its balance and is moving by hopping from war to war. And at last the time has arrived when woman must step in and impart her life rhythm to this reckless movement of power.** For woman's function is the passive function of the soil, which not only helps the tree to grow but keeps its growth within limits. Our civilisation must also have its passive element, broad and deep and stable. It must not be mere growth but harmony of growth.

Woman can bring her fresh mind and all her power of sympathy to this new task of building up a spiritual civilisation. She must restore the lost social balance by putting the full weight of the woman into the creation of the human world.

●

Q. What do you think of the modern woman's clamour for equality of status?[1]

1. These conversations took place between Sri Dilip Kumar Roy and Tagore, and the former has recorded them in his *Among the Great*.

Ans. I have always held that, essentially, woman is not man's competitor but his complement. This may sound somewhat old-fashioned, but an undeniable experience that becomes richer with the stamp and seal of time on its brow.

Q. Does that mean that she is to be debarred from claiming equal rights with men?

Ans. No—not that. All I mean is: she must not forget that her life has a real mission which is not the duplicate of her partner's, of course she is there to co-operate with him—to give him her comradeship, often her guidance as well, but she would do well to remember that co-operation doesn't amount to imitation. In other words, she must find her proper place in society and not rush to fill somebody else's. And this she can achieve only by being true to her nature—her *swadharma.*

Q. But why may she not aspire to share man's work in his own sphere?

Ans. Because her nature is unsuited for it; she could never be at home in the sphere of masculine rough and tumble activities. For woman's function works passively, subterraneously, like the roots of a tree, while man's fulfilment consists in spreading himself out like the branches through growth, adventure, activity.

Q. Is this not simply another way of saying that there is a fundamental difference between man and woman?

Ans. Of course. If woman had been but an exact counterpart of man, with exactly the same part to play, life as we know it would have ceased to exist long ago. But fortunately, woman is not man's replica but his fellow-pilgrim in their joint journey through life—and that is why the march still continues. Woman is so well saddled by Nature with the qualities which man lacks, like humility, restraint, self abnegation, etc. It is these qualities which have imparted stability to the restless world of masculine creation.

Q. There are some who say that woman is incapable of creation in any but the inferior plane, and therefore must always play the second fiddle to man in the superior spheres of life.

Ans. I cannot even conceive of assigning such an undignified function to woman... Woman's function in life is not really confined to the physical plane; she is as indispensable to man's mental creation as man is to her physical. It is only because on the mental plane she works unseen, behind the screen, that we do not visualise her contribution at this stage. But that is only because we are unimaginative.

Q. What you say amounts then to this: that woman's way of self-fulfilment must differ from man's?

Ans. Roundly, yes. The chief thing to remember is, that woman cannot have been created by Nature to tread the same beaten track as man, mouthing the identical slogans. The banks of a river are not intended to serve the same purpose as its current. And it is because the two are dissimilar, that the river continues to flow.

Q. The essential needs of the two sexes must also be very dissimilar then?

Ans. Unquestionably.

Q. In what way, precisely?

Ans. For one thing, man can be more at home with the non-human qualities than woman, can be more easily impersonal, even anti-social if you like. Woman is by temperament taken up with the personal, the human, the social side of our nature... Her grace and charm and sweetness—that is, her *hladini* qualities are necessary to our very existence, and this is no mere poetising but an incontestable experience of our everyday life... Although man needs freedom and space—*mukti*—more fundamentally than woman, who needs nest building as urgently, she can never find complete fulfilment in mere empty space.

Q. Do not both man and woman need it equally?

Ans. I did not imply woman has no such need. What I meant was that woman's need for emotion and 'earthwardness' is greater than man's, or to put it differently, while womanhood finds its completest fulfilment through love and home, man's perfect fulfilment needs a more generous margin of freedom, of comparative detachment. Man at his highest is essentially an aspirer after the infinite.

Q. But surely woman also has similar aspiration?

Ans. Of course, she has. Her salvation too must lie in the direction of the infinite, —that goes without saying, only, her method of attaining it is different from man's. For she too must touch the Infinite, the Eternal, though not, like him—through *mukti*—expansion and detachment—but through *bandhan*—bonds and concentration. The impulse which enabled Buddha to abandon his wife Gopa in quest of the infinite, is a true impulse for man, but not for woman.

Q. You mean Gopa was essentially incapable of giving up Buddha to attain such an end?

Ans. Precisely.

Q. But why must that be?

Ans. Because Gopa was a woman. Her nature could neither hanker after nor thrive in the void of the utter renunciation and detachment which Buddha accepted.

Q. But aren't there women too, whose nature...

Ans. Of course there are. But that is simply another way of saying that there are women whose nature is essentially masculine just as there are men whose nature is essentially feminine. But neither of these types is a true representative of its sex, and may well be looked upon as somewhat of a freak.

Q. Do you mean perhaps that love is more or less unnecessary to man?

Ans. Emotional fervour is the very backbone of woman's make-up, while with man it is simply a beacon-light in his life's voyage—a wonderful light if you will, but still not the be-all-and-end-all of his existence, as it is with woman.

●

I have passed through various experiences of fire and shadow, the warp and woof with which providence weaves the strange webs of human personality. But one thing I can say with honest pride; that I have never made light of the love of a woman no matter how she has loved me. I have always been grateful for it all, always looked upon it as a grace—a favour. For I have experienced again and again that every feminine love, no matter of what quality, leaves behind it a legacy of flowers in our soul, a harvest of dreams that would never have been born but for her showers of tenderness. Her gift of blooms may fade with time, yes, but the memory of their fragrance, never.

... matter how long ... lives ...
... for it all ...
... I have compared ...
... naturally ...
... of flowers ...
... have been born ...
... bloom may fade ...
... fragrance ...

A Thinker *Par Excellence*

Ignored So Far

1

The Nature of Reality

Tagore Talks to Einstein

A conversation that took place on July 14, 1930, at Einstein's residence in Germany.

Einstein: Do you believe in the Divine as isolated from the world?

Tagore: Not isolated. The infinite personality of man comprehends the universe. There cannot be anything that cannot be subsumed under the human personality, and this proves that the truth of the universe is human truth.

I have taken a scientific fact to explain this. Matter is composed of protons and electrons, with gaps between them, but matter may seem to be solid without the links of space that unify the individual electrons and protons. Similarly, humanity is composed of individuals, yet they have their interconnection of human relationships, which give living unity to man's world. The entire universe is linked up with us, as individuals, in a similar manner; it is a human universe.

I have pursued this thought through art, literature, and the religious consciousness of men.

Einstein: There are two different conceptions of the nature of the universe: 1. the world as unity dependent on humanity; 2. the world as a reality independent of the human factor.

Tagore: When our universe is in harmony with man,

the Eternal, we know it as truth, we feel it as beauty.

Einstein: This is the purely human conception of the universe.

Tagore: There can be no other conception. This world is a human world—the scientific view of it is the view of the scientific man. Therefore, the world apart from us does not exist; it is a relative world depending for its reality upon our consciousness. There is a standard of reason and enjoyment that gives it truth, the standard of the eternal man whose experiences are through our experiences.

Einstein: This is a realisation of the human entity.

Tagore: Yes, one eternal entity. We have to realise it through our emotions and activities. We realise the supreme man, who has no individual limitations, through our limitations. Science is concerned with that which is not confined to individuals; it is the impersonal human deeper needs: our individual consciousness of truth gains universal significance. Religion applies values to truth, and we know truth as good through our own harmony with it.

Einstein: Truth, then, or beauty, is not independent of man?

Tagore: No.

Einstein: It there were no human beings any more, the Apollo Belvedere would no longer be beautiful?

Tagore: No.

Einstein: I agree with this conception in regard to beauty, but not in regard to truth.

Tagore: Why not? Truth is realised through man.

Einstein: I cannot prove that I am right, but that is my religion.

Tagore: Beauty is found in the ideal of perfect harmony which is in the Universal Being, and truth is the perfect comprehension of the universal mind. We individuals approach truth through our own mistakes and blunders, through our accumulated experiences, through our illumined consciousness. How, otherwise, can we know it?

Einstein: I cannot prove that scientific truth must be

conceived as a truth that is valid independent of humanity; but I believe it firmly. I believe, for instance, that the Pythagorean theorem in geometry states something that is approximately true, independent of the existence of man. In any case, if there is a reality independent of man, there is also a truth relative to this reality; and the negation of the first engenders a negation of the existence of the latter.

Tagore: Truth, which is one with the Universal Being, must essentially be human; otherwise, whatever we individuals realise as true can never be called truth, at least the truth which is described as scientific and which can be reached only through the process of logic, in other words, through the medium of human thought. According to Hindu philosophy there is Brahman, the Absolute Truth, which cannot be conceived by the isolated individual or described in words, but can be realised only when the individual merges himself completely in its infinity. But such a truth cannot belong to science. The nature of the truth we are discussing is an appearance, that is to say what appears to be true to the human mind and therefore is human may be called *maya* or illusion.

Einstein: So, according to your conception, which may be the Hindu concerption, it is not the illusion of the individual but of humanity as a whole.

Tagore: In science we go through the discipline of eliminating the personal limitations of our individual minds and thus reach that comprehension of truth which is in the mind of the universal man.

Einstien: The initial problem is whether truth is independent of our consciousness.

Tagore: What we call truth lies in rational harmony between the subjective and objective aspects of reality, both of which belong to the superpersonal man.

Einstien: Even in our everyday life, we feel compelled to ascribe a reality independent of man to the objects we use. We do this to connect the experiences of our senses in a reasonable way. For instance, if nobody is in this house, yet that table remains where it is.

Tagore: Yes, it remains outside the individual mind, but not outside the universal mind. The table that I perceive is perceptible by the same kind of consciousness that I possess.

Einstein: Our natural point of view in regard to the existence of truth apart from humanity cannot be explained or proved, but it is a belief that nobody is without, not even primitive beings. We attribute to truth a superhuman objectivity; it is indispensable to us, this reality that is independent of our existence and our experience and our mind, though we cannot say what it means.

Tagore: Science has proved that the table as a solid object is an appearance, and therefore that which the human mind perceives as a table would not exist if that mind were naught. At the same time it must be admitted that the fact that the ultimate physical reality of the table is nothing but a multitude of separate revolving centres of electric force which also belong to the human mind.

In the apprehension of truth there is an eternal conflict between the universal human mind and the same mind confined in the individual. The perpetual process of reconciliation is being carried on in our science, in our philosophy, and in our ethics. In any case, if there be any truth absolutely unrelated to humanity, then for us it is absolutely nonexistent.

Einstein: Then I am more religious than you are.

Tagore: My religion lies in the reconciliation of the superpersonal man, the universal human spirit, with my own individual being. This was the subject of my Hibbert Lectures, which I called *The Religion of Man*.

2

Nation As Evil: A Critique of Modern Times

Man's history is being shaped according to the difficulties it encounters. These have offered us problems and claimed their solutions from us, the penalty of non-fulfilment being death or degradation. These difficulties have been different in different peoples of the earth, and in the manner of our overcoming them lies our distinction.

The Scythians of the earlier period of Asiatic history had to struggle with the scarcity of their natural resources. The easiest solution that they could think of was to organise their whole population, men, women, and children, into bands of robbers. And they were irresistible to those who were chiefly engaged in the constructive work of social co-operation.

But fortunately for man the easiest path is not his truest path. If his nature were not as complex as it is, if it were as simple as that of a pack of hungry wolves, then, by this time, those hordes of marauders would have overrun the whole earth. But man, when confronted with difficulties, has to acknowledge that he is man, that he has his responsibilities to the higher faculties of his nature, by ignoring which he may achieve success that is immediate, perhaps, but that will become a death-trap to him. For, what are obstacles to the lower creatures are opportunities to the higher life of man.

To India has been given her problem from the beginning of history—it is the race problem. Races ethnologically different have in this country come into close contact. This fact has been and still continues to be the most important one in our history. **It is our mission to face it and prove our humanity by dealing with it in the fullest truth.** Until we fulfil our mission all other benefits will be denied us.

There are other peoples in the world who have to overcome obstacles in their physical surroundings, or the menace of their powerful neighbours. They have organised their power till they are not only reasonably free from the tyranny of Nature and human neighbours, but have a surplus of it left in their hands to employ against others. But in India, our difficulties being internal, **our history has been the history of continual social adjustment and not that of organised power for defence and aggression.**

Neither the colourless vagueness of cosmopolitanism, nor the fierce self-idolatry of nation-worship, is the goal of human history. And India **has been trying to accomplish her task through social regulation of differences, on the one hand, and the spiritual recognition of unity on the other.** She has made grave errors in setting up the boundary walls too rigidly between races, in perpetuating in her classifications the results of inferiority; often she has crippled her children's minds and narrowed their lives in order to fit them into her social forms; but for centuries new experiments have been made and adjustments carried out.

Her mission has been like that of a hostess who has to provide proper accommodation for numerous guests, whose habits and requirements are different from one another. This gives rise to infinite complexities whose solution depends not merely upon tactfulness but upon sympathy and true realisation of the unity of man. Towards this realisation have worked, from the early times of the Upanishads up to the present moment, a series of great spiritual teachers, whose one object has been to set at naught all differences of man by the overflow of our consciousness of God. In fact, **our history has not been of the rise and fall of kingdoms, of fights for political supremacy.** In our country records of these days have been despised and forgotten, for they in no way represent the true history of our people. **Our history is that of our social life and attainment of spiritual ideals.**

But we feel that our task is not yet done. The world-flood has swept over our country, new elements have been introduced, and wider adjustments are waiting to be made.

We feel this all the more, because the teaching and example of the West have entirely run counter to what we think was given to India to accomplish. In the West the national machinery of commerce and politics turns our neatly compressed bales of humanity which have their use and high market value; but they are bound in iron hoops, labelled and separated with scientific care and precision. Obviously God made man to be human; but this modern product has such marvellous square-cut finish, savouring of gigantic manufacture, that the Creator will find it difficult to recognise it as a thing of spirit and a creature made in His own divine image.

Take it in whatever spirit you like, here is India, of about fifty centuries at least, who tried to live peacefully and think deeply, the India devoid of all politics, the India of no nations, whose one ambition has been to know this world as of soul, to live here every moment of her life in the meek spirit of adoration, in the glad consciousness of an eternal and personal relationship with it. It was upon this remote portion of humanity, childlike in its manner, with the wisdom of the old, that the Nation of the West burst in.

Through all the fights and intrigues and deceptions of her earlier history India had remained aloof. Because her homes, her fields, her temples of worship, her schools, where her teachers and students lived together in the atmosphere of simplicity and devotion and learning, her village self-government with its simple laws and peaceful administration—all these truly belonged to her. But her thrones were not her concern. They passed over her head like clouds, now tinged with purple gorgeousness, now black with the threat of thunder. Often they brought devastations in their wake, but they were like catastrophes of nature whose traces are soon forgotten.

But this time it was different. It was not a mere drift over her surface of life—drift of cavalry and foot soldiers, richly caprisoned elephants, white tents and canopies, strings of patient camels bearing the loads of royalty, bands of kettle-drums and flutes, marble domes of mosques, palaces and tombs, like the bubbles of the foaming wine of extravagance; stories of treachery and loyal devotion, of changes of fortune, of dramatic surprises of fate. This time it was the Nation of the West driving its tentacles of machinery deep down into the soil.

Therefore I say to you, it is we who are called as witnesses to give evidence as to what our Nation has been to humanity. **We had known the hordes of Moghul and Pathans who invaded India, but we had known them as human races, with their own religions and customs, likes and dislikes—we had never known them as a nation.** We loved and hated them as the occasions arose; we fought for them and against them, talked with them in a language which was theirs as well as our own, and guided the destiny of the Empire in which we had our active share. But this time we had to deal, not with kings, not with human races, but with a nation—we, who are no nation ourselves.

A nation, in the sense of the political and economic union of a people, is that aspect which a whole population assumes when organised for a mechanical purpose. Society as such has no ulterior purpose. It is an end in itself. It is a spontaneous self-expression of man as a social being. It is a natural regulation of human relationships, so that men can develop ideals of life in co-operation with one another. It has also a political side, but this is only for a special purpose. It is for self-preservation. It is merely the side of power, not of human ideals. And in the early days it had its separate place in society, restricted to the professionals. But when with the help of science and the perfecting of organisation this power begins to grow and brings in harvests of wealth, then it crosses its boundaries with amazing rapidity. For then it goads all its neighbouring societies with greed of material prosperity, and consequent mutual jealousy, and by the fear of each other's growth into powerfulness. The time comes when it can stop no longer, for the competition grows keener, organisation grows vaster, and selfishness attains supremacy. Trading upon the greed and fear of man, it occupies more and more space in society, and at last becomes its ruling forces.

When this organisation of politics and commerce becomes all-powerful at the cost of the harmony of the higher social life, then it is an evil day for humanity. Our only intimate experience of the Nation is with the British Nation, and as far as the government by the Nation goes there are reasons to believe that it is one of the best. We have to consider that **the West is necessary to the East. We are complementary to each other because of our different outlooks upon life which have given us different aspects of truth.** Therefore if it be true that the spirit of the West has come upon our fields in the guise of a storm it is nevertheless scattering living seeds that are immortal. And when in India we become able to assimilate in our life what is permanent in Western civilisation we shall be in the position to bring about a reconciliation of these two great worlds.

We have to recognise that the history of India does not belong to one particular race but to a process of creation to which various races of the world contributed—the Dravidians and the Aryans, the ancient Greeks and the Persians, the Mohammedans of the West and those of central

Asia. Now at last has come the turn of the English to become true to this history and bring to it the tribute of their life, and we neither have the right nor the power to exclude this people from the building of the destiny of India. Therefore, what I say about the Nation has more to do with the history of Man than specially with that of India.

This history has come to a stage when the moral man, the complete man, is more and more giving way, almost without knowing it, to make room for the political and the commercial man, the man of the limited purpose. This process, aided by the wonderful progress in science, is assuming gigantic proportion and power, causing the upset of man's moral balance, obscuring his human side under the shadow of soul-less organisation. We have felt its iron grip at the root of our life, and for the sake of humanity we must stand up and give warning to all, that this nationalism is a cruel epidemic of evil that is sweeping over the human world of the present age, and eating into its moral vitality.

The British race has produced great-hearted men, thinkers of great thoughts, doers of great deeds. It has given rise to a great literature. I know that these people love justice and freedom, and hate lies. They are clean in their minds, frank in their manners, true in their friendships; in their behaviour they are honest and reliable. The personal experience which I have had of their literary men has roused my admiration not merely for their power of thought or expression but for their chivalrous humanity.

During the government of the former days there have been instances of tyranny, injustice, and extortion. They caused sufferings and unrest from which we are glad to be rescued. The protection of law is not only a boon, but it is a valuable lesson to us. It is teaching us the discipline which is necessary for the stability of civilisation and for continuity of progress. **We are realising through it that there is a universal standard of justice to which all men,**

irrespective of their caste and colour, have their equal claim.

Moral law is the law of humanity, and the exclusive civilisation which thrives upon others who are barred from its benefit carries its own death-sentence in its moral limitations.

Of all things in Western civilisation, those which **this Western Nation has given us in a most generous measure are law and order**. While the small feeding-bottle of our education is nearly dry, and sanitation sucks its own thumb in despair, the military organisation, the magisterial offices, the police, the Criminal Investigation Department, the secret spy system, attain to an abnormal girth in their waists, occupying every inch of our country. This is to maintain order. But is not this order merely a negative good? **Is it not for giving people's life greater opportunities for the freedom of development?** Its perfection is the perfection of an egg-shell, whose true value lies in the security it affords to the chick and its nourishment and not in the convenience it offers to the person at the breakfast table.

But mere administration is unproductive, it is not creative, not being a living thing. It is a steam-roller, formidable in its weight and power, having its uses, but it does not help the soil to become fertile.

It is no consolation to us to know that the weakening of humanity from which the present age is suffering is not limited to the subject races, and its ravages are even more radical because they get insidious and voluntary in peoples who are hypnotized into believing that they are free. This bartering of your higher aspirations of life for profit and power has been your own free choice, and I leave you there, at the wreckage of your soul, contemplating your protuberant prosperity. But will you never be called to answer for organising the instincts of self-aggrandisement of whole peoples into perfection and calling it good? I ask you what disaster has there ever been in the history of man, in its darkest period, like this terrible disaster of the Nation fixing its fangs deep into the naked flesh of the world, taking permanent precautions against its natural relaxation?

You, the people of the West, who have manufactured this abnormality, can you imagine the desolating despair of this haunted world of suffering man possessed by the ghastly abstraction of the organising man? Can you put yourself into the position of the peoples who seem to have been doomed to an eternal damnation of their own humanity, who not only must suffer continual curtailment of their manhood, but even raise their voices in paeans of praise for the benignity of a mechanical apparatus in its interminable parody of providence?

The Nation, with all its paraphernalia of power and prosperity, its flags and pious hymns, its blasphemous prayers in the churches, and the literary mock thunders of its patriotic bragging, cannot hide the fact that **the Nation is the greatest evil for the Nation, that all its precautions are against it, and any new birth of its fellows in the world is always followed in its mind by the dread of a new peril.** Its one wish is to trade on the feebleness of the rest of the world, like some insects that are bred in the paralysed flesh of victims kept just enough alive to make them toothsome and nutritious. Therefore it is ready to send its poisonous fluid into the vitals of the other living peoples, who, not being nations, are harmless.

For the sake of your own salvation, I say, they shall *live,* and this is truth. It is extremely bold of me to say so, but I assert that man's world is a moral world, not because we blindly agree to believe it, but because it is so in truth which would be dangerous for us to ignore.

Man with his mental and material power far outgrowing his moral strength, is like an exaggerated giraffe whose head has suddenly shot up miles away from the rest of him, making normal communication difficult to establish. This greedy head, with its huge dental organisation, has been munching all the topmost foliage of the world, but the nourishment is too late in reaching his digestive organs, and his heart is suffering from want of blood. Of this present disharmony in man's nature the West seems to have been blissfully unconscious.

Man in his fullness is not powerful, but perfect. When we are fully human, we cannot fly at one another's throats; our instincts of social life, our traditions of moral ideals stand in the way.

The logic of the Nation will never heed the voice of truth and goodness. It will go on its ring-dance of moral corruption, linking steel unto steel, and machine unto machine; trampling under its tread all the sweet flowers of simple faith and the living ideals of man. We must not forget that the scientific organisations vastly spreading in all directions are strengthening our power, but not our humanity.

Man, the person, must protest for his very life against the heaping up of things where there should be the heart, and systems and policies where there should flow living human relationship.

We of no nations of the world whose heads have been bowed to the dust, will know that this dust is more sacred than the bricks which build the pride of power. For this dust is fertile of life, and of beauty and worship. We shall thank God that we were made to wait in silence through the night of despair, had to bear the insult of the proud and the strong man's burden, yet all through it, though our hearts quaked with doubt and fear, never could we blindly believe in the salvation which machinery offered to man, but we held fast to our trust in God and the truth of the human soul.

3

Races: An India-America Parallelism

Our real problem in India is not political. It is social. This is a condition not only prevailing in India, but among all nations. I do not believe in an exclusive political interest. Politics in the West have dominated Western ideals, and we in India are trying to imitate them. We have to remember that in Europe, where peoples had their racial unity from the beginning, and where natural resources were insufficient for the inhabitants, the civilisation has naturally taken the character of political and commercial aggressiveness. For, on the one hand they had no internal complications, and on the other they had to deal with neighbours who were strong and rapacious. To have perfect combination among themselves and a watchful attitude of animosity against others was taken as the solution of their problems. In former days they organised and plundered, in the present age the same spirit continues—and they organise and exploit the whole world.

But from the earliest beginnings of history India has had her own problem constantly before her—it is the race problem. Each nation must be conscious of its mission, and we, in India, must realise that we cut a poor figure when we are trying to be political, simply because we have not yet been finally able to accomplish what was set before us by our providence.

In spite of our great difficulty, however, India has done something. She has tried to make an adjustment of races, to acknowledge the real differences between them where these exist, and yet seek for some basis of unity. This basis has come through our saints, like Nanak, Kabir, Chaitanya and others, preaching one God to all races of India.

In finding the solution of our problem we shall have helped to solve the world problem as well. What India has been, the whole world is now. The whole world is becoming one country through scientific facility. And the moment is arriving when you must also find a basis of unity which is not political. If India can offer to the world her solution, it will be a contribution to humanity. There is only one history—the history of man. All national histories are merely chapters in the larger one. And we are content in India to suffer for such a great cause.

Each individual has his self-love. Therefore, his brute instinct leads him to fight with others in the sole pursuit of his self-interest. But man has also his higher instincts of sympathy and mutual help. The people who are lacking in this higher moral power and who therefore cannot combine in fellowship with one another must perish or live in a state of degradation. **Only those peoples have survived and achieved civilisation who have this spirit of co-operation strong in them.** So we find that from the beginning of history men had to choose between fighting with one another and combining, between serving their own interest or the common interest of all.

In our early history, when the geographical limits of each country and also the facilities of communication were small, this problem was comparatively small in dimension. It was sufficient for men to develop their sense of unity within their area of segregation. In those days they combined among themselves and fought against others. But it was this moral spirit of combination which was the true basis of their greatness, and this fostered their art, science and religion. At that early time the most important fact that man had to take count of was the fact of the members of one particular race of men coming in close contact with one another. Those who truly grasped this fact through their higher nature made their mark in history.

The most important fact of the present age is that all the different races of men have come close together. And again we are confronted with two alternatives. The problem is whether the different groups of peoples shall go on fighting with one another or find out some true basis of reconciliation and mutual help; whether it will be interminable competition or co-operation.

I have no hesitation in saying that those who are gifted with the moral power of spiritual unity, who have the least feeling of enmity against aliens, and the sympathetic insight to place themselves in the position of others, will be the fittest to take their permanent place in the age that is lying before us, and those who are constantly developing their instinct of fight and intolerance of aliens will be eliminated. For this is the problem before us, and we have to prove our humanity by solving it through the help of our higher nature. The gigantic organisations for hurting others and warding off their blows, for making money by dragging others back, will not help us. On the contrary, by their crushing weight, their enormous cost and their deadening effect upon living humanity, they will seriously impede our freedom in the larger life of a higher civilisation.

During the evolution of Nation the moral culture of brotherhood was limited by geographical boundaries, because at that time those boundaries were true. Now they have become imaginary lines of tradition divested of the qualities of real obstacles. So the time has come when man's moral nature must deal with this great fact with all seriousness or perish. The first impulse of this change of circumstance has been the churning up of man's baser passions of greed and cruel hatred. If this persists indefinitely, and armaments go on exaggerating themselves to unimaginable absurdities, and machines and storehouses envelop this fair earth with their dirt and smoke and ugliness, then it will end in a conflagration of suicide. Therefore, man will have to exert all his power of love and clarity of vision to make another great moral adjustment which will comprehend the whole world of men and not merely the fractional groups of nationality. The call has come to every individual in the present age to prepare himself and his surroundings for this dawn of a new era, when man shall discover his soul in the spiritual unity of all human beings.

If it is given at all to the West to struggle out of these tangles of the lower slopes to the spiritual summit of humanity then I cannot but think that it is the special mission of America to fulfil this hope of God and man. They are the country of expectation, desiring something else than what is. Europe has her subtle habits of mind and her conventions. But America, has come to no conclusion. I realise how much America is untrammelled by the traditions of the past, and I can appreciate that experimentalism is a sign of America's youth. The foundation of her glory is in the future, rather than in the past; and if one is gifted with the power of clairvoyance, one will be able to love the America that is to be.

In America national habits and traditions have not had time to spread their clutching roots round their hearts. They have constantly felt and complained of their disadvantages when they compared their nomadic restlessness with the settled traditions of Europe—the Europe which can show her picture of greatness to the best advantage because she can fix it against the background of the past. But in this present age of transition, when a new era of civilisation is sending its trumpet-call to all peoples of the world across an unlimited future, this very freedom of detachment will enable them to accept its invitation and to achieve the goal for which Europe began her journey but lost herself midway. For she was tempted out of her path by her pride of power and greed of possession.

A parallelism exists between America and India—the parallelism of welding together into one body various races.

In my country we have been seeking to find out something common to all races, which will prove their real unity. No nation looking for a mere political or commercial basis for unity will find such a solution sufficient. Men of thought and power will discover the spiritual unity, will realise it, and preach it.

The educated Indian at present is trying to absorb some lessons from history contrary to the lessons of our ancestors. The East, in fact, is attempting to take unto itself a history, which is not the outcome of its own living. Japan, for example, thinks she is getting powerful through adopting Western methods.

We must know for certain that there is a future before us and that future is waiting for those who are rich in moral ideals and not in mere things. And it is the privilege of man to work for fruits that are beyond his immediate reach, and to adjust his life not in slavish conformity to the examples of some present success or even to his own prudent past, limited in its aspiration, but to an infinite future bearing in its heart the ideals of our highest expectation.

We must recognise that it is providential that the West has come to India. I have great faith in human nature, and I think the West will find its true mission. The West must not make herself a curse to the world by using her power for her own selfish needs, but, by teaching the ignorant and helping the weak, she should save herself.

4

India's Chief Problem: Caste

An unusually instructive analysis which, though too late, should draw every thinking Indian's attention today. In it lies the solution to our chief social-political-economic problem.

I will draw your attention to the difficulties India has had to encounter and her struggle to overcome them. Her problem is the problem of the world in miniature. India is too vast in its area and too diverse in its races. It is many countries packed in one geographical receptacle. It is just the opposite of what Europe truly is, namely, one country made into many. Thus Europe in its culture and growth has had the advantage of the strength of the many as well as the strength of the one. India, on the contrary, being naturally many, yet adventitiously one, has all along suffered from the looseness of its diversity and the feebleness of its unity.

A true unity is like a round globe, it rolls on, carrying its burden easily; but diversity is a many- cornered thing which has to be dragged and pushed with all force. Be it said to the credit of India that this diversity was not her own creation; she has had to accept it as a fact from the beginning of her history. In America and Australia, Europe has simplified their problem by almost exterminating the original population. Even in the present age this spirit of extermination is making itself manifest, in the inhospitable shutting out of aliens, by those who themselves were aliens in the lands they now occupy. But India tolerated difference of races from the first, and that spirit of toleration has acted all through her history.

Her caste system is the outcome of this spirit of toleration. For India has all along been trying experiments in evolving a social unity within which all the different peoples could be held together, while fully enjoying the freedom of maintaining their own differences. The tie has been as loose as possible, yet as close as the circumstances permitted. This has produced something like a United States of a social federation, whose common name is Hinduism.

India had felt that diversity of races there must be and should be, whatever may be its drawback, and you can never coerce nature into your narrow limits of convenience without paying one day very dearly for it. In this India was right; but what she failed to realise was that in human beings differences are not like the physical barriers of mountains, fixed for ever—they are fluid with life's flow, they are changing their courses and their shapes and volume.

Therefore **in her caste retardations India recognised differences, but not the mutability which is the law of life. In trying to avoid collisions she set up boundaries of immovable walls, thus giving to her numerous races the negative benefit of peace and order but not the positive opportunity of expansion and movement.** She accepted nature where it produces diversity, but ignored it where it uses that diversity for its world-game of infinite permutations and combinations. She treated life in all truth where it is manifold, but insulted it where it is ever moving. Therefore Life departed from her social system and in its place she is worshipping with all ceremony the magnificent cage of countless compartment that she has manufactured.

The same thing happened where she tried to ward off the collisions of trade interests. **She associated different trades**

and professions with different castes. This had the effect of allowing for good the interminable jealousy and hatred of competition—the competition which breeds cruelty and makes the atmosphere thick with lies and deception. In this also India laid all her emphasis upon the law of heredity, ignoring the law of mutation, and thus gradually reduced arts into crafts and genius into skill.

However, in her caste system India in all seriousness accepted her responsibility to solve the race problem in such a manner as to avoid all friction, and yet to afford each race freedom within its boundaries. Let us admit India has not in this achieved a full measure of success. But this one must also concede, that the West being more favourably situated as to homogeneity of races, has never given her attention to this problem, and whenever confronted with it she has tried to make it easy by ignoring it altogether.

India also thought she knew human nature when she strongly barricaded her race distinctions by the fixed barriers of social gradations. But we have found out to our cost that human nature is not what it seems, but what it is in truth; which is in its infinite possibilities. And when we in our blindness insult humanity for its ragged appearance, it sheds its disguise to disclose to us that we have insulted our God. The degradation which we cast upon others in our pride or self-interest degrades our own humanity—and this is the punishment which is most terrible, because we do not detect it till it is too late. In India the production of commodities was brought under the law of social adjustments. Its basis was co-operation, having for its object the perfect satisfaction of social needs. But in the West it is guided by the impulse of competition, whose end is the gain of wealth for individuals. But the individual is like the geometrical line: it is length without breadth. It has not got the depth to be able to hold anything permanently. Therefore, its greed or gain can never come to finality. In its lengthening process of growth it can cross other lines and cause entanglements, but will ever go on missing the ideal of completeness in its thinness of isolation.

In all our physical appetites we recognise a limit. We know that to exceed that limit is to exceed the limit of health. But has this lust for wealth and power no bounds beyond which is death's dominion? In these national carnivals of materialism are not the Western peoples spending most of their vital energy in merely producing things and neglecting the creation of ideals? And can a civilisation ignore the law of moral health and go on in its endless process of inflation by gorging upon material things? Man in his social ideals naturally tries to regulate his appetites, subordinating them to the higher purpose of his nature. But in the economic world our appetites follow no other restrictions but those of supply and demand which can be artificially fostered, affording individuals opportunities for indulgence in an endless feast of grossness. In India our social instincts imposed restrictions upon our appetites—maybe it went to the extreme of repression—but in the West the spirit of economic organisation with no moral purpose goads the people into the perpetual pursuit of wealth; but has this no wholesome limit?

The ideals that strive to take form in social institutions have two objects. One is to regulate our passions and appetites for the harmonious development of man, and the other is to help him to cultivate disinterested love for his fellow-creatures. Therefore, society is the expression of those moral and spiritual aspirations of man which belong to his higher nature.

Our food is creative, it builds our body; but not so wine, which stimulates. Our social ideals create the human world, but when our mind is diverted from them to greed of power then in that state of intoxication we live in a world of abnormality where our strength is not health and our liberty is not freedom. Therefore, political freedom does not give us freedom when our mind is not free. An automobile does not create freedom of movement, because it is a mere machine. When I myself am free I can use the automobile for the purpose of my freedom.

We must never forget in the present times that those people who have got their political freedom are not necessarily free, they are merely powerful. The passions which are unbridled in them are creating huge organisations of slavery in the disguise of freedom. Those who have made the gain of money their highest end are unconsciously selling their life and soul to rich persons or to the combinations that represent money. Those who are enamoured of their political power and gloat over their extension of dominion over foreign races gradually surrender their own freedom and humanity to the organisations necessary for holding other peoples in slavery. In the so-called free countries the majority of the people are not free; they are driven by the minority to a goal which is not even known to them. This becomes possible only because people do not acknowledge moral and spiritual freedom as their object. They create huge eddies with their passions, and they feel dizzily inebriated with the mere velocity of their whirling movement, taking that to be freedom. But the doom which is waiting to overtake them is as certain as death—for man's truth is moral truth and his emancipation is in the spiritual life.

The general opinion of the majority of the nationalists in India is that we have come to a final completeness in our social and spiritual ideals, the task of the constructive work of society having been done several thousand years before we were born, and that now we are free to employ all our activities in the political direction. We never dream of blaming our social inadequacy as the origin of our present helplessness, for **we have accepted as the creed of our nationalism that this social system has been perfected for all times to come by our ancestors, who had the superhuman vision of all eternity and supernatural power for making infinite provision for future ages. Therefore, for all our miseries and shortcomings, we hold responsible the historical surprises that burst upon us from outside.** This is the reason why we think that our one task is to build a political miracle of freedom upon the quicksand of social slavery. In fact we want to dam up the true course of our own historical stream, and only borrow power from the sources of other peoples' history.

Those of us in India who have come under the delusion that mere political freedom will make us free have accepted their lessons from the West as the gospel truth and lost their faith in humanity. We must remember whatever weakness we cherish in our society will become the source of danger in politics. The same inertia which leads us to our idolatry of dead farms in social institutions will create in our politics prison-houses with immovable walls. The narrowness of sympathy which makes it possible for us to impose upon a considerable portion of humanity the galling yoke of inferiority will assert itself in our politics in creating the tyranny of injustice.

The basis of nationalism is wanting. The very people who are upholding these ideals are themselves the most conservative in their social practice. Nationalists say, for example, look at Switzerland where, in spite of race differences, the people have solidified into a nation. Yet, remember that in Switzerland the races can mingle, they can intermarry, because they are of the same blood. In India there is no common birthright. And when we talk of Western Nationality we forget that the nations there do not have that physical repulsion, one for the other, that we have between different castes. Have we an instance in the whole world where a people who are not allowed to mingle their blood shed their blood for one another except by coercion or for mercenary purposes? And can we ever hope that these moral barriers against our racial amalgamation will not stand in the way of our political unity?

Then again we must give full recognition to this fact that **our social restrictions are still tyrannical, so much so as to make men cowards.** If a man tells me that he has heterodox ideas, but that he cannot follow them because he would be socially ostracised, I excuse him for having to live a life of untruth, in order to live at all. **The social habit of mind which impels us to make the life of our fellow-being, a burden to them where they differ from us even in such a thing as their choice of food, is sure to persist** in our political organisation and result in creating engines of coercion to crush every rational difference which is the sign of life. And tyranny will only add to the inevitable lies and hypocrisy in our political life. Is the mere name of freedom so valuable that we should be willing to sacrifice for its sake our moral freedom?

The intemperance of our habits does not immediately show its effects when we are in the vigour of our youth. But it gradually consumes that vigour, and when the period of decline sets in then we have to settle accounts and pay off our debts, which leads us to insolvency. In the West they are still able to carry their head high, though their humanity is suffering every moment from its dipsomania of organising power. India also in the heyday of her youth could carry in her vital organs the dead weight of her social organisations stiffened to rigid perfection, but it has been fatal to her, and has produced a gradual paralysis of her living nature.

And this is the reason why the educated community of India has become insensible of her social needs. They are taking the very immobility of our social structures as the sign of their perfection—and because the healthy feeling of pain is dead in the limbs of our social organism, they delude themselves into thinking that it needs no ministration. Therefore, they think that all their energies need their only scope in the political field. It is like a man whose legs have become shrivelled and useless, trying to delude himself that these limbs have grown still because they have attained their ultimate salvation, and all that is wrong about him is the shortness of his sticks.

5

India: Forest-Created Thought Culture

The civilisation of ancient Greece was nurtured within city walls. In fact, **all the modem civilisations have their cradles of brick and mortar.**

These walls leave their mark deep in the minds of men. They set up a principle of 'divide and rule' in our mental outlook, which begets in us a habit of securing all our conquests by fortifying them and separating them from one another. We divide nation and nation, knowledge and knowledge, man and nature. It breeds in us a strong suspicion of whatever is beyond the barriers we have built, and everything has to fight hard for its entrance into our recognition.

When the first Aryan invaders appeared in India it was a vast land of forests, and the newcomers rapidly took advantage of them. These forests afforded them shelter from the fierce heat of the sun and the ravages of tropical storms, pastures for cattle, fuel for sacrificial fire, and materials for building cottages. And the different Aryan clans with their patriarchal heads settled in the different forest tracts which had some special advantage of natural protection, and food and water in plenty.

Thus in India it was in the forests that our civilisation had its birth and it took a distinct character from this origin and environment. It was surrounded by the vast life of nature, was fed and clothed by her, and had the closest and most constant intercourse with her varying aspects.

Such a life, it may be thought, tends to have the effect of dulling human intelligence and dwarfing the incentives to progress by lowering the standards of existence. But in ancient India we find that the circumstances of forest life did not overcome man's mind, and did not enfeeble the current of his energies, but only gave to it a particular direction. Having been in constant contact with the living growth of nature, his mind was free from the desire to extend his dominion by erecting boundary walls around his acquisitions.

His aim was not to acquire but to realise, to enlarge his consciousness by growing with and growing into his surroundings. He felt that truth is all-comprehensive, that there is no such thing as absolute isolation in existence, and the only way of attaining truth is through the interpenetration of our being into all objects. To realise this great harmony between man's spirit and the spirit of the world was the endeavour of the forest-dwelling sages of ancient India.

In later days there came a time when these primeval forests gave way to cultivated fields, and wealthy cities sprang up on all sides. Mighty kingdoms were established, which had communications with all the great powers of the world. But even in the heyday of its material prosperity the heart of India ever looked back with adoration upon the early ideal of strenuous self-realisation, and the dignity of the simple life of the forest hermitage, and drew its best inspiration from the wisdom stored there.

The West seems to take pride in thinking that it is subduting nature; as if we are living in a hostile world where we have to wrest everything we want from an unwilling and alien arrangement of things. This sentiment is the product of the city-wall habit and training of mind.

For in the city life man naturally directs the concentrated light of his mental vision upon his own life and works, and this creates an artificial dissociation between himself and the Universal Nature within whose bosom he lies.

But in India the point of view was different; it included the world with the man as one great truth. India put all her emphasis on the harmony that exists between the individual and the universal. She felt we could have no communication whatever with our surroundings if they were absolutely foreign to us. Man's complaint against nature is that he has to acquire most of his necessaries by his own efforts. Yes, but his efforts are not in vain; he is reaping success every day, and that shows there is a rational connection between him and nature, for we never can make anything our own except that which is truly related to us.

We can look upon a road from two different points of view. One regards it as dividing us from the object of our desire; in that case we count every step of our journey over it as something attained by force in the face of obstruction. The other sees it as the road which leads us to our destination; and as such it is part of our goal. It is already the beginning of our attainment, and by journeying over it we can only gain that which it itself offers to us.

In the West the prevalent feeling is that nature belongs exclusively to inanimate things and to beasts, that there is a sudden unaccountable break where human-nature begins. According to it, everything that is low in the scale of beings is merely nature, and whatever has the stamp of perfection on it, intellectual or moral, is human-nature. It is like dividing the bud and the blossom into two separate categories, and putting their grace to the credit of two different and antithetical principles. But the Indian mind never has any hesitation in acknowledging its kinship with nature, its unbroken relation with all.

The fundamental unity of creation was not simply a philosophical speculation for India; it was her life-object to realise this great harmony in feeling and in action. With meditation and service, with a regulation of her life, she cultivated her consciousness in such a way that everything had a spiritual meaning to her. The earth, water and light, fruits and flowers, to her were not merely physical phenomena to be turned to use and then left aside. They were necessary to her in the attainment of her ideal of perfection, as every note is necessary to the completeness of the symphony. India intuitively felt that the essential fact of this world has a vital meaning for us; we have to be fully alive to it and establish a conscious relation with it.

The man of science knows, in one aspect, that the world is not merely what it appears to be to our senses; he knows that earth and water are really the play of forces that manifest themselves to us as earth and water—how, we can but partially apprehend. Likewise, the man who has his spiritual eyes open knows that the ultimate truth about earth and water lies in our apprehension of the eternal will which works in time and takes shape in the forces we realise under those aspects. This is not mere knowledge, as science is, but it is a perception of the soul by the soul. This does not lead us to power, as knowledge does, but it gives us joy, which is the product of the union of kindred things.

The man whose acquaintance with the world does not lead him deeper than science leads him, will never understand what it is that the man with the spiritual vision finds in these natural phenomena. The water does not merely cleanse his limbs, but it purifies his heart; for it touches his soul. The earth does not merely hold his body, but it gladdens his mind; for its contact is more than a physical contact—it is a living presence. When a man does not realise his kinship with the world, he lives in a prison-house whose walls are alien to him. When he meets the eternal spirit in all objects, then is he emancipated, for then he discovers the fullest significance of the world into which he is born; then he finds himself in perfect truth, and his harmony with the all is established.

In India men are enjoined to be fully awake to the fact that they are in the closest relation to things around them, body and soul, and that they are to hail the morning sun, the flowing water, the fruitful earth, as the manifestation of the same living truth which holds them in its embrace. Thus the text of our everyday meditation is the Gayatri, a verse which is considered to be the epitome of all the Vedas. By its help we try to realise the essential unity of the world with the conscious soul of man; we learn to perceive the unity held together by the one Eternal Spirit, whose power creates the earth, the sky, and the stars, and at the same time irradiates our minds with the light of a consciousness that moves and exists in unbroken continuity with the outer world.

India knew that when by physical and mental barriers we violently detach ourselves from the inexhaustible life of nature; when we become merely man, not man-in-the-universe, we create bewildering problems, and having shut off the source of their solution, we try all kinds of artificial methods each of which brings its own crop of interminable difficulties. When man leaves his resting-place in universal nature, when he walks on the single rope of humanity, it means either a dance or a fall for him, he has ceaselessly to strain every nerve and muscle to keep his balance at each step, and then, in the intervals of his weariness, he fulminates against Providence and feels a secret pride and satisfaction in thinking that he has been unfairly dealt with by the whole scheme of things.

But this cannot go on for ever. Man must realise the wholeness of his existence, his place in the infinite; he must know that hard as he may strive he can never create his honey within the cells of his hive, for the perennial supply of his life food is outside their walls. He must know that when man shuts himself out from the vitalising and purifying touch of the infinite, and falls back upon himself for his sustenance and his healing, then he goads himself into madness, tears himself into shreds, and eats his own substance.

Deprived of the background of the whole, his poverty loses its one great quality, which is simplicity, and becomes squalid and shamefaced. His wealth is no longer magnanimous; it grows merely extravagant. His appetites do not minister to his life, keeping to the limits of their purpose; they become an end in themselves and set fire to his life and play the fiddle in the lurid light of the conflagration. Then it is that in our self-expression we try to startle and not to attract; in art we strive for originality and lose sight of the truth which is old and yet ever new; in literature we miss the complete view of man which is simple and yet great. Man appears instead as a psychological problem, or as the embodiment of a passion that is intense because abnormal, being exhibited in the glare of a fiercely emphatic artificial light.

When man's consciousness is restricted only of the immediate vicinity of his human self, the deeper roots of his nature do not find their permanent soil, his spirit is ever on the brink of starvation, and in the place of healthful strength he substitutes rounds of stimulation. Then it is that man misses his inner perspective and measures his greatness by its bulk and not by its vital link with the infinite, judges his activity by its movement and not by the repose of perfection—the repose which is in the starry heavens, in the everflowing rhythmic dance of creation.

The first invasion of India has its exact parallel in the invasion of America by the European settlers. They also were confronted with primeval forests and fierce struggle with aboriginal races. But this struggle between man and man and man and nature lasted till the very end; they never came to any terms. In India the forests which were the habitation of barbarians became the sanctuary of sages, but in America these great living cathedrals of nature had no deeper significance to man. They brought wealth and power to him, and perhaps at times they ministered to his enjoyment of beauty, and inspired a solitary poet. They never acquired a sacred association in the hearts of men as the site of some great spiritual reconcilement where man's soul had its meeting-place with the soul of the world.

I do not for a moment wish to suggest that things should have been otherwise. It would be an utter waste of opportunities if history were to repeat itself exactly in the same manner in every place. It is best for the commerce of the spirit that people differently situated should bring their different products into the market of humanity, each of which is complementary and necessary to the others. All that I wish to say is that **India at the outset of her career met with a special combination of circumstances which was not lost upon her.** She had, according to her opportunities, thought and pondered, striven and suffered, dived into the depths of existence, and achieved something which surely cannot be without its value to people whose evolution in history took a different way altogether.

Civilisation is a kind of mould that each nation is busy making for itself to shape its men and women according to its best ideal. All its institutions, its legislature, its standard of approbation and condemnation, its conscious and unconscious teachings tend toward that object. **The modern civilisation of the West, by all its organised efforts, is trying to turn out men perfect in physical, intellectual, and moral efficiency.** There the vast energies of the nations are employed in extending man's power over his surroundings, and people are combining and straining every faculty to possess and to turn to account all that they can lay their hands upon, to overcome every obstacle on their path of conquest. They are ever disciplining themselves to fight nature and other races; their armaments are getting more and more stupendous every day; their machines, their appliances, their organisations go on multiplying at an amazing rate. This is a splendid achievement, no doubt, and a wonderful manifestation of man's masterfulness, which knows no obstacle and has for its object the supremacy of himself over everything else.

The ancient civilisation of India had its own ideal of perfection towards which its efforts were directed. **Its aim was not attaining power, and it neglected to cultivate to the utmost its capacities, and to organise men for defensive and offensive purposes, for co-operation in the acquisition of wealth and for military and political ascendancy.** The ideal that India tried to realise led her best men to the isolation of a contemplative life, and the treasures that she gained for mankind by penetrating into the mysteries of reality cost her dear in the sphere of worldly success. Yet, this also was a sublime achievement, it was a supreme manifestation of that human aspiration which knows no limit, and which has for its object nothing less than the realisation of the Infinite.

There were the virtuous, the wise, the courageous; there were the statesmen, kings and emperors of India; but whom amongst all these classes did she look up to and choose to be the representative of men?

They were the rishis. What were the rishis? They who having attained the supreme soul in knowledge were filled with wisdom, and having found him in union with the soul were in perfect harmony with the inner self; they having realised him in the heart were free from all selfish desires, and having experienced him in all the activities of the world, had attained calmness.

Thus the state of realising our relationship with all, of entering into everything through union with God, was considered in India to be the ultimate end and fulfilment of humanity.

Man can destroy and plunder, earn and accumulate, invent and discover, but he is great because his soul comprehends all. It is dire destruction for him when he envelopes his soul in a dead shell of callous habits, and when a blind fury of works whirls round him like an eddying duststorm, shutting out the horizon. That indeed kills the very spirit of his being, which is the spirit of comprehension.

Essentially man is not a slave either of himself or of the world; but he is a lover. His freedom and fulfilment is in love, which is another name for perfect comprehension. By this power of comprehension, this permeation of his being, he is united with the all-pervading Spirit, who is also the breath of his soul. Where a man tries to raise himself to eminence by pushing and jostling all others, to achieve a distinction by which he prides himself to be more than everybody else, there he is alienated from that Spirit. This is why the Upanishads describe those who have attained the goal of human life as *'peaceful'*[1] and as *'at-one with-God'*,[2] meaning that they are in perfect harmony with man and nature, and therefore in undisturbed union with God.

It fills me with great joy and a high hope for the future of humanity when I realise that there was a time in the remote past when our poet-prophets stood under the lavish sunshine of an Indian sky and greeted the world with the glad recognition of kindred. It was not an anthropomorphic hallucination. It was not seeing man reflected everywhere in grotesquely exaggerated images, and witnessing the human drama acted on a gigantic scale in nature's arena of flitting lights and shadows. On the contrary, it meant crossing the limiting barriers of the individual, to become more than man, to become one with the All. It was not a mere play of the imagination, but it was the liberation of consciousness from all the mystifications and exaggerations of the self.

This is the noble heritage from our forefathers waiting to be claimed by us as our own, this ideal of the supreme freedom of consciousness. It is not merely intellectual or emotional, it has an ethical basis, and it must be translated into action.

1. *Prashantah.*
2. *Yuktatminah.*

6

Beauty Everywhere

Things in which we do not take joy are either a burden upon our minds to be got rid of at any cost; or they are useful, and therefore in temporary and partial relation to us, becoming burdensome when their utility is lost; or they are like wandering vagabonds, loitering for a moment on the outskirts of our recognition, and then passing on. **A thing is only completely our own when it is a thing of joy to us.**

The greater part of this world is to us as if it were nothing. But we cannot allow it to remain so, for thus it belittles our own self. The entire world is given to us, and all our powers have their final meaning in the faith that by their help we are to take possession of our patrimony.

But what is the function of our sense of beauty in this process of the extension of our consciousness? Is it there to separate truth into strong lights and shadows, and bring it before us in its uncompromising distinction of beauty and ugliness? It that were so, then we should have to admit that this sense of beauty creates a dissension in our universe and sets up a wall of hindrance across the highway of communication that leads from each individual thing to all things.

But that cannot be true. As long as our realisation is incomplete, a division necessarily remains between things known and unknown, pleasant and unpleasant. But in spite of the dictum of some philosophers man does not accept any arbitrary and absolute limit to his knowable world. Every day his science is penetrating into the region formerly marked in his map as unexplored or inexplorable. Our sense of beauty is similarly engaged in ever pushing on its conquests. Truth is everywhere, therefore everything is the object of our knowledge. Beauty is omnipresent, therefore everything is capable of giving us joy.

In the early days of his history man took every thing as a phenomenon of life. His science of life began by creating a sharp distinction between life and non-life. But as it is proceeding farther and farther the line of demarcation between the animate and inanimate is growing more and more dim. In the beginning of our apprehension these sharp lines of contrast are helpful to us, but as our comprehension becomes clearer they gradually fade away.

The Upanishads have said that all things are created and sustained by an infinite joy. To realise this principle of creation we have to start with a division—the division into the beautiful and the non-beautiful. Then the apprehension of beauty has to come to us with a vigorous blow to awaken our consciousness from its primitive lethargy, and it attains its object by the urgency of the contrast. Therefore, our first acquaintance with beauty is in her dress of motley colours, that affects us with its stripes and feathers, nay, with its disfigurements. But as our acquaintance ripens, the apparent discords are resolved into modulations of rhythm. At first we detach beauty from its surroundings, we hold it apart from the rest, but at the end we realise its harmony with all. Then the music of beauty has no more need of exciting us with loud noise; it renounces violence, and appeals to our heart with the truth that it is meekness which inherits the earth.

In some stage of our growth, in some period of our

history, we try to set up a special cult of beauty, and pare it down to a narrow circle, so as to make it a matter of pride for a chosen few. Then it breeds in its votaries affectations and exaggerations, as it did with the Brahmins in the time of the decadence of Indian civilisation, when the perception of the higher truth fell away and superstitions grew up unchecked.

In the history of aesthetics there also comes an age of emancipation when the recognition of beauty in things great and small becomes easy, and when we see it more in the unassuming harmony of common objects than in things startling in their singularity. So much so, that we have to go through the stages of reaction when in the representation of beauty we try to avoid everything that is obviously pleasing and that has been crowned by the sanction of convention. We are then tempted in defiance to exaggerate the commonness of commonplace things, thereby making them aggressively uncommon.

To restore harmony we create the discords which are a feature of all reactions. We already see in the present age the sign of this aesthetic reaction, which proves that man has at last come to know that it is only the narrowness of perception which sharply divides the field of his aesthetic consciousness into ugliness and beauty. When he has the power to see things detached from self-interest and from the insistent claims of the lust of the senses, then alone can he have the true vision of the beauty that is everywhere. Then only can he see that what is unpleasant to us is not necessarily unbeautiful, but has its beauty in truth.

When we say that beauty is everywhere we do not mean that the word ugliness should be abolished from our language, just as it would be absurd to say that there is no such thing as untruth. Untruth there certainly is, not in the system of the universe, but in our power of comprehension, as its negative element. In the same manner there is ugliness in the distorted expression of beauty in our life and in our art which comes from our imperfect realisation of Truth. To a certain extent we can set our life against the law of truth which is in us and which is in all, and likewise we can give rise to ugliness by going counter to the eternal law of harmony which is everywhere.

Through our sense of truth we realise law in creation, and **through our sense of beauty we realise harmony in the universe.** When we recognise the law in nature we extend our mastery over physical forces and become powerful; when we recognise the law in our moral nature we attain mastery over self and become free. In like manner the more we comprehend the harmony in the physical world the more our life shares the gladness of creation, and our expression of beauty in art becomes more truly catholic. As we become conscious of the harmony in our soul, our apprehension of the blissfulness of the spirit of the world becomes universal, and the expression of beauty in our life moves in goodness and love towards the infinite.

This is the ultimate object of our existence, that we must ever know that "beauty is truth, truth beauty'; we must realise the whole world in love, for love gives it birth, sustains it, and takes it back to its bosom. We must have that perfect emancipation of heart which gives us the power to stand at the innermost centre of things and have the taste of that fulness of disinterested joy which belongs to Brahma.

Music is the purest form of art, and therefore the most direct expression of beauty, with a form and spirit which is one and simple, and least encumbered with anything extraneous. We seem to feel that the manifestation of the infinite in the finite forms of creation is music itself, silent and visible. The evening sky, tirelessly repeating the starry constellation, seems like a child struck with wonder at the mystery of its own first utterance, lisping the same word over and over again, and listening to it in unceasing joy. When in the rainy night of July the darkness is thick upon the meadows and the pattering rain draws veil upon veil over the stillness of the slumbering earth, this monotony of the rain patter seems to be the darkness of sound itself. The gloom of the dim and dense line of trees, the thorny bushes scattered on the bare earth like floating heads of swimmers with bedraggled hair, the smell of the damp grass and the wet earth, the spire of the temple rising above the undefined mass of blackness grouped around the village huts—everything seems like notes rising from the heart of the night, mingling and losing themselves in the one sound of ceaseless rain filling the sky.

Therefore the true poets, they who are seers, seek to express the universe in terms of music. They rarely use symbols of painting to express the unfolding of forms, the mingling of endless lines and colours that goes on every moment on the canvas of the blue sky.

They have their reason. For the man who paints must have canvas, brush, and colour-box. The first touch of his brush is very far from the complete idea. And then when the work is finished and the artist is gone, the widowed picture stands alone, the incessant touches of love of the creative hand are withdrawn.

But the singer has everything within him. The notes come out from his very life. They are not materials gathered from outside. His idea and his expression are brother and sister; very often they are born as twins. In music the heart reveals itself immediately; it suffers not from any barrier of alien material.

Therefore, though music has to wait for its completeness like any other art, yet at every step it gives out the beauty of the whole. As the material of expression even words are barriers, for their meaning has to be construed by thought. But music never has to depend upon any obvious meaning; it expresses what no words can ever express.

What is more, music and the musician are inseparable. When the singer departs, his singing dies with him; it is in eternal union with the life and joy of the master.

This world-song is never for a moment separated from its singer. It is not fashioned from any outward material. It is his joy itself taking never-ending form. It is the great heart sending the tremor of its thrill over the sky.

There is a perfection in each individual strain of this music, which is the revelation of completion in the incomplete. No one of its notes is final, yet each reflects the infinite.

What does it matter if we fail to derive the exact meaining of this great harmony? Is it not like the hand meeting the string and drawing out at once all its tones at the touch? It is the language of beauty, the caress, that comes from the heart of the world and straightway reaches our heart.

Last night, in the silence which pervaded the darkness, I stood alone and heard the voice of the singer of eternal melodies. When I went to sleep I closed my eyes with this last thought in my mind, that even when I remain unconscious in slumber the dance of life will still go on in the hushed arena of my sleeping body, keeping step with the stars. The heart will throb, the blood will leap in the veins, and the millions of living atoms of my body will vibrate in tune with the note of the harp-string that thrills at the touch of the master.

A Few Great Stories

Classic

1

Kabuliwallah

(This famous story was also filmed.)

My five years' old daughter Mini cannot live without chattering. I really believe that in all her life she has not wasted a minute in silence. Her mother is often vexed at this, and would stop her prattle, but I would not. To see Mini quiet is unnatural, and I cannot bear it long. And so my own talk with her is always lively.

One morning, for instance, when I was in the midst of the seventeenth chapter of my new novel, my little Mini stole into the room, and putting her hand into mine, said: 'Father! Ramdayal the door-keeper calls a crow a krow! He doesn't know anything, does he?'

Before I could explain to her the differences of language in this world, she was embarked on the full tide of another subject. 'What do you think, Father? Bhola says there is an elephant in the clouds, blowing water out of his trunk, and that is why it rains!'

And then, darting off anew, while I sat still making ready some reply to this last saying: 'Father! what relation is Mother to you?'

'My dear little sister in law!' I murmured involuntarily to myself, but with a grave face contrived to answer: 'Go and play with Bhola, Mini! I am busy!

The window of my room overlooks the road. The child had seated herself at my feet near my table, and was playing softly, drumming on her knees. I was hard at work on my seventeenth chapter, where Pratap Singh, the hero, had just caught Kanchanlata, the heroine, in his arms, and was about to escape with her by the third-storey window of the castle, when all of a sudden Mini left her play, and ran to the window, crying: 'A Kabuliwallah! A Kabuliwallah!' Sure enough in the street below was a Kabuliwallah, passing slowly along. He wore the loose soiled clothing of his people, with a tall turban; there was a bag on his back, and he carried boxes of grapes in his hand.

I cannot tell what were my daughter's feelings at the sight of this man, but she began to call him loudly. 'Ah!' I thought, 'he will come in, and my seventeenth chapter will never be finished!' At which exact moment the Kabuliwallah turned, and looked up at the child. When she saw this, overcome by terror, she fled to her mother's protection, and disappeared. She had a blind belief that inside the bag, which the big man carried, there were perhaps two or three other children like herself. The pedlar meanwhile entered my doorway, and greeted me with a smiling face.

So precarious was the position of my hero and my heroine, that my first impulse was to stop and buy something, since the man had been called. I made some small purchases, and a conversation began about Abdurrahman, the Russians, the English, and the Frontier Policy.

As he was about to leave, he asked: 'And where is the little girl, sir?'

And I, thinking that Mini must get rid of her false fear, had her brought out.

She stood by my chair, and looked at the Kabuliwallah

and his bag. He offered her nuts and raisins, but she would not be tempted, and only clung the closer to me, with all her doubts increased.

This was their first meeting.

One morning, however, not many days later, as I was leaving the house, I was startled to find Mini, seated on a bench near the door, laughing and talking, with the great Kabuliwallah at her feet. In all her life, it appeared, my small daughter had never found so patient a listener, save her father. And already the corner of her little sari was stuffed with almonds and raisins, the gift of her visitor. 'Why did you give her those?' I said, and taking out a half rupee coin, I handed it to him. The man accepted the money without demur, and slipped it into his pocket.

Alas, on my return an hour later, I found the unfortunate coin had made twice its own worth of trouble! For the Kabuliwallah had given it to Mini, and her mother catching sight of the bright round object, had pounced on the child with: 'Where did you get that coin?'

'The Kabuliwallah gave it to me,' said Mini cheerfully.

'The Kabuliwallah gave it to you!" cried her mother much shocked. '0 Mini! how could you take it from him?'

I, entering at the moment, saved her from impending disaster, and proceeded to make my own inquiries.

It was not the first or second time, I found, that the two had met. The Kabuliwallah had overcome the child's first terror by a judicious bribery of nuts and almonds, and the two were now great friends.

They had many quaint jokes, which afforded them much amusement. Seated in front of him, looking down on his gigantic frame in all her tiny dignity, Mini would ripple her face with laughter, and begin: '0 Kabuliwallah! Kabuliwallah! what have you got in your bag?'

And he would reply, in the nasal accents of the mountaineer: 'An elephant!' Not much cause for merriment, perhaps; but how they both enjoyed the witticism! And for me, this child's talk with a grown-up man had always in it something strangely fascinating.

Then the Kabuliwallah, not to be behindhand, would take his turn: "Well, little one, and when are you going to the father-in-law's house?'

Now most small Bengali maidens have heard long ago about the father-in-law's house; but we, being a little newfangled, had kept these things from our child, and Mini at this question must have been a triffle bewildered. But she would not show it, and with ready tact replied: 'Are you going there?'

Amongst men of the Kabuliwallah's class, however, it is well-known that the words *father-in-law's house* have a double meaning. It is a euphemism for jail, the place where we are well cared for, at no expense to ourselves. In this sense would the sturdy pedlar take my daughter's question. 'Ah,' he would say, shaking his fist at an invisible policeman, 'I will thrash my father-in-law!' Hearing this, and picturing the poor discomfited relative. Mini would go off into peals of laughter, in which her formidable friend would join.

These were autumn mornings, the very time of year when kings of old went forth to conquest; and I, never stirring from my little corner in Calcutta, would let my mind wander over the whole world. At the very name of another country, my heart would go out to it, and at the sight of a foreigner in the streets, I would fall to weaving a network or dreams—the mountains, the glens, and the forests of his distant home, with his cottage in its setting, and the free and independent life of faraway wilds. Perhaps the scenes of travel conjure themselves up before me, and pass and repass in my imagination all the more vividly, because I lead such a vegetable existence that a call to travel would fall upon me like a thunderbolt. In the presence of this Kabuliwallah I was immediately transported to the foot of arid mountain peaks, with narrow little defiles twisting in and out amongst their towering heights. I could see the string of camels bearing the merchandise, and the company of turbanned merchants carrying some of their queer old firearms, and some of their spears, journeying downwards towards the plains. I could see — But at some such point Mini's mother would intervene, imploring me to 'beware of that man.'

Mini's mother is unfortunately a very timid lady. Whenever she hears a noise in the street, or sees people coming towards the house, she always jumps to the conclusion that they are either thieves, or drunkards, or snakes, or tigers, or malaria or cockroaches, or caterpillars, or an English sailor. Even after all these years of experience, she is not able to overcome her terror. So she was full of doubts about the Kabuliwallah, and used to beg me to keep a watchful eye on him.

I tried to laugh her fear gently away, but then she would turn round on me seriously, and ask me solemn questions.

Were children never kidnapped?

Was it, then, not true that there was slavery in Kabul?

Was it so very absurd that this big man should be able to carry off a tiny child?

I urged that, though not impossible, it was highly improbable. But this was not enough, and her dread persisted. As it was indefinite, however, it did not seem right to forbid the man the house, and the intimacy went on unchecked.

Once a year in the middle of January Rahmun, the Kabuliwallah, was in the habit of returning to his country, and as the time approached he would be very busy, going from house to house collecting his debts. This year, however, he could always find time to come and see Mini. It would have seemed to an outsider that there was some conspiracy between the two, for when he could not come in the morning, he would appear in the evening.

Even to me it was a little tartling now and then, in the corner of a dark room, suddenly to surprise this tall, loose-garmented, much bebagged man; but when Mini would run in smiling, with her 'O Kabuliwallah! Kabuliwallah!' and the two friends, so far apart in age, would subside into their old laughter and their old jokes, I felt reassured.

One morning, a few days before he had made up his mind to go, I was correcting my proof sheets in my study. It was chilly weather. Through the window the rays of the sun touched my feet, and the slight warmth was very welcome. It was almost eight o'clock, and the early pedestrains were returning home with their heads covered. All at once I heard an uproar in the street, and, looking out, saw Rahmun being led away bound between two policemen, and behind them a crowd of curious boys. There were, bloodstains on the clothes of the Kabuliwallah, and one of the policemen carried a knife.

Hurrying out, I stopped them, and inquired what it all meant. Partly from one, partly from another, I gathered that a certain neighbour had owed the pedlar something for a Rampuri shawl, but had falsely denied having bought it, and that in the course of the quarrel Rahmun had struck him. Now in the heat of his excitement, the prisoner began calling his enemy all sorts of names, when suddenly in a verandah of my house appeared my little Mini, with her usual exclamation: 'O Kabuliwallah! Kabuliwallah!' Rahmun's face lighted up as he turned to her. He had no bag under his arm today, so she could not discuss the elephant with him. She at once therefore proceeded to the next question: 'Are you going to the father-in-law's house?' Rahmun laughed and said: 'Just there I am going, little one!' Then seeing that the reply did not amuse the child, he held up his fettered hands. 'Ah,' he said, 'I would have thrashed that old father-in-law, but my hands are bound!"

On a charge of murderous assault, Rahmun was sentenced to some years' imprisonment.

Time passed, and he was not remembered. The accustomed work in the accustomed place was ours, and the thought of the once free mountaineer spending his years in prison seldom or never occurred to us. Even my lighthearted Mini, I am ashamed to say, forgot her old friend. New companions filled her life. As she grew older, she spent more of her time with girls. So much time indeed did she spend with them that she came no more, as she used to do, to her father's room. I was scarcely on speaking terms with her.

Years had passed. It was once more autumn and we had made arrangements for our Mini's marriage. It was to take place during the Puja Holidays. With Durga returning to Kailas, the light of our home also was to depart to her husband's house, and leave her father's in the shadow.

The morning was bright. After the rains, there was a sense of ablution in the air, and the sun-rays looked like pure gold. So bright were they that they gave a beautiful radiance even to the sordid brick walls of our Calcutta lanes. Since early dawn today the wedding-pipes had been sounding, and at each beat my own heart throbbed. The wail of the tune, Bhairavi, seemed to intensify my pain at the approaching separation. My Mini was to be married tonight.

From early morning noise and bustle had pervaded the house. In the courtyard the canopy had to be slung on its bamboo poles; the chandeliers with their tinkling sound must be hung in each room and verandah. There was no end of hurry and excitement. 1 was sitting in my study, looking through the accounts, when someone entered, saluting respectfully, and stood before me. It was Rahmun the Kabuliwallah. At first I did not recognise him. He had no bag, nor the long hair, nor the same vigour that he used to have. But he smiled, and I knew him again.

'When did you come, Rahmun?' I asked him.

'Last evening,' he said, 'I was released from jail.'

The words struck harsh upon my ears. I had never before talked with one who had wounded his fellow, and my heart shrank within itself when I realised this, for I felt that the day would have been better-omened had he not turned up.

'There are ceremonies going on,' I said, 'and I am busy. Could you perhaps come another day?'

At once he turned to go; but as he reached the door he hesitated, and said: 'May I not see the little one, sir, for a moment?'

It was his belief that Mini was still the same. He had

pictured her running to him as she used, calling 'O Kabuliwallah! Kabuliwallah!' He had imagined too that they would laugh and talk together, just as of old. In fact, in memory of former days he had brought, carefully wrapped up in paper, a few almonds and raisins and grapes, obtained somehow from a countryman, for his own little fund was dispersed.

I said again: 'There is a ceremony in the house, and you will not be able to see anyone today.'

The man's face fell. He looked wistfully at me for a moment, said 'Good morning,' and went out.

I felt a little sorry, and would have called him back, but I found he was returning of his own accord. He came close up to me holding out his offerings, and said: 'I brought these few things, sir, for the little one. Will you give them to her?"

I took them and was going to pay him, but he caught my hand and said: 'You are very kind, sir! Keep me in your mind. Do not offer me money!—You have a little girl: I too have one like her in my own home. I think of her, and bring fruits to your child—not to make a profit for myself.'

Saying this, he put his hand inside his big loose robe, and brought out a small and dirty piece of paper. With great care he unfolded it, and smoothed it out with both hands on my table. It bore the impression of a little hand. Not a photograph. Not a drawing. The impression of an ink-smeared hand laid flat on the paper. This touch of his own little daughter had been always on his heart, as he had come year after year to Calcutta to sell his wares in the streets.

Tears came to my eyes. I forgot that he was a poor Kabuli fruitseller, while I was — But no, what was I more than he? He also was a father.

That impression of the hand of his little Parbati. in her distant mountain home reminded me of my own little Mini.

I sent for Mini immediately from the inner apartment. Many difficulties were raised, but I would not listen. Clad in the red silk of her wedding-day, with the sandal paste on her forehead, and adorned as a young bride, Mini came, and stood bashfully before me.

The Kabuliwallah looked a little staggered at the apparition. He could not revive their old friendship. At last he smiled and said: 'Little one, are you going to your father-in-law's house?'

Mini now understood the meaning of the word 'father-in-law,' and she could not reply to him as of old. She flushed up at the question, and stood before him with her bridelike face turned down.

I remembered the day when the Kabuliwallah and my Mini had first met, and I felt sad. When she had gone, Rahmun heaved a deep sigh, and sat down on the floor. The idea had suddenly come to him that his daughter too must have grown in this long time, and that he would have to make friends with her anew. Assuredly he would not find her as he used to know her. And besides, what might not have happened to her in these eight years?

The marriage-pipes sounded, and the mild autumn sun streamed round us. But Rahmun sat in the little Calcutta lane, and saw before him the barren mountains of Afghanistan.

I took out a bank-note and gave it to him, saying: 'Go back to your own daughter, Rahmun, in your own country, and may the happiness of your meeting bring good fortune to my child!'

Having made this present, I had to curtail some of the festivities. I could not have the electric lights I had intended, nor the military band, and the ladies of the house were despondent at it. But to me the wedding-feast was all the brighter for the thought that in a distant land a long-lost father met again with his only child.

1892 **—Tr. by Sister Nivedita**

2

Hungry Stones

My kinsman and myself were returning to Calcutta from our Puja trip when we met the man in a train. From his dress and bearing we took him at first for an up-country Muslim but we were puzzled as we heard him talk. He discoursed upon all subjects so confidently that you might think the Disposer of All Things consulted him at all times in all that He did. Hitherto we had been perfectly happy, as we did not know that secret and unheard-of forces were at work, that the Russians had advanced close to us, that the English had deep and secret policies, that confusion among the native chiefs had come to a head. But our newly acquired friend said with a sly smile: 'There happen more things in heaven and earth, Horatio, than are reported in your newspapers.'

As we had never stirred out of our homes before, the demeanour of the man struck us dumb with wonder. Be the topic ever so trivial, he would quote science, or comment on the Vedas, or repeat quatrains from some Persian poet; and as we had no pretence to a knowledge of science or the Vedas or Persian, our admiration for him went on increasing, and my kinsman, a Theosophist, was firmly convinced that our fellow-passenger must have been supernaturally inspired by some strange 'magnetism' or 'occult power,' by an 'astral body' or something of that kind. He listened to the tritest saying that fell from the lips of our extraordinary companion with devotional rapture, and secretly took down notes of his conversation. I fancy that the extraordinary man saw this, and was a little pleased with it.

When the train reached the junction, we assembled in the waiting-room for the connection. It was then 10 P.M., and as the train, we heard, was likely to be very late, owing to something wrong in the lines, I spread my bed on the table and was about to lie down for a comfortable doze, when the extraordinary person deliberately set about spinning the following yarn. Of course, I could get no sleep that night.

When, owing to a disagreement about some questions of administrative policy, I threw up my post at Junagarh, and entered the service of the Nizam of Hyderabad, they appointed me at once, as a strong young man, collector of cotton duties at Barich.

Barich is a lovely place. The river Susta 'chatters over stony ways and babbles on the pebbles,' tripping, like a skilful dancing girl, in through the woods below the lonely hills. A flight of 150 steps rises from the river, and above that flight, on the river's brim and at the foot of the hills, there stands a solitary marble palace. Around it there is no habitation of man—the village and cotton mart of Barich being far off.

About 250 years ago the Emperor Mahmud Shah II had built this lonely palace for his pleasure and luxury. In his days jets of rose-water spurted from its fountains, and on the cold marble floors of its spray-cooled rooms young Persian damsels would sit, their hair dishevelled before bathing, and, splashing their soft naked feet in the clear water of the reservoirs, would sing, to the tune of the guitar, the gazals of their vineyards.

The fountains play no longer; the songs have ceased; no longer do snowwhite feet step gracefully on the snowy marble. It is but the vast and solitary quarters of cess-collectors like us, men oppressed with solitude and deprived of the society of women. Now, Karim Khan, the old clerk of my office, warned me repeatedly not to take up my abode there. 'Pass the day there, if you like,' said he, 'but never stay the night.' I passed it off with a light laugh. The servants said that they would work till dark, and go away at night. I gave my ready assent. The house had such a bad name that even thieves would not venture near it after dark.

At first the solitude of the deserted palace weighed upon me like a nightmare. I would stay out, and work hard as long as possible, then return home at night jaded and tired, go to bed and fall asleep.

Before a week had passed, the place began to exert a weird fascination upon me. It is difficult to describe or to induce people to believe, but I felt as if the whole house was like a living organism slowly and imperceptibly digesting me by the action of some stupefying gastric juice.

Perhaps the process had begun as soon as I set my foot in the house, but I distinctly remember the day on which 1 first was conscious of it.

It was the beginning of summer, and the market being dull I had no work to do. A little before sunset I was sitting in an armchair near the water's edge below the steps. The Susta had shrunk and sunk low; a broad patch of sand on the other side glowed with the hues of evening; on this side the pebbles at the bottom of the clear shallow waters were glistening. There was not a breath of wind anywhere, and the still air was laden with an oppressive scent from the spicy shrubs growing on the hills close by.

As the sun sank behind the hill-tops a long dark curtain fell upon the stage of day, and the intervening hills cut short the time in which light and shade mingle at sunset. I thought of going out for a ride, and was about to get up when I heard a footfall on the steps behind. I looked back, but there was no one.

As I sat down again, thinking it to be an illusion, I heard many footfalls, as if a large number of persons were rushing down the steps. A strange thrill of delight, slightly tinged with fear, passed through my frame, and though there was not a figure before my eyes, methought I saw a bevy of joyous maidens coming down the steps to bathe in the Susta in that summer evening. Not a sound was in the valley, in the river, or in the palace, to break the silence, but I distinctly heard the maidens' gay and mirthful laugh, like the gurgle of a spring gushing forth in a hundred cascades, as they ran past me, in quick playful pursuit of each other, towards the river, without noticing me at all. As they were invisible to me, so I was, as it were, invisible to them. The river was perfectly calm, but I felt that its still, shallow, and clear waters were stirred suddenly by the splash of many an arm jingling with bracelets, that the girls laughed and dashed and spattered water at one another, that the feet of the fair swimmers tossed the tiny waves up in showers of pearl.

I felt a thrill at my heart—I cannot say whether the excitement was due to fear or delight or curiosity. I had a strong desire to see them more clearly, but nothing was visible before me. I thought I could catch all that they said if I only strained my ears; but however hard I strained them, I heard nothing but the chirping of the cicadas in the woods. It seemed as if a dark curtain of 250 years was hanging before me, and I would fain lift a corner of it trembling and peer through, though the assembly on the other side was completely enveloped in darkness.

The oppressive closeness of the evening was broken by a sudden gust of wind, and the still surface of the Susta rippled and curled like the hair of a nymph, and from the woods wrapt in the evening gloom there came forth a simultaneous murmur, as though they were awakening from a black dream. Call it reality or dream, the momentary glimpse of that invisible mirage reflected from a far-off world, 250 years old, vanished in a flash. The mystic forms that brushed past me with their quick unbodied steps, and loud, voiceless laughter, and threw themselves into the river, did not go back wringing their dripping robes as they went. Like fragrance wafted away by the wind they were dispersed by a single breath of the spring.

Then I was filled with a lively fear that it was the Muse

that had taken advantage of my solitude and possessed me—the witch had evidently come to ruin a poor devil like myself making a living by collecting cotton duties. I decided to have a good dinner—it is the empty stomach that all sorts of incurable diseases find an easy prey. I sent for my cook and gave orders for a rich, sumptuous mughlai dinner, redolent of spices and ghee.

Next morning the whole affair appeared a queer fantasy. With a light heart I put on a sola hat like the sahebs, and drove out to my work. I was to have written my quarterly report that day, and expected to return late; but before it was dark I was strangely drawn to my house—by what I could not say—I felt they were all waiting, and that I should delay no longer. Leaving, my report unfinished I rose, put on my sola hat, and startling the dark, shady, desolate path with the rattle of my carriage, I reached the vast silent palace standing on the gloomy skirts of the hills.

On the first floor the stairs led to a very spacious hall, its roof stretching wide over ornamental arches resting on three rows of massive pillars, and groaning day and night under the weight of its own intense solitude. The day had just closed, and the lamps had not yet been lighted. As I pushed the door open a great bustle seemed to follow within, as if a throng of people had broken up in confusion, and rushed out through the doors and windows and corridors and verandas and rooms, to make its hurried escape.

As I saw no one I stood bewildered, my hair on end in a kind of ecstatic delight, and a faint scent of *attar* and unguents almost effaced by age lingered in my nostrils. Standing in the darkness of that vast desolate hall between the rows of those ancient pillars, I could hear the gurgle of fountains slashing on the marble floor, a strange tune on the guitar, the jingle of ornaments and the tinkle of anklets, the clang of bells tolling the hours, the distant note of nahabat, the din of the crystal pendants of chandeliers shaken by the breeze, the song of *bulbuls* from the cages in the corridors, the cackle of storks in the gardens, all creating round me a strange unearthly music.

Then I came under such a spell that this intangible,

inaccessible, unearthly vision appeared to be the only reality in the world—and all else a mere dream. That I, that is to say, Mr. So-and-so, the eldest son of So-and-so of blessed memory, should be drawing a monthly salary of Rs. 450 by the discharge of my duties as collector of cotton duties, and driving in my dog-cart to my office every day in a short coat and sola hat, appeared to me to be such an astonishingly ludicrous illusion that I burst into a horse-laugh, as I stood in the gloom of that vast silent hall.

At that moment my servant entered with a lighted kerosene lamp in his hand. I do not know whether he thought me mad, but it came back to me at once that I was in very deed Mr. So-and-so, son of So-and so of blessed memory, and that, while our poets, great and small, alone could say whether inside or outside the earth there was a region where unseen fountains perpetually played and fairy guitars, struck by invisible fingers, sent forth an eternal harmony, this at any rate was certain, that I collected duties at the cotton market at Barich, and earned thereby Rs. 450 per mensem as my salary. I laughed in great glee at my curious illusion, as I sat over the newspaper at my camp-table, lighted by the kerosene lamp.

After I had finished my paper and eaten my mughlai dinner, I put out the lamp, and lay down on my bed in a small side-room. Through the open window a radiant star, high above the Avalli hills skirted by the darkness of their woods, was gazing intently from millions and millions of miles away in the sky at Mr. Collector lying on a humble camp-bed. I wondered and felt amused at the idea, and do not know when I fell asleep or how long I slept; but I suddenly awoke with a start, though I heard no sound and saw no intruder—only the steady bright star on the hill-top had set, and the dim light of the new moon was stealthily entering the room through the open window, as if ashamed of its intrusion.

I saw nobody, but felt as if someone was gently pushing

me. As I awoke she said not a word, but beckoned me with her five fingers bedecked with rings to follow her cautiously. I got up noiselessly, and, though not a soul save myself was there in the countless apartments of that deserted palace with its slumbering sounds and waking echoes, I feared at every step lest any one should wake up. Most of the rooms of the palace were always kept closed, and I had never entered them.

I followed breathless and with silent steps my invisible guide—I cannot now say where. What endless dark and narrow passages, what long corridors, what silent and solemn audience-chambers and close secret cells I crossed!

Though I could not see my fair guide, her form was not invisible to my mind's eye—an Arab girl, her arms, hard and smooth as marble, visible through her loose sleeves, a thin veil falling on her face from the fringe of her cap, and a curved dagger at her waist! Methought that one of the thousand and one Arabian Nights had been wafted to me from the world of romance, and that at the dead of night I was wending my way through the dark narrow alleys of slumbering Baghdad to a trysting-place fraught with peril.

At last my fair guide stopped abruptly before a deep blue screen, and seemed to point to something below. There was nothing there, but a sudden dread froze the blood in my heart—methought I saw there on the floor at the foot of the screen a terrible negro eunuch dressed in rich brocade, sitting and dozing with outstretched legs, with a naked sword on his lap. My fair guide lightly tripped over his legs and held up a fringe of the screen. I could catch a glimpse of a part of the room spread with a Persian carpet—some one was sitting inside on a bed—I could not see her, but only caught a glimpse of two exquisite feet in gold-embroidered slippers, hanging out from loose saffron-coloured paijamas and placed idly on the orange-coloured velvet carpet. On one side there was a bluish crystal tray on which a few apples, pears, oranges, and bunches of grapes in plenty, two small cups, and a gold-tinted decanter were evidently awaiting the guest. A fragrant intoxicating vapour, issuing from a strange sort of incense that burned within, almost overpowered my senses.

As with trembling heart I made an attempt to step across the outstretched legs of the eunuch, he woke up suddenly with a start, and the sword fell from his lap with a sharp clang on the marble floor.

A terrific scream made me jump, and I saw I was sitting on that camp-bed of mine sweating heavily; and the crescent moon looked pale in the morning light like a weary sleepless patient at dawn; and our crazy Meher Ali was crying out, as is his daily custom, 'Keep away! Keep away!!' while he went along the lonely road.

Such was the abrupt close of one of my Arabian Nights; but there were yet a thousand nights left.

Then followed a great discord between my days and nights. During the day I would go to my work worn and tired, cursing the bewitching night and her empty dreams, but as night came my daily life with its bonds and shackles of work would appear a petty, false, ludicrous vanity.

After nightfall I was caught and overwhelmed in the snare of a strange intoxication. I would then be transformed into some unknown persona of a bygone age, playing my part in unwritten history; and my short English coat and tight breeches did not suit me in the least. With a red velvet cap on my head, loose paijamas, an embroidered vest, a long flowing silk gown, and coloured handkerchiefs scented with *attar*. I would complete my elaborate toilet, sit on a high-cushioned chair, and replace my cigarette with a many-coiled *narghileh* filled with rose-water, as if in eager expectation of a strange meeting with the beloved one.

I have no power to describe the marvellous incidents that unfolded themselves as the gloom of the night deepened. I felt as if in the curious apartments of that vast edifice the fragments of a beautiful story, which I could follow for some distance, but of which I could never see the end, flew about in a sudden gust of the vernal breeze. And all the same I would wander from room to room in pursuit of them the whole night long.

Amid the eddy of these dream-fragments, amid the smell of henna and the twanging of the guitar, amid the waves of air charged with fragrant spray, I would catch like a flash of lightning the momentary glimpse of a fair damsel. She it was who had saffron-coloured paijamas, white ruddy soft feet in gold-embroidered slippers with curved toes, a close-fitting bodice wrought with gold, a red cap, from which a golden frill fell on her snowy brow and cheeks.

She had maddened me. In pursuit of her I wandered from room to room, from path to path among the bewildering maze of alleys in the enchanted dreamland of the nether world of sleep.

Sometimes in the evening, while arraying myself carefully as a prince of the blood-royal before a large mirror, with a candle burning on either side, I would see a sudden reflection of the Persian beauty by the side of my own. A swift turn of her neck, a quick eager glance of intense passion and pain glowing in her large dark eyes, just a suspicion of speech on her dainty red lips, her figure, fair and slim, crowned with youth like a blossoming creeper, quickly uplifted in her graceful tilting gait, a dazzling flash of pain and craving and ecstasy, a smile and a glance and a blaze of jewels and silk, and she melted away.

A wild gust of wind, laden with all the fragrance of hills and woods, would put out my light, and I would fling aside my dress and lie down on my bed, eyes closed and body thrilling with delight, and there around me in the breeze, amid all the perfume of the woods and hills, floated through the silent gloom many a caress and many a kiss and many a tender touch of hands, and gentle murmurs in my ears, and fragrant breaths on my brow; or a sweetly-perfumed kerchief was wafted again and again on my cheeks. Then slowly a mysterious serpent would twist her stupefying coils about me; and heaving a heavy sigh, I would lapse into insensibility, and then into a profound slumber.

One evening I decided to go out on my horse—I do not know who implored me to stay—but I would listen to no entreaties that day. My English hat and coat were resting on a rack, and I was about to take them down when a sudden whirlwind, crested with the sands of the Susta and the dead leaves of the Avalli hills, caught them up, and whirled them round and round, while a loud peal of merry laughter rose higher and higher, striking all the chords of mirth till it died away in the land of sunset.

I could not go out for my ride, and the next day I gave up my queer English coat and hat for good.

That day again at dead of night I heard the stifled heart-breaking sobs of someone—as if below the bed, below the floor, below the stony foundation of that gigantic palace, from the depths of a dark damp grave, a voice piteously cried and implored me: 'Rescue me! Break through these doors of hard illusion, deathlike slumber and fruitless dreams, place me by your side on the saddle, press me to your heart, and, riding through hills and woods and across the river, take me to the warm radiance of your sunny rooms above!'

Who am I? Oh, how can I rescue thee? What drowning beauty, what incarnate passion shall I drag to the shore from this wild eddy of dreams? O lovely ethereal apparition! Where did thou flourish and when? By what cool spring, under the shade of what date-groves wast thou bom—in the lap of what homeless wanderer in the desert? What Bedouin snatched thee from thy mother's arms, an opening bud plucked from a wild creeper, placed thee on a horse swift as lightning, crossed the burning sands, and took thee to the slave-market of what royal city? And there, what officer of the Badshah, seeing the glory of thy bashful blossoming youth, paid for thee in gold, placed thee in a golden palanquin, and offered thee as a present for the seraglio of his master? And O, the history of that place! The music of the *sareng* the jingle of anklets, the occasional flash of daggers and the glowing wine of Shiraz poison, and the piercing flashing glance! What infinite grandeur, what endless servitude! The slave-girls to thy right and left waved the chowrie, as diamonds flashed from their bracelets; the Badshah, the king of kings, fell on his knees at thy snowy feet in bejewelled shoes, and outside the terrible Abyssinian eunuch, looking like a messenger of death, but clothed like an angel, stood with a naked sword in his hand! Then, O, thou flower of the desert, swept away by the bloodstained dazzling ocean of grandeur, with its foam of jealousy, its rocks and shoals of intrigue, on what shore of cruel death wast thou cast, or in what other land more splendid and more cruel?

Suddenly at this moment that crazy Meher Ali screamed out: 'Keep away ! Keep away!! All is false! All is false!!' I opened my eyes and saw that it was already light. My peon came and handed me my letters, and the cook waited with a *salaam* for my orders.

I said: 'No, I can stay here no longer.' That very day I packed up, and moved to my office. Old Karim Khan smiled a little as he saw me. I left nettled, but said nothing, and left to my work.

As evening approached I grew absent-minded; I felt as if I had an appointment to keep; and the work of examining the cotton accounts seemed wholly useless; even the Nizamat of the Nizam did not appear to be of much worth. Whatever belonged to the present, whatever was moving and acting and working for bread seemed trivial, meaningless, and contemptible.

I threw my pen down, closed my ledgers, got into my dog-cart, and drove away. I noticed that it stopped of itself at the gate of the marble palace just at the hour of twilight. With quick steps I climbed the stairs, and entered the room.

A heavy silence was reigning within. The dark rooms were looking sullen as if they had taken offence. My heart was full of contrition, but there was no one to whom I could lay it bare, or of whom I could ask forgiveness. I wandered about the dark rooms with a vacant mind. I wished I had a guitar to which I could sing to the unknown: 'O fire, the poor moth that made a vain effort to fly away has come back to thee! Forgive it but this once, burn its wings and consume it in thy flame!'

Suddenly two tear-drops fell from overhead on my brow. Dark masses of clouds overcast the top of the Avalli hills that day. The gloomy woods and the sooty waters of the Susta were waiting in terrible suspense and in an ominous calm. Suddenly land, water, and sky shivered, and a wild tempest-blast rushed howling through the distant pathless woods, showing its lightning-teeth like a raving maniac who had broken his chains. The desolate halls of the palace banged their doors, and moaned in the bitterness of anguish.

The servants were all in the office, and there was no one to light the lamps. The night was cloudy and moonless. In the dense gloom within I could distinctly feel that a woman was lying on her face on the carpet below the bed—clasping and tearing her long dishevelled hair with desperate fingers. Blood was trickling down her fair brow, and she was now laughing a hard, harsh, mirthless laugh, now bursting into violent wringing sobs, now rending her bodice and striking at her bare bosom, as the wind roared in through the open window, and the rain poured in torrents and soaked her through and through.

All night there was no cessation of the storm or of the passionate cry. I wandered from room to room in the dark, with unavailing sorrow. Whom could I console when no one was by? Whose was this intense agony of sorrow? Whence arose this inconsolable grief?

And the mad man cried out: 'Keep away! Keep away!! All is false! All is false!!'

I saw that the day had dawned, and Meher Ali was going round and round the palace with his usual cry in that dreadful weather. Suddenly it came to me that perhaps he also had once lived in that house, and that, though he had gone mad, he came there every day, and went round and round, fascinated by the weird spell cast by the marble demon.

Despite the storm and rain I ran to him and asked: 'Ho, Meher Ali, what is false?'

The man answered nothing, but pushing me aside went round and round with his frantic cry, like a bird flying fascinated about the jaws of a snake, and made a desperate effort to warn himself by repeating: 'Keep away! Keep away!! All is false! All is false!!'

I ran like a mad man through the pelting rain to my office, and asked Karim Khan: 'Tell me the meaning of all this!'

What I gathered from that old man was this: That at one time countless unrequited passions and unsatisfied longings and lurid flames of wild blazing pleasure raged within that palace, and that the curse of all the heartaches and blasted hopes had made its every stone thirsty and hungry, eager to swallow up like a famished ogress any living man who might chance to approach. Not one of those who lived there for three consecutive nights could escape these cruel jaws, save Meher Ali, who had escaped at the cost of his reason.

I asked: 'Is there no means whatever of my release?' The old man said: 'There is only one means, and that is very difficult. I will tell you what it is, but first you must hear the history of a young Persian girl who once lived in that pleasure-dome. A stranger or a more bitterly heart-rending tragedy was never enacted on this earth.'

Just at this moment the coolies announced that the train was coming. So soon? We hurriedly packed up our luggage, as the train steamed in. An English gentleman, apparently just aroused from slumber, was looking out of a first-class carriage endeavouring to read the name of the station. As soon as he caught sight of our fellow-passenger he cried, 'Hallo,' and took him into his own compartment. As we got into a second-class carriage, we had no chance of finding out who the man was nor what was the end of his story.

I said: 'The man evidently took us for fools and imposed upon us out of fun. The story is pure fabrication from start to finish.' The discussion that followed ended in a lifelong rupture between my theosophist kinsman and myself.

1895 **—Tr. by Pannalal Basu**

3

After the Glory

Once upon a time the Babus of Nayanjore were famous landholders. They were noted for their princely extravagance. They would tear off the rough border of their Dacca muslin, because it rubbed against their skin. They could spend thousands of rupees over the wedding of a kitten. On a certain grand occasion it is said that in order to turn night into day they lighted numberless lamps and showered silver threads from the sky to imitate sunlight.

Those were the days before the flood. The flood came. The line of succession among these old-world Babus, with their lordly habits, could not continue for long. Like a lamp with too many wicks burning, the oil flared away quickly, and the light went out.

Kailas Babu, our neighbour, is the last relic of this extinct magnificence. Before he grew up, his family had very nearly reached its lowest ebb. When his father died, there was one dazzling outburst of funeral extravagance, and then insolvency. The property was sold to liquidate the debt. What little ready money was left over was altogether insufficient to keep up the past ancestral splendours.

Kailas Babu left Nayanjore and came to Calcutta. His son

did not remain long in this world of faded glory. He died, leaving behind him an only daughter.

In Calcutta we are Kailas Babu's neighbours. Curiously enough our own family history is just the opposite to his. My father got his money by his own exertions, and prided himself on never spending a penny more than was needed. His clothes were those of a working man. And his hands also. He never had any inclination to earn the title of Babu by extravagant display, and I myself, his only son, owe him gratitude for that. He gave me the very best education, and I was able to make my way in the world. I am not ashamed of the fact that I am a self-made man. Crisp banknotes in my safe are dearer to me than a long pedigree in an empty family chest.

I believe this was why I disliked seeing Kailas Babu drawing his heavy cheques on the public credit from the bankrupt bank of his ancient Babu reputation, I used to fancy that he looked down on me, because my father had earned money with his own hands.

I ought to have noticed that no one showed any vexation towards Kailas Babu except myself. Indeed it would have been difficult to find an old man who did less harm than he. He was always ready with his kindly little acts of courtesy in times of sorrow and joy. He would join in all the ceremonies and religious observances of his neighbours. His familiar smile would greet young and old alike. His politeness in asking details about domestic affairs was untiring. The friends who met him in the street were perforce ready to be buttonholed, while a long string of questions of this kind followed one another from his lips:

'My dear friend, I am delighted to see you. Are you quite well? How is Shashi? And Dada—is he all right? Do you know, I've only just heard that Madhu's son has got fever. How is he? Have you heard? And Hari Charan Babu—I have not seen him for a long time—I hope he is not ill. What's the matter with Rakhal? And, er—er, how are the ladies of your family?'

Kailas Babu was spotlessly neat in his dress on all occasions, though his supply of clothes was sorely limited. Every day he used to air his shirts and vests and coats and trousers carefully, and put them out in the sun, along with his bed-quilt, his pillow-case, and the small carpet on which he always sat. After airing them he would shake them, and brush them, and put them on the rock. His little bits of furniture made his small room decent, and hinted that there was more in reserve if needed. Very often, for want of a servant, he would shut up his house for a while. Then he would iron out his shirts and linen with his own hands, and do other little menial tasks. After this he would open his door and receive his friends again.

Though Kailas Babu, as I have said, had lost all his landed property, he had still some family heirlooms left. There was a silver cruet for sprinkling scented water, a filigree box for otto-of-roses, a small gold salver, a costly ancient shawl, and the old-fashioned ceremonial dress and ancestral turban. These he had rescued with the greatest difficulty from the moneylenders' clutches. On every suitable occasion he would bring them out in state, and thus try to save the world-famed dignity of the Babus of Nayanjore. At heart the most modest of men, in his daily speech he regarded it as a sacred duty, owed to his rank, to give free play to his family pride. His friends would encourage this trait in his character with kindly good humour, and it gave them great amusement.

The neighbourhood soon learnt to call him their Thakur Dada. They would flock to his house, and sit with him for hours together. To prevent his incurring any expense, one or other of his friends would bring him tobacco, and say: 'Thakur Dada, this morning some tobacco was sent to me from Gaya. Do take it, and see how you like it.'

Thakur Dada would take it, and say it was excellent. He would then go on to tell of a certain exquisite tobacco which they once smoked in the old days at Nayanjore at the cost of a guinea an ounce.

'I wonder,' he used to say, 'I wonder if anyone would like to try it now. I have some left, and can get it at once.'

Everyone knew that, if they asked for it, then somehow or

other the key of the cupboard would be missing; or else Ganesh, his old family servant, had put it away somewhere.

'You never can be sure,' he would add, 'where things go to when servants are about. Now, this Ganesh of mine—I can't tell you what a fool he is, but I haven't the heart to dismiss him.'

Ganesh, for the credit of the family, was quite ready to bear all the blame without a word.

One of the company usually said at this point: 'Never mind, Thakur Dada. Please don't trouble to look for it. This tobacco we're smoking will do quite well. The other would be too strong.'

Then Thakur Dada would be relieved, and settle down again, and the talk would go on.

When his guests got up to go, Thakur Dada would accompany them to the door, and say to them on the doorstep: 'Oh, by the way, when are you all coming to dine with me?'

One or other of us would answer: 'Not just yet, Thakur Dada, not just yet. We'll fix a day later.'

'Quite right,' he would answer. 'Quite right. We had much better wait till the rains come. It's too hot now. And a grand rich dinner such as I should want to give you would upset us in weather like this.'

But when the rains did come, everyone was very careful not to remind him of his promise. If the subject was brought up, some friend would suggest gently that it was very inconvenient to get about when the rains were so severe, that it would be much better to wait till they were over. And so the game went on.

His poor lodging was much too small for his position, and we used to condole with him about it. His friends would assure him they quite understood his difficulties: it was next to impossible to get a decent house in Calcutta. Indeed, they had all been looking out for years for a house to suit him, but, I need hardly add, no friend had been foolish enough to find one. Thakur Dada used to say, after a long sigh of resignation: 'Well, well, I suppose I shall have to put up with this house after all.' Then he would add with a genial smile: 'But, you know, I could never bear to be away from my friends. I must be near you. That really compensates for everything.'

Somehow I felt all this very deeply indeed. I suppose the real reason was, that when a man is young, stupidity appears to him the worst of crimes. Kailas Babu was not really stupid. In ordinary business matters everyone was ready to consult him. But with regard to Nayanjore his utterances were certainly void of common sense. Because, out of amused affection for him, no one contradicted his impossible statements, he refused to keep them in bounds. When people recounted in his hearing the glorious history of Nayanjore with absurd exaggerations, he would accept all they said with the utmost gravity, and never doubted, even in his dreams, that anyone could disbelieve it.

When I sit down and try to analyse the thoughts and feelings that I had towards Kailas Babu, I see that there was a still deeper reason for my dislike. I will now explain.

Though I am the son of a rich man, and might have wasted time at college, my industry was such that I took my M.A. degree in Calcutta University when quite young. My moral character was flawless. In addition, my outward appearance was so handsome, that if I were to call myself beautiful, it might be thought a mark of self-estimation, but could not be considered an untruth.

There could be no question that among the young men of Bengal I was regarded by parents generally as a very eligible match. I was myself quite clear on the point, and had determined to obtain my full value in the marriage market. When I pictured my choice, I had before my mind's eye a wealthy father's only daughter, extremely beautiful and highly educated. Proposals came pouring in to me from far and near; large sums in cash were offered. I weighed these offers with rigid impartiality, in the delicate scales of my own estimation. But there was no one fit to be my partner. I became convinced, with the poet Bhabavuti, that

In this world's endless time and boundless space, One may
be born at last to match my sovereign grace.

But in this puny modern age, and this contracted space of modern Bengal, it was doubtful if the peerless creature existed as yet.

Meanwhile my praises were sung in many tunes, and in different metres, by designing parents.

Whether I was pleased with their daughters or not, this worship which they offered was never unpleasing. I used to regard it as my proper due, because I was so good. We are told that when the gods withhold their boons from mortals they still expect their worshippers to pay them fervent honour, and are angry if it is withheld. I had that divine expectance strongly developed in myself.

I have already mentioned that Thakur Dada had an only grand-daughter. I had seen her many times, but had never mistaken her for beautiful. No thought had ever entered my mind that she would be a possible partner for myself. All the same, it seemed quite certain to me that some day or other Kailas Babu would offer her, with all due worship, as an oblation at my shrine. Indeed—this was the secret of my dislike—I was thoroughly annoyed that he had not done it already.

I heard he had told his friends that the Babus of Nayanjore never craved a boon. Even if the girl remained unmarried, he would not break the family tradition. It was this arrogance of his that made me angry. My indignation smouldered for some time. But I remained perfectly silent, and bore it with the utmost patience, because I was so good.

As lightning accompanies thunder, so in my character a flash of humour was mingled with the mutterings of my wrath. It was, of course, impossible for me to punish the old man merely to give vent to my rage; and for a long time I did nothing at all. But suddenly one day such an amusing plan came into my head, that I could not resist the temptation of carrying it into effect.

I have already said that many of Kailas Babu's friends used to flatter the old man's vanity to the full. One, who was a retired Government servant, had told him that whenever he saw the Chota Lord Sahib he always asked for the latest news about the Babus of Nayanjore, and the Chota Lord had been heard to say that in all Bengal the only really respectable families were those of the Maharaja of Burdwan and the Babus of Nayanjore. When this monstrous falsehood was told to Kailas Babu he was extremely gratified, and often repeated the story. And wherever after that he met this Government servant in company he would ask, along with other questions:

'Oh! er—by the way, how is the Chota Lord Sahib? Quite well, did you say? Ah, yes, I am so delighted to hear it! And the dear Mem Sahib, is she quite well too? Ah, yes! and the little children—are they quite well also? Ah, yes! that's very good news! Be sure and give them my compliments when you see them.'

Kailas Babu would constantly express his intention of going some day and paying a visit to the Sahib. But it may be taken for granted that many Chota Lords and Burra Lords also would come and go, and much water would pass down the Hooghly, before the family coach of Nayanjore would be furnished up to pay a visit to Government House.

One day I took Kailas Babu aside, and told him in a whisper: 'Thakur Dada, I was at the Levee yesterday, and the Chota Lord happened to mention the Babus of Nayanjore. I told him that Kailas Babu had come to town. Do you know, he was terribly hurt because you hadn't called. He told me he was going to put etiquette on one side, and pay you a private visit himself this very afternoon.'

Anybody else could have seen through this plot of mine in a moment. And, if it had been directed against another person, Kailas Babu would have understood the joke. But after all he had heard from his friend the Government servant, and after all his own exaggerations, a visit from the Lieutenant-Governor seemed the most natural thing in the world. He became highly nervous and excited at my news. Each detail of the coming visit exercised him greatly—most of all his own ignorance of English. How on earth was that difficulty to be met? I told him there was no difficulty at all: it was aristocratic not to know English: and, besides, the Lieutenant-Governor always brought an interpreter with him, and he had expressly mentioned that this visit was to be private.

About midday, when most of our neighbours are at work, and the rest are asleep, a carriage and pair stopped before the lodging of Kailas Babu. Two flunkeys in livery came up the stairs, and announced in a loud voice, 'The Chota Lord Sahib has arrived.' Kailas Babu was ready, waiting for him, in his old-fashioned ceremonial robes and ancestral turban, and Ganesh was by his side, dressed in his master's best suit of clothes for the occasion. When the Chota Lord Sahib was announced, Kailas Babu ran panting and puffing and trembling to the door, and led in a friend of mine, in disguise, with repeated salaams, bowing low at each step, and walking backward as best he could. He had his old family shawl spread over a hard wooden chair, and he asked the Lord Sahib to be seated. He then made a high-flown speech in Urdu, the ancient Court language of the Sahibs, and presented on the golden salver a string of gold mohurs, the last relics of his broken fortune. The old family servant Ganesh, with an expression of awe bordering on terror, stood behind with the scent-sprinkler, drenching the Lord Sahib, touching him gingerly from time to time with the otto-of-roses from the filigree box.

Kailas Babu repeatedly expressed his regret at not being able to receive His Honour Bahadur with all the ancestral magnificence of his own family estate at Nayanjore. There he could have welcomed him properly with due ceremonial. But in Calcutta he was a mere stranger and sojourner—in fact a fish out of water.

My friend, with his tall silk hat on, very gravely nodded. I need hardly say that according to English custom the hat ought to have been removed inside the room. But my friend did not dare to take it off for fear of detection; and Kailas Babu and his old servant Ganesh were sublimely unconscious of the breach of etiquette.

After a ten minutes' interview, which consisted chiefly of nodding the head, my friend rose to his feet to depart. The two flunkeys in livery, as had been planned beforehand, carried off in state the string of gold mohurs, the gold salver, the old ancestral shawl, the silver scent-sprinkler, and the otto-of roses filigree box; they placed them ceremoniously in the carriage. Kailas Babu regarded this as the usual habit of Chota Lord Sahibs.

I was watching all the while from the next room. My sides were aching with suppressed laughter. When I could hold myself in no longer, I rushed into a further room, suddenly to discover, in a comer, a young girl sobbing as if her heart would break. When she saw my uproarious laughter she stood upright in passion, flashing the lightning of her big dark eyes in mine, and said with a tear-choked voice: 'Tell me! What harm has my grandfather done to you? Why have you come to deceive him? Why have you come here? Why—'

She could say no more. She covered her face with her hands, and broke into sobs.

My laughter vanished in a moment. It had never occurred to me that there was anything but a supremely funny joke in this act of mine, and here I discovered that I had given the cruellest pain to this tenderest little heart. All the ugliness of my cruelty rose up to condemn me. I slunk out of the room in silence, like a kicked dog.

Hitherto I had only looked upon Kusum, the granddaughter of Kailas Babu, as a somewhat worthless commodity in the marriage market, waiting in vain to attract a husband. But now I found, with a shock of surprise, that in the comer of that room a human heart was beating.

The whole night through I had very little sleep. My mind was in a tumult. On the next day, very early in the morning, I took all those stolen goods back to Kailas Babu's lodgings, wishing to hand them over in secret to the servant Ganesh. I waited outside the door, and, not finding any one, went upstairs to Kailas Babu's room. I heard from the passage Kusum asking her grandfather in the most winning voice: 'Dada, dearest, do tell me all that the Chota Lord Sahib said to you yesterday. Don't leave out a single word. I am dying to hear it all over again.'

And Dada needed no encouragement. His face beamed over with pride as he related all manner of praises which the Lord Sahib had been good enough to utter concerning the ancient families of Nayanjore. The girl was seated before him, looking up into his face, and listening with rapt attention. She was determined, out of love for the old man, to play her part to the full.

My heart was deeply touched, and tears came to my eyes. I stood there in silence in the passage, while Thakur Dada finished all his embellishments of the Chota Lord Sahib's wonderful visit. When he left the room at last, I took the stolen goods and laid them at the feet of the girl and came away without a word.

Later in the day I called again to see Kailas Babu himself. According to our ugly modern custom, I had been in the habit of making no greeting at all to this old man when I came into the room. But on this day I made a low bow, and touched his feet. I am convinced the old man thought that the coming of the Chota Lord Sahib to his house was the cause of my new politeness. He was highly gratified by it, and an air of benign severity shone from his eyes. His friends had flocked in, and he had already begun to tell again at full length the story of the Lieutenant-Governor's visit with still further adornments of a most fantastic kind. The interview was already becoming an epic, both in quality and in length.

When the other visitors had taken their leave, I made my proposal to the old man in a humble manner. I told him that, 'though I could never for a moment hope to be worthy of marriage connection with such an illustrious family, yet... etc. etc.'

When I made clear my proposal of marriage, the old man embraced me, and broke out in a tumult of joy: 'I am a poor man, and could never have expected such great good fortune.'

That was the first and last time in his life that Kailas Babu confessed to being poor. It was also the first and last time in his life that he forgot, if only for a single moment, the ancestral dignity that belongs to the Babus of Nayanjore.

1895 **—Tr. by C.F. Andrews**

4

Homecoming

Phatik Chakravorti was ringleader among the boys of the village. A new mischief got into his head. There was a heavy log lying on the mud-flat of the river waiting to be shaped into a mast for a boat. He decided that they should all work together to shift the log by main force from its place and roll it away. The owner of the log would be angry and surprised, and they would all enjoy of the fun. Everyone seconded the proposal, and it was carried unanimously.

But just as the fun was about to begin, Makhan, Phatik's younger brother, sauntered up, and sat down on the log in front of them all without a word. The boys were puzzled for a moment. He was pushed, rather timidly, by one of the boys and told to get up: but he remained quite unconcerned. He appeared like a young philosopher mediating on the futility of games. Phatik was furious. 'Makhan,' he cried, 'if you don't get down this minute, I'll thrash you!'

Makhan only moved to a more comfortable position.

Now, if Phatik was to keep his regal dignity before the public, it was clear he ought to carry out his threat. But his courage failed him at the crisis. His fertile brain, however, rapidly seized upon a new manoeuvre which would discomfit his brother and afford his followers an added amusement. He gave the word of command to roll the log and Makhan over together. Makhan heard the order, and made it a point of honour to stick on. But he overlooked the fact, like those who attempt earthly fame in other matters, that there was peril in it.

The boys began to heave at the log with all their might, calling out, 'One, two, three, go.' At the word 'go' the log went; and with it went Makhan's philosophy, glory and all.

All the other boys shouted themselves hoarse with delight. But Phatik was a little frightened. He knew what was coming. And, sure enough, Makhan rose from Mother Earth blind as Fate and screaming like the Furies. He rushed at Phatik and scratched his face and beat him and kicked him, and then went crying home. The first act of the drama was over.

Phatik wiped his face, and sat down on the edge of a sunken barge on the river-bank, and began to chew a piece of grass. A boat came up to the landing, and a middle-aged man, with grey hair and dark moustache, stepped on shore. He saw the boy, sitting there doing nothing, and asked him where the Chakravortis lived. Phatik went on chewing the grass, and said: 'Over there,' but it was quite impossible to tell where he pointed. The stranger asked him again. He swung his legs to and fro on the side of the barge, and said: 'Go and find out,' and continued to chew the grass as before.

But now a servant came down from the house and told Phatik his mother wanted him. Phatik refused to move. But the servant was the master on this occasion. He took Phatik up roughly, and carried him, kicking and struggling in impotent rage.

When Phatik came into the house, his mother saw him. She called out angrily: 'So you have been hitting Makhan again?'

Phatik answered indignantly; 'No, I haven't; who told you that?'

His mother shouted: 'Don't tell lies! You have.'

Phatik said suddenly: 'I tell you, I haven't. You ask Makhan!' But Makhan thought it best to stick to his previous statement. He said: 'Yes, mother. Phatik did hit me.'

Phatik's patience was already exhausted. He could not bear this injustice. He rushed at Makhan and hammered him with blows: 'Take that,' he cried, 'and that, and that, for telling lies.'

His mother took Makhan's side in a moment, and pulled Phatik away, beating him with her hands. When Phatik pushed her aside, she shouted out: 'What! you little villain! would you hit your own mother?'

It was just at this critical juncture that the grey-haired stranger arrived. He asked what was the matter. Phatik looked sheepish and ashamed.

But when his mother stepped back and looked at the stranger, her anger was changed to surprise. For she recognised her brother, and cried: 'Why, Dada! Where have you come from?'

As she said these words, she bowed to the ground and touched his feet. Her brother had gone away soon after she had married, and he had started business in Bombay. His sister had lost her husband while he was in Bombay. Bishamber had now come back to Calcutta, and had at once made enquiries about his sister. He had then hastened to see her as soon as he found out where she was.

The next few days were full of rejoicing. The brother asked after the education of the two boys. He was told by his sister that Phatik was a perpetual nuisance. He was lazy, disobedient, and wild. But Makhan was as good as gold, as quite as a lamb, and very fond of reading. Bishamber kindly offered to take Phatik off his sister's hands, and educate him with his own children in Calcutta. The widowed mother readily agreed. When his uncle asked Phatik if he would like to go to Calcutta with him, his joy knew no bounds, and he said: 'Oh, yes, uncle!' in a way that made it quite clear that he meant it.

It was an immense relief to the mother to get rid of Phatik. She had a prejudice against the boy, and no love was lost between the two brothers. She was in daily fear that he would either drown Makhan some day in the river, or break his head in a fight, or run him into some danger or other. At the same time she was somewhat distressed to see Phatik's extreme eagerness to get away.

Phatik, as soon as all was settled, kept asking his uncle every minute when they were to start. He was on pins and needles all day long with excitement, and lay awake most of the night. He bequeathed to Makhan, in perpetuity, his fishing-rod, his big kite, and his marbles. Indeed, at this time of departure his generosity towards Makhan was unbounded.

When they reached Calcutta, Phatik made the acquaintance of his aunt for the first time. She was by no means pleased with this unnecessary addition to her family. She found her own three boys quite enough to manage without taking anyone else. And to bring a village lad of fourteen into their midst was terribly upsetting. Bishamber should really have thought twice before committing such an indiscretion.

In this world of human affairs there is no worse nuisance than a boy at the age of fourteen. He is neither ornamental nor useful. It is impossible to shower affection on him as on a little boy; and he is always getting in the way. If he talks with a childish lisp he is called a baby, and if he answers in a grown-up way he is called impertinent. In fact any talk at all from him is resented. Then he is at the unattractive, growing age. He grows out of his clothes with indecent haste; his voice grows hoarse and breaks and quavers; his face grows suddenly angular and unsightly. It is easy to excuse the shortcomings of early childhood, but it is hard to tolerate even unavoidable lapses in a boy of fourteen. The lad himself becomes painfully self-conscious. When he talks with elderly people he is either unduly forward, or else so unduly shy that he appears ashamed of his very existence.

'Yet it is at this very age when in his heart of hearts a young lad most craves for recognition and love; and he becomes the devoted slave of anyone who shows him consideration. But none dare openly love him, for that would be regarded as undue indulgence, and therefore bad for the boy. So, what with scolding and chiding, he becomes very much like a stray dog that has lost his master.

For a boy of fourteen his own home is the only Paradise. To live in a strange house with strange people is little short of torture, while the height of bliss is to receive the kind looks of women, and never to be slighted by them.

It was anguish to Phatik to be the unwelcome guest in his aunt's house, despised by this elderly woman, and slighted on every occasion. If she ever asked him to do anything for her, he would be so overjoyed that he would overdo it; and then she would tell him not to be so stupid, but to get on with his lessons.

The cramped atmosphere of neglect in his aunt's house oppressed Phatik so much that he felt that he could hardly breathe. He wanted to go out into the open country and fill his lungs and breathe freely. But there was no open country to go to. Surrounded on all sides by Calcutta houses and walls, he would dream night after night of his village home, and long to be back there. He remembered the glorious meadow where he used to fly his kite all day long; the broad river-banks where he would wander about the livelong day singing and shouting for joy; the narrow brook where he could go and dive and swim at any time he liked.

He thought of his band of boy companions over whom he was despot; and, above all, the memory of that tyrant mother of his, who had such a prejudice against him, occupied him day and night. A kind of physical love like that of animals; a longing to be in the presence of the one who is loved; an inexpressible wistfulness during absence; a silent cry of the inmost heart for the mother, like the lowing of a calf in the twilight—this love, which was almost an animal instinct, agitated the shy, nervous, lean, uncouth and ugly boy. No one could understand it, but it preyed upon his mind continually.

There was not a more backward boy in the whole school than Phatik. He gaped and remained silent when the teacher asked him a question, and like an overladen ass patiently suffered all the blows that came down on his back. When other boys were out at play, he stood wistfully by the window and gazed at the roofs of the distant houses. And if by chance he espied children playing on the open terrace of any roof, his heart would ache with longing.

One day he summoned up all his courage, and asked his uncle: 'Uncle, when can I go home?'

His uncle answered: 'Wait till the holidays come.'

But the holidays would not come till November, and there was a long time still to wait.

One day Phatik lost his lesson-book. Even with the help of books he had found it very difficult indeed to prepare his lesson. Now it was impossible. Day after day the teacher would cane him unmercifully. His condition became so abjectly miserable that even his cousins were ashamed to own him. They began to jeer and insult him more than the other boys. He went to his aunt at last, and told her that he had lost his book.

His aunt pursed her lips in contempt, and said: 'You great clumsy, country lout. How can I afford, with all my family, to buy you new books five times a month?'

That night, on his way back from school, Phatik had a bad headache with a fit of shivering. He felt he was going to have an attack of malarial fever. His one great fear was that he would be a nuisance to his aunt.

The next morning Phatik was nowhere to be seen. All searches in the neighbourhood proved futile. The rain had been pouring in torrents all night, and those who went out in search of the boy got drenched through to the skin. At last Bishamber asked help from the police.

At the end of the day a police van stopped at the door before the house. It was still raining and the streets were all flooded. Two constables brought out Phatik in their arms and placed him before Bishamber. He was wet through from head to foot, muddy all over, his face and eyes flushed red with fever, and his limbs all trembling. Bishamber carried him in his arms, and took him into the inner apartments. When his wife saw him, she exclaimed; 'What a heap of trouble this boy has given us. Hadn't you better send him home?'

Phatik heard her words, and sobbed out loud: 'Uncle, I was just going home; but they dragged me back again.'

The fever rose very high, and all that night the boy was delirious. Bishamber brought in a doctor. Phatik opened his eyes flushed with fever, and looked up to the ceiling, and said vacantly: 'Uncle, have the holidays come yet? May I go home?'

Bishamber wiped the tears from his own eyes, and took Phatik's lean and burning hands in his own, and sat by him through the night. The boy began again to mutter. At last his voice became excited: 'Mother,' he cried, 'don't beat me like that! Mother! I am telling the truth!'

The next day Phatik became conscious for a short time. He turned his eyes about the room, as if expecting someone to come. At last, with an air of disappointment, his head sank back on the pillow. He turned his face to the wall with a deep sigh.

Bishamber knew his thoughts, and, bending down his head, whispered: 'Phatik, I have sent for your mother.'

The day went by. The doctor said in a troubled voice that the boy's condition was very critical.

Phatik began to cry out: 'By the mark!—three fathoms. By the mark—four fathoms. By the mark—' He had heard the sailor on the river-steamer calling out the mark on the plumbline. Now he was himself plumbing an unfathomable sea.

Later in the day Phatik's mother burst into the room like a whirlwind, and began to toss from side to side and moan and cry in a loud voice.

Bishamber tried to calm her agitation, but she flung herself on the bed, and cried: 'Phatik, my darling, my darling.'

Phatik stopped his restless movements for a moment. His hands ceased beating up and down. He said: 'Eh?'

The mother cried again: 'Phatik, my darling, my darling.'

Phatik very slowly turned his head and, without seeing anybody, said: 'Mother, the holidays have come.

1893

—Tr. by C.F. Andrews

5

The Brahmin

It was a night of full moon early in the month of Phalgun, The youthful spring was everywhere sending forth its breeze laden with the fragrance of mango-blossoms. The melodious notes of an untiring *papiha,* concealed within the thick foliage of an old *lichi* tree by the side of a tank, penetrated a sleepless bedroom of the Brahmin Mukerji family. There Hemanta now restlessly twisted a lock of his wife's hair round his finger, now beat her bangles against her wristlet until it tinkled, now pulled at the chaplet of flowers about her head, and left it hanging over her face. His mood was that of an evening breeze which played about a favourite flowering shrub, gently shaking her now this side, now that, in the hope of rousing her to animation.

But Kusum sat motionless, looking out of the open window, with eyes immersed in the moonlit depth of never-ending space beyond. Her husband's caresses were lost on her.

At last Hemanta clasped both the hands of his wife, and, shaking them gently, said: 'Kusum, where are you? A patient search through a big telescope would reveal you only as a small speck—you seem to have receded so far away. O, do come closer to me, dear. See how beautiful the night is.'

Kusum turned her eyes from the void of space towards

her husband, and said slowly: 'I know a mantra which could in one moment shatter this spring night and the moon into pieces.'

'If you do,' laughed Hemanta, 'pray don't utter it. If any mantra of yours could bring three or four Saturdays during the week, and prolong the nights till 5 P.M. the next day, say it by all means.'

Saying this, he tried to draw his wife a little closer to him. Kusum, freeing herself from the embrace, said: 'Do you know, tonight I feel a longing to tell you what I promised to reveal only on my death-bed. Tonight I feel that I could endure whatever punishment you might inflict on me.'

Hemanta was on the point of making a jest about punishments by reciting a verse from Jayadeva, when the sound of an angry pair of slippers was heard approaching rapidly. They were the familiar footsteps of his father, Harihar Mukerji, and Hemanta, not knowing what it meant, was in a flutter of excitement.

Standing outside the door Harihar roared out: 'Hemanta, turn your wife out of the house immediately.'

Hemanta looked at his wife, and detected no trace of surprise in her features. She merely buried her face within the palms of her hands, and, with all the strength and intensity of her soul, wished that she could then and there melt into nothingness. It was the same *papiha* whose song floated into the room with the south breeze, and no one heard it. Endless are the beauties of the earth—but alas, how easily everything is twisted out of shape.

Returning from without, Hemanta asked his wife: 'Is it true?'

'It is,' replied Kusum.

'Why didn't you tell me long ago?'

'I did try many a time, and I always failed. I am a wretched woman.'

'Then tell me everything now.'

Kusum gravely told her story in a firm unshaken voice. She waded barefooted through fire, as it were, with slow unflinching steps, and nobody knew how much she was scorched. Having heard her to the end, Hemanta rose and walked out.

Kusum thought that her husband had gone, never to return to her again. It did not strike her as strange. She took it as naturally as any other incident of everyday life—so dry and apathetic had her mind become during the last few moments. Only the world and love seemed to her as a void and make-believe from beginning to end. Even the memory of the protestations of love, which her husband had made to her in days past, brought to her lips a dry, hard, joyless smile, like a sharp cruel knife which had cut through her heart. She was thinking, perhaps, that the love which seemed to fill so much of one's life, which brought in its train such fondness and depth of feeling, which made even the briefest separation so exquisitely painful and a moment's union so intensely sweet, which seemed boundless in its extent and eternal in its duration, the cessation of which could not be imagined even in births to come—that this was that love! So feeble was its support!

No sooner does the priesthood touch it than your 'eternal' love crumbles into a handful of dust! Only a short while ago Hemanta had whispered to her: 'What a beautiful night!' The same night was not yet at an end, the same *papiha* was still warbling, the same south breeze still blew into the room, making the bed-curtain shiver; the same moonlight lay on the bed next the open window, sleeping like a beautiful heroine exhausted with gaiety. All this was unreal! Love was more falsely dissembling than she herself!

The next morning Hemanta, fagged after a sleepless night, and looking like one distracted, called at the house of Peari Sankar Ghosal. 'What news, my son?' Peari Sankar greeted him.

Hemanta, flaring up like a big fire, said in a trembling

voice: 'You have defiled our caste. You have brought destruction upon us. And you will have to pay for it.' He could say no more; he felt choked.

'And you have preserved my caste, prevented my ostracism from the community, and patted me on the back affectionately!' said Peari Sankar with a slight sarcastic smile.

Hemanta wished that his Brahmin-fury could reduce Peari Sankar to ashes in a moment, but his rage burnt only himself. Peari Sankar sat before him unscathed, and in the best of health.

'Did I ever do you any harm?' demanded Hemanta in a broken voice.

'Let me ask you one question,' said Peari Sankar. 'My daughter, my only child—what harm had she done your father? You were very young then, and probably never heard. Listen, then. Now, don't you excite yourself. There is much humour in what I am going to relate.

'You were quite small when my son-in-law Nabakanta ran away to England after stealing my daughter's jewels. You might remember the commotion in the village when he returned as a barrister five years later. Or, perhaps, you were unaware of it, as you were at school in Calcutta at the time. Your father, arrogating to himself the headship of the community, declared that if I sent my daughter to her husband's home, I must renounce her for good, and never again allow her to cross my threshold. I fell at your father's feet, and implored him, saying: 'Brother, save me this once. I will make the boy swallow cow-dung, and go through the *prayaschitta* ceremony. Do take him back into caste.' But your father remained obdurate. For my part, I could not disown my only child, and, bidding good-bye to my village and my kinsmen, I betook myself to Calcutta. There, too, my troubles followed me. When I had made every arrangement for my nephew's marriage, your father stirred up the girl's people, and they broke the match off. Then I took a solemn vow that, if there was a drop of Brahmin blood flowing in my veins, I would avenge myself. You understand the business to some extent now, don't you? But wait a little longer. You will enjoy it, when I tell you the whole story; it is interesting.

'When you were attending college, one Bipradas Chatterji used to live next door to your lodgings. The poor fellow is dead now. In his house lived a child-widow called Kusum, the destitute orphan of a Kayastha gentleman. The girl was very pretty, and the old Brahmin desired to shield her from the hungry gaze of college students. But for a young girl to throw dust in the eyes of her old guardian was not at all a difficult task. She often went to the top of the roof, to hang her washing out to dry, and, I believe, you found your own roof best suited for your studies. Whether you two spoke to each other, and when on your respective roofs, I cannot tell, but the girl's behaviour excited suspicion in the old man's mind. She made frequent mistakes in her household duties, and, like Parvati, Lord Shiva's spouce engaged in her devotions, began gradually to renounce food and sleep. Some evenings she would burst into tears in the presence of the old gentleman, without any apparant reason.

'At last he discovered that you two saw each other from the roofs pretty frequently, and that you even went the length of absenting yourself from college to sit on the roof at midday with a book in your hand, so fond had you grown suddenly of solitary study. Bipradas came to me for advice, and told me everything, 'Uncle,' said I to him, 'for a long while you have cherished a desire to go on a pilgrimage to Benares. You had better do it now, and leave the girl in my charge. I will take care of her.'

'So he went, I lodged the girl in the house of Sripati Chatterji, passing him off as her father. What happened next is known to you. I feel a great relief today, having told you everything from the beginning. It sounds like a romance, doesn't it? I think of turning it into a book, and getting it printed. But I am not a writing-man myself. They say my nephew has some aptitude that way—I will get him to write it for me. But the best thing would-be, if you would collaborate with him, because the conclusion of the story is not known to me so far.'

Without paying much attention to the concluding remarks of Peari Sankar, Hemanta asked: 'Did not Kusum object to this marriage?'

'Well,' said Peari Sankar, 'it is very difficult to guess. You know, my boy, how women's minds are constituted. When they say "no", they mean "yes." During the first few days after her removal to the new home, she went almost crazy at not seeing you. You, too, seemed to have discovered her new address somehow, as you used to lose your way after starting for college, and loiter about in front of Sripati's house. Your eyes did not appear to be exactly in search of the Presidency College, as they were directed towards the barred windows of a private house, through which nothing but insects and the hearts of moon-struck young men could obtain access. I felt very sorry for you both. I could see that your studies were being seriously interrupted, and that the plight of the girl was pitiable also. One day I called Kusum to me, and said: "Listen to me, daughter. I am an old man, and you need feel no delicacy in my presence. I know whom you desire at heart. The young man's condition is hopeless too. I wish I could bring about your union." At this Kusum suddenly melted into tears, and ran away. On several evenings after that, I visited Sripati's house, and, calling Kusum to me, discussed with her matters relating to you, and so I succeeded in gradually overcoming her shyness. At last, when I said that I would try to bring about a marriage, she asked me: "How can it be?" "Never mind," I said, "I would pass you off as a Brahmin maiden." After a good deal of argument, she begged me to find out whether you would approve of it. "What nonsense!" replied I, "the boy is well-nigh mad as it were—what's the use disclosing all these complications to him? Let the ceremony be over smoothly and then—all's well that ends well. Especially, as there is not the slightest risk of its ever leaking out, why go out of the way to make a fellow miserable for life?"

'I do not know whether the plan had Kusum's assent or not. At times she wept, and at other times she remained silent. If I said, "Let us drop it then," she would become very restless. When things were in this state, I sent Sripati to you with the proposal of marriage; you consented without a moment's hesitation. Everything was settled.

'Shortly before the day fixed, Kusum became so obstinate that I had the greatest difficulty in bringing her round again. "Do let it drop, Uncle," she said to me constantly. "What do you mean, you silly child," I rebuked her; "how can we back out now, when everything has been settled?"

' "Spread a rumour that I am dead," she implored. "Send me away somewhere."

' "What would happen to the young man then?" said I. "He is now in the seventh heaven of delight, expecting that his long-cherished desire would be fulfilled tomorrow; and today you want me to send him the news of your death? The result would be that tomorrow I should have to bear news of his death to you, and the same evening your death would be reported to me. Do you imagine, child, that I am capable of committing a girl-murder and a Brahmin-murder at my age?"

'Eventually the happy marriage was celebrated at the auspicious moment, and I felt relieved of a burdensome duty which I owed to myself. What happened afterwards you know best.'

'Couldn't you stop after having done us an irreparable injury?' burst out Hemanta after a short silence. 'Why have you told the secret now?'

With the utmost composure, Peari Sankar replied: 'When I saw that all arrangements had been made for the wedding of your sister, I said to myself: "Well, I have fouled the caste of one Brahmin, but that was only from a sense of duty. Here, another Brahmin's caste is imperilled, and this time it is my plain duty to prevent it." So I wrote to them saying that I was in a position to prove that you had taken the daughter of a Sudra to wife.'

Controlling himself with a gigantic effort, Hemanta said: 'What will become of this girl whom I shall abandon now? Would you give her food and shelter?'

'I have done what was mine to do,' replied Peari Sankar calmly. 'It is no part of my duty to look after the discarded wives of other people. Anybody there? Get a glass of coconut

milk for Hemanta Babu with ice in it. And some *pan* too.'
Hemanta rose, and took his departure without waiting for this ...urious hospitality.

...t was the fifth night of the waning of the moon— and the ...t was dark. No birds were singing. The *lichi* tree by the ...k looked like a smudge of ink on a background of shadeless deep. The south wind was blindly roaming about in the darkness like a sleep-walker. The stars in the sky with vigilant unblinking eyes were trying to penetrate the darkness, in their effort to fathom some profound mystery.

No light shone in the bedroom. Hemanta was sitting on the side of the bed next the open window, gazing at the darkness in front of him. Kusum lay on the floor, clasping her husband's feet with both her arms, and her face resting on them. Time stood like an ocean hushed into stillness. On the background of eternal night, Fate seemed to have painted this one single picture for all time—annihilation on every side, the judge in the centre of it, and the guilty one at his feet.

The sound of slippers was heard again. Approaching the door, Harihar Mukerji said: 'You have had enough time—I can't allow you more. Turn the girl out of the house.'

Kusum, as she heard this, embraced her husband's f... with all the ardour of a lifetime, covered them with kisses, ... touching her forehead to them reverentially, withdrew he...

Hemanta rose, and walking to the door, said: 'Fa... won't forsake my wife.'

'What!' roared out Harihar, 'would you lose you...

' I don't care for caste,' was Hemanta's calm rep... you too I renounce.'

1892

—Tr. by Prabhat K. M...

6

Kadambini's Story

The widow in the house of Saradasankar, the Ranihat zemindar, had no kinsmen of her father's family. One after another all had died. Nor had she in her husband's
anyone she could call her own, neither husband nor
child of her brother-in-law Saradasankar was her
For a long time after his birth, his mother had been
the widow, his aunt Kadambini, had fostered him.
fosters another's child, her love for him is all the
use she has no claim upon him—no claim of
but simply the claim of love. Love cannot prove
ocument which society accepts, and does not
merely worships with double passion its
ure. Thus all the widow's thwarted love
little child.
Kadambini died suddenly. For some
beating. Everywhere else the world
is gentle little breast, suffering with
still for ever.
ssed by the police, four of the
ook away the body, without
ing-ground of Ranihat was

milk for Hemanta Babu with ice in it. And some *pan* too.'

Hemanta rose, and took his departure without waiting for this luxurious hospitality.

It was the fifth night of the waning of the moon— and the night was dark. No birds were singing. The *lichi* tree by the tank looked like a smudge of ink on a background of shadeless deep. The south wind was blindly roaming about in the darkness like a sleep-walker. The stars in the sky with vigilant unblinking eyes were trying to penetrate the darkness, in their effort to fathom some profound mystery.

No light shone in the bedroom. Hemanta was sitting on the side of the bed next the open window, gazing at the darkness in front of him. Kusum lay on the floor, clasping her husband's feet with both her arms, and her face resting on them. Time stood like an ocean hushed into stillness. On the background of eternal night, Fate seemed to have painted this one single picture for all time—annihilation on every side, the judge in the centre of it, and the guilty one at his feet.

The sound of slippers was heard again. Approaching the door, Harihar Mukerji said: 'You have had enough time—I can't allow you more. Turn the girl out of the house.'

Kusum, as she heard this, embraced her husband's feet with all the ardour of a lifetime, covered them with kisses, and touching her forehead to them reverentially, withdrew herself.

Hemanta rose, and walking to the door, said: 'Father, I won't forsake my wife.'

'What!' roared out Harihar, 'would you lose your caste?'

' I don't care for caste,' was Hemanta's calm reply. 'Then you too I renounce.'

1892 **—Tr. by Prabhat K. Mukhopadhyaya**

6

Kadambini's Story

The widow in the house of Saradasankar, the Ranihat zemindar, had no kinsmen of her father's family. One after another all had died. Nor had she in her husband's family anyone she could call her own, neither husband nor son. The child of her brother-in-law Saradasankar was her darling. For a long time after his birth, his mother had been very ill, and the widow, his aunt Kadambini, had fostered him. If a woman fosters another's child, her love for him is all the stronger because she has no claim upon him—no claim of kinship, that is, but simply the claim of love. Love cannot prove its claim by any document which society accepts, and does not wish to prove it; it merely worships with double passion its life's uncertain treasure. Thus all the widow's thwarted love went out towards this little child.

One night in Sravan Kadambini died suddenly. For some reason her heart stopped beating. Everywhere else the world held on its course; only in this gentle little breast, suffering with love, the watch of time stood still for ever.

Lest they should be harassed by the police, four of the zemindar's Brahmin servants took away the body, without ceremony, to be burned. The burning-ground of Ranihat was very far from the village. There was a hut beside a tank, a huge banian near it, and nothing more. Formerly a river, now completely dried up, ran through the ground, and a part of the water-course had been dug out to make a tank for the performance of funeral rites. The people considered the tank as part of the river and reverenced it as such.

Taking the body into the hut, the four men sat down to wait for the wood. The time seemed so long that two of the four grew restless, and went to see why it did not come. Nitai and Gurucharan being gone, Bidhu and Banamali remained to watch over the body.

It was a dark night of Sravan. Heavy clouds hung in a starless sky. The two men sat silent in the dark room. Their matches and lamp were useless. The matches were damp, and would not light for all their efforts, and the lantern went out. After a long silence, one said: 'Brother, it would be good if we had a bowl of tobacco. In our hurry we brought none.'

The other answered: 'I can run and bring all we want.'

Understanding why Banamali wanted to go, Bidhu said: 'I dare say! Meanwhile, I suppose I am to sit here alone!'

Conversation ceased again. Five minutes seemed like an hour. In their minds they cursed the two who had gone to fetch the wood, and they began to suspect that they sat gossiping in some pleasant nook. There was no sound anywhere, except the incessant noise of frogs and crickets from the tank. Then suddenly they fancied that the bed shook slightly, as if the dead body had turned on its side. Bidhu and Banamali trembled, and began muttering: 'Ram, Ram.' A deep sigh was heard in the room. In a moment the watchers leapt out of the hut, and raced for the village.

After running about three miles, they met their colleagues coming back with a lantern. As a matter of fact, they had gone to smoke, and knew nothing about the wood. But they declared that a tree had been cut down, and that, when it was split up, it would be brought along at once. Then Bidhu and Banamali told them what had happened in the hut. Nitai and Gurucharan scoffed at the story, and abused Bidhu and Banamali angrily for leaving their duty.

Without delay all four returned to the hut. As they entered, they saw at once that the body was gone; nothing but an empty bed remained. They stared at one another. Could a jackal have taken it? But there was no scrap of clothing anywhere. Going outside, they saw that on the mud that had collected at the door of the hut there were a woman's tiny footprints, newly made. Saradasankar was no fool, and they could hardly persuade him to believe in this ghost story. So after much discussion the four decided that it would be best to say that the body had been burnt.

Towards dawn, when the men with the wood arrived they were told that, owing to their delay, the work had been done without them; there had been some wood in the hut after all. No one was likely to question this, since a dead body is not such a valuable property that anyone would steal it.

Everyone knows that, even when there is no sign, life is often secretly present, and may begin again in an apparently dead body. Kadambini was not dead; only the machine of her life had for some reason suddenly stopped.

When consciousness returned, she saw dense darkness on all sides. It occurred to her that she was not lying in her usual place. She called out 'Sister,' but no answer came from the darkness. As she sat up, terror-stricken, she remembered her death-bed, the sudden pain at her breast, the beginning of a choking sensation. Her elder sister-in-law was warming some milk for the child, when Kadambini became faint, and fell on the bed, saying with a choking voice: 'Sister, bring the child here. I am worried.' After that everything was black, as when an inkpot is upset over an exercise-book. Kadambini's memory and consciousness, all the letters of the world's book, in a moment became formless.

The widow could not remember whether the child, in the

sweet voice of love, called her 'Auntie,' as if for the last time, or not; she could not remember whether, as she left the world she knew for death's endless unknown journey, she had received a parting gift of affection, love's passage-money for the silent land. At first, I fancy, she thought the lonely dark place was the House of Yama, where there is nothing to see, nothing to hear, nothing to do, only an eternal watch. But when a cold damp wind drove through the open door, and she heard the croaking of frogs, she remembered vividly and in a moment all the rains of her short life, and could feel her kinship with the earth. Then came a flash of lightning, and she saw the tank, the banian, the great plain, the far-off trees. She remembered how at full moon she had sometimes come to bathe in this tank, and how dreadful death had seemed when she saw a corpse on the burning-ground.

Her first thought was to return home. But then she reflected: 'I am dead. How can I return home? That would bring disaster on them. I have left the kingdom of the living; I am my own ghost!' If this were not so, she reasoned, how could she have got out of Saradasankar's well-guarded zenana, and come to this distant burning-ground at midnight? Also, if her funeral rites had not been finished, where had the men gone who should burn her? Recalling her death-moment in Saradasankar's brightly-lit house, she now found herself alone in a distant, deserted, dark burning-ground. Surely she was no member of earthly society! Surely she was a creature of horror, of ill-omen, her own ghost!

At this thought, all the bonds were snapped which bound her to the world. She felt that she had marvellous strength, endless freedom. She could do what she liked, go where she pleased. Mad with the inspiration of this new idea, she rushed from the hut like a gust of wind, and stood upon the burning-ground. All trace of shame or fear had left her.

But as she walked on and on, her feet grew tired, her body weak. The plain stretched on endlessly; here and there were paddy-fields; sometimes she found herself standing knee-deep in water.

At the first glimmer of dawn she heard one or two birds cry from the bamboo-clumps by the distant houses. Then terror seized her. She could not tell in what new relation she stood to the earth and to living folk. So long as she had been on the plain, on the burning-ground, covered by the dark night of *sraban*, so long she had been fearless, a denizen of her own kingdom. By daylight the homes of men filled her with fear. Men and ghosts dread each other, for their tribes inhabit different banks of the river of death.

Her clothes were clotted in the mud; strange thoughts and walking by night had given her the aspect of a mad-woman; truly, her apparition was such that folk might have been afraid of her, and children might have stoned her or run away. Luckily, the first to catch sight of her was a traveller. He came up, and said: 'Mother, you look a respectable woman. Wherever are you going, alone and in this guise?'

Kadambini, unable to collect her thoughts, stared at him in silence. He could not think that she was still in touch with the world, that she looked like a respectable woman, that a traveller was asking her questions.

Again the man said: 'Come, mother, I will see you home. Tell me where you live.'

Kadambini thought. To return to her father-in-laws house would be absurd, and she had no father's house. Then she remembered the friend of her childhood. She had not seen Jogmaya since the days of her youth, but from time to time they had exchanged letters. Occasionally there had been quarrels between them, as was only right, since Kadambini wished to make it clear that her love for Jogmaya was unbounded, while her friend complained that Kadambini did not return a love equal to her own. They were both sure that, if they once met, they would be inseparable.

Kadambini said to the traveller: 'I will go to Sripati's house at Nisindapur.'

As he was going to Calcutta, Nisindapur, though not near, was on his way. So he took Kadambini to Sripati's house, and the friends met again. At first they did not recognise one another, but gradually each recognised the features of the other's childhood.

'What luck!' said Jogmaya. 'I never dreamt that I should see you again. But how have you come here, sister? Your father-in-law's folk surely didn't let you go!'

Kadambini remained silent, and at last said: 'Sister, do not ask about my father-in-law. Give me a corner, and treat me as a servant: I will do your work.'

'What?' cried Jogmaya. 'Keep you like a servant! Why, you are my closest friend, you are my'... and so on and so on.

Just then Sripati came in. Kadambini stared at him for some time, and then went out very slowly. She kept her head uncovered, and showed not the slightest modesty or respect. Jogmaya, fearing that Sripati would be prejudiced against her friend, began an elaborate explanation. But Sripati, who readily agreed to anything Jogmaya said, cut short her story, and left his wife uneasy in her mind.

Kadambini had come, but she was not at one with her friend: death was between them. She could feel no intimacy for others so long as her existence perplexed her and consciousness remained. Kadambini would look at Jogmaya, and brood. She would think: 'She has her husband and her work, she lives in a world far away from mine. She shares affection and duty with the people of the world; I am an empty shadow. She is among the living; I am in eternity.'

Jogmaya also was uneasy, but could not explain why. Women do not love mystery, because, though uncertainty may be transmuted into poetry, into heroism, into scholarship, it cannot be turned to account in household work. So, when a woman cannot understand a thing, she either destroys and forgets it, or she shapes it anew for her own use; if she fails to deal with it in one of these ways, she loses her temper with it. The greater Kadambini's abstraction became, the more impatient was Jogmaya with her, wondering what trouble weighed upon her mind.

Then a new danger arose. Kadambini was afraid of herself; yet she could not flee from herself. Those who fear ghosts fear those who are behind them; wherever they cannot see there is fear. But Kadambini's chief terror lay in herself, for she dreaded nothing external. At the dead of night, when alone in her room, she screamed; in the evening, when she saw her shadow in the lamplight, her whole body shook. Watching her tearfulness, the rest of the house fell into a sort of terror. The servants and Jogmaya herself began to see ghosts.

One midnight Kadambini came out from her bedroom weeping, and wailed at Jogmaya's door: 'Sister, sister, let me lie at your feet! Do not put me by myself!'

Jogmaya's anger was no less than her fear. She would have liked to drive Kadambini from the house that very second. The good-natured Sripati, after much effort, succeeded in quieting their guest, and put her in the next room.

Next day Sripati was unexpectedly summoned to his wife's apartments. She began to upbraid him: 'You, do you call yourself a man? A woman runs away from her father-in-law, and enters your house; a month passes, and you haven't hinted that she should go away, nor have I heard the slightest protest from you. I should take it was a favour if you would explain yourself. You men are all alike.'

Men, as a race, have a natural partiality for womankind in general, for which women themselves hold them accountable. Although Sripati was prepared to touch Jogmaya's body and swear that his kind feeling towards the helpless but beautiful Kadambini was no whit greater than it should be, he could not prove it by his behaviour. He thought that her father-in-law's people must have treated this forlorn widow abominably, if she could bear it no longer, and was driven to take refuge with him. As she had neither father nor mother, how could he desert her? So saying, he let the matter drop, for he had no mind to distress Kadambini by asking her unpleasant questions.

His wife, then, tried other means of attack upon her sluggish lord, until at last he saw that for the sake of peace he must send word to Kadambini's father-in-law. The result of a letter, he thought, might not be satisfactory; so he resolved to go to Ranihat, and act on what he leamt.

Sripati went, and Jogmaya on her part said to Kadambini: 'Friend, it hardly seems proper for you to stop here any longer. What will people say?'

Kadambini stared solemnly at Jogmaya, and said: 'What have I to do with people?'

Jogmaya was astounded. Then she said sharply: 'If you have nothing to do with people, we have. How can we explain the detention of a woman belonging to another house?'

Kadambini said: 'Where is my father-in-law's house?'

'Confound it!' thought Jogmaya. 'What will the wretched woman say next?'

Very slowly Kadambini said: 'What have I to do with you? Am I of the earth? You laugh, weep, love; each grips and holds his own; I merely look. You are human, I a shadow. I cannot understand why God has kept me in this world of yours.'

So strange were her look and speech that Jogmaya understood something of her drift, though not all. Unable either to dismiss her, or to ask her any more questions, she went away, oppressed with thought.

•

It was nearly ten o'clock at night when Sripati returned from Ranihat. The earth was drowned in torrents of rain. It seemed that the downpour would never stop, that the night would never end.

Jogmaya asked: 'Well?'

'I've lots to say to you.'

So saying, Sripati changed his clothes, and sat down to supper; then he lay down for a smoke. His mind was perplexed.

His wife stifled her curiosity for a long time; then she came to his couch and demanded:

'What did you hear?'

'That you have certainly made a mistake.'

Jogmaya was nettled. Women never make mistakes, or, if they do, a sensible man never mentions them; it is better to take them on his own shoulders. Jogmaya snapped: 'May I hear how?'

Sripati replied: 'The woman you have taken into your house is not your Kadambini.'

Hearing this, she was greatly annoyed, especially since it was her husband who said it. 'What! I don't know my own friend? I must come to you to recognise her! You are clever, indeed!'

Sripati explained that there was no need to quarrel about his cleverness. He could prove what he said. There was no doubt that Jogmaya's Kadambini was dead.

Jogmaya replied: 'Listen! you've certainly made some huge mistake. You've been to the wrong house, or are confused as to what you have heard. Who told you to go yourself? Write a letter, and everything will be cleared up.'

Sripati was hurt by his wife's lack of faith in his executive ability; he produced all sorts of proof, without result. Midnight found them still asserting and contradicting. Although they were both agreed now that Kadambini should be got out of the house, although Sripati believed that their guest had deceived his wife all the time by a pretended acquintance, and Jogmaya that she was a prostitute, yet in the present discussion neither would acknowledge defeat. By degrees their voices became so loud that they forgot that Kadambini was sleeping in the next room.

The one said: 'We're in a nice fix! I tell you, I heard it with my own ears!' And the other answered angrily: 'What do I care about that? I can see with my own eyes, surely.'

At length Jogmaya said: 'Very well. Tell me when Kadambini died.' She thought that if she could find a discrepancy between the day of death and the date of some letter from Kadambini, she could prove that Sripati erred.

He told her the date of Kadambini's death, and they both saw that it fell on the very day before she came to their house.

Jogmaya's heart trembled, and even Sripati was not unmoved.

Just then the door flew open; a damp wind swept in and blew the lamp out. The darkness rushed after it, and filled the whole house. Kadambini stood in the room. It was nearly one o'clock, and the rain was pelting outside.

Kadambini spoke: 'Friend, I am your Kadambini, but I am no longer living. I am dead.'

Jogmaya screamed with terror; Sripati could not speak.

'But, save in being dead, I have done you no wrong. If I have no place among the living, I have none among the dead. Oh! where shall I go?' Crying as if to wake the sleeping Creator in the dense night of rain, she asked again: 'Oh! where shall I go?'

So saying, Kadambini left her friend fainting in the dark house, and went out into the world, seeking her place.

It is hard to say how Kadambini reached Ranihat. At first she showed herself to no one, but spent the whole day in a ruined temple, starving. When the untimely afternoon of the rains was pitch-black, and people huddled into their houses for fear of the impending storm, Kadambini came forth. Her heart trembled as she reached her father-in-law's house; and when, drawing a thick veil over her face, she entered, none of the doorkeepers objected, since they took her for a servant. And the rain was pouring down, and the wind howled.

The mistress, Saradasankar's wife, was playing cards with her widowed sister. A servant was in the kitchen, the sick child was sleeping in the bedroom. Kadambini, escaping everyone's notice, entered this room. I do not know why she had come to her father-in-law's house; she herself did not know; she felt only that she wanted to see her child again. She had no thought where to go next, or what to do.

In the lighted room she saw the child sleeping, his fists clenched, his body wasted with fever. At the sight of him, her heart became parched and thirsty. If only she could press that tortured body to her breast! Immediately the thought followed: 'I do not exist. Who would see it? His mother loves company, loves gossip and cards. All the time that she left me in charge, she was herself free from anxiety, nor was she troubled about him in the least. Who will look after him now as I did?'

The child turned on his side, and cried, half-asleep: 'Auntie, give me water.' Her darling had not yet forgotten his auntie! In a fever of excitement, she poured out some water, and, taking him to her breast, she gave it to him.

As long as he was asleep, the child felt no strangeness in taking water from the accustomed hand. But when Kadambini satisfied her longstarved longing, and kissed him and began rocking him asleep again, he awoke and embraced her. 'Did you die, Auntie?' he asked,

'Yes, darling.'

'And you have come back? Do not die again.'

Before she could answer disaster overtook her. One of the maid servants coming in with a cup of sago dropped it, and fell down. At the crash the mistress left her cards, and entered the room. She stood like a pillar of wood, unable to flee or speak. Seeing all this, the child, too, became terrified, and burst out weeping; 'Go away? Auntie,' he said, 'go away!'

Now at last Kadambini understood that she had not died. The old room, the old things, the same child, the same love, all returned to their living state, without change or difference between her and them. In her friend's house she had felt that her childhood's companion was dead. In her child's room she knew that the boy's 'Auntie' was not dead at all. In anguished tones she said: 'Sister, why do you dread me? See, I am as you knew me.'

Her sister-in-law could endure no longer, and fell into a faint. Saradasankar himself entered the zenana. With folded hands, he said piteously: 'Is this right? Satish is my only son. Why do you show yourself to him? Are we not your own kin? Since you went, he has wasted away daily; his fever has been incessant; day and night he cries: 'Auntie, Auntie.' You have left the world; break these bonds of maya. We will perform all funeral honours.'

Kadambini could bear no more. She said: 'Oh, I am not

dead, I am not dead. Oh, how can I persuade you that I am not dead? I am living, living!' She lifted a brass pot from the ground and dashed it against her forehead. The blood ran from her brow. 'Look!' she cried, 'I am Living!' Saradasankar stood like an image; the child screamed with fear, the two fainting women lay still.

Then Kadamabini, shouting 'I am not dead, I am not dead,' went down the steps to the zenana well, and plunged in. From the upper story Saradasankar heard the splash.

All night the rain poured; it poured next day at dawn, was pouring still at noon. By dying, Kadambini had given proof that she was not dead.

1892 **—Tr. by Edward Thompson**